THE NEAL'S YARD BAKERY
WHOLEFOOD COOKBOOK

THE NEAL'S YARD BAKERY
WHOLEFOOD COOKBOOK

Rachel Haigh

DORLING KINDERSLEY
LONDON

Editorial Director Pamela Norris
Editors Joanna Lorenz, Miren Lopategui
Art Director Roger Bristow
Designers Jane Warring, Tessa Richardson-Jones

Photography by Geoff Dann
Illustrations by Eric Thomas, Robert Micklewright,
David Ashby and Vanessa Luff
Stylist Sue Brown

First published in Great Britain in 1986 by
Dorling Kindersley Publishers Limited,
9 Henrietta Street, London WC2E 8PS

First published as a Dorling Kindersley paperback 1988

British Library Cataloguing in Publication Data

Haigh, Rachel
    The Neal's Yard Bakery wholefood cookbook.
    1. Cookery (Natural foods)
    I. Title   II. Neal's Yard Bakery
    641.5'637   TX741
    ISBN 0-86318-190-2

The publishers would like to thank the Controller of
Her Majesty's Stationery Office for permission to
reproduce some of the nutritional information in the
charts from The Composition of Foods and The
Supplementary Booklet Immigrant Foods.

The publishers would like to thank Jimmy Tsao, Josephine
and staff for all their help, and would also like to thank the
following for the loan of some of the items which appear in
the photographs of this book : Neal Street East, 5 Neal Street,
London ; David Mellor, 26 James Street, London ;
Elizabeth David, 46 Bourne Street, London.

Typeset by Chambers Wallace Ltd, London
Printed and bound in Italy by Lego
Reproduced in Singapore

CONTENTS

PREFACE

This book is based on the extensive experience of the Neal's Yard Bakery Co-operative in preparing, cooking and selling wholefoods.

Neal's Yard is a small triangular area in Covent Garden in London, surrounded by high Victorian warehouse buildings which were formerly part of London's main wholesale fruit and vegetable market. What makes Neal's Yard remarkable are the distinctive and original businesses which occupy these buildings.

Narrow alleyways lead into the Yard, which is full of plants and bustling activity. Situated along two sides of the triangle are the businesses: the Dairy, Flour Mill, Bakery, Apothecary, Soup and Salad Bar, Organic Fruit and Vegetable Shop and Alternative Therapy Rooms. The Neal's Yard Wholefood Warehouse is situated at the entrance to one of the alleyways.

The Yard was started by Nicolas Saunders, who bought the semi-derelict buildings in the mid-seventies and set up the original Neal's Yard Warehouse. He actively encouraged and helped others to start up most of the businesses operating in the Yard. These businesses are in fact quite separate, although compatible with Nicolas Saunders' original aim of providing in one area both natural health care and a complete range of wholefoods.

The Neal's Yard Bakery Co-operative incorporates the Flour Mill, Bakery and Restaurant in Neal's Yard and the Wholefood Warehouse in Portobello Road in West London. The Co-operative specializes in the sale of high quality wholefoods and the business itself is organized along unconventional lines. The Bakery was set up in 1978 by Clare Taylor with a group of her friends and former workmates, and it was formally registered as a co-operative in 1980. In 1981 it bought the Neal's Yard Flour Mill and in 1983 opened its own wholefood warehouse in Portobello Road. Each member of the Co-operative shares in the ownership of the business and takes an equal part in all its operations. This means that all jobs are shared, from breadmaking and serving customers to administration and management decisions.

This book is the result of countless requests from customers for wholefood information and for the recipes from the Restaurant. Many of the dishes served daily at the Bakery Restaurant are included and there is also a wide range of other dishes, reflecting the diversity of modern vegetarian cookery. All the recipes have been scaled down to a quantity suitable for domestic use and have been carefully tested for accuracy. The first part of the book is a detailed reference section, providing invaluable information on wholefoods.

As people are becoming more and more aware of the importance of wholefoods in a balanced diet, there is increasing curiosity about the food we eat: where it comes from, how it is grown, what processing (if any) is needed for its production and the different ways in which it can be prepared and presented. It is hoped that this book will succeed in answering most of these questions.

The information and recipes in this book were collated by Rachel Haigh, a founder member of the Neal's Yard Bakery Co-operative. Simon Blackley, also a founder member, contributed the sections on grains and flours.

INTRODUCTION

Why eat wholefoods?

Wholefoods are foods which have not been over-refined or -processed, which have not been subjected to chemicals in their production and which do not contain harmful additives.

As a result of modern technology, the concept of eating foods in a whole, natural state has been seriously eroded. We can now eat banana-flavoured desserts which contain no bananas, buy fruit which is large and glossy as a result of chemical nutrients and chickens which have been artificially fattened by the use of hormones. We can also keep naturally perishable foodstuffs for weeks without danger of mould or decay and separate out the very heart of a grain of wheat. These are remarkable scientific and technological advances, but what is happening to the nutritional value of the foods themselves?

The economic pressures of large-scale agriculture have led to the increasing use, particularly in the 'developed' world, of a wide range of chemicals. Drugs are added to animal feed, artificial fertilizers are added to the soil and herbicides, insecticides and fungicides are sprayed over crops. It has been widely claimed that this has greatly increased yields. Aerial crop-spraying with weedkillers, for example, is clearly more efficient and economic than the traditional, labour-intensive method of walking the field and plucking out the weeds by hand. However, the costs of these chemicals both in terms of the environment and of human health are only now beginning to be appreciated.

Many of the chemicals are poisonous in large quantities. Some, such as DDT, have already been banned in many countries. Others, such as inorganic nitrate (used as a fertilizer), are still used in high concentrations. The use of these chemical fertilizers is addictive, so that the fertilizers used now, for instance, often need to be 20 times stronger than 5 years previously. This can result in total depletion of the soil and pollution of ground water and streams. Herbicides and pesticides get into the food chain and end up on our plates, along with the other chemicals left in or on the foods themselves.

The long-term dangers of eating foods grown with the help of chemicals may not be fully understood, but it is widely accepted that there is a connection between modern agricultural practices and the recent increase in degenerative and debilitative diseases. There is no doubt that wherever possible it is safer to eat wholefoods made from organically grown plants.

Another source of chemicals in the modern diet is processed and refined food. Food additives now include flavourings, preservatives, stabilizers, antioxidants, sweeteners, colourants and bleaching agents. Although natural additives have been used in food for centuries, as many as 3,000 additives are now available to food manufacturers, many derived from chemicals.

Since 1951, the consumption of food additives has more than doubled, and it has been documented that the average adult living in a Western society currently consumes about 2 kilos (4 lb) of additives a year. Although many additives are now tested before use, their long-term effects are unknown. The evidence increasingly suggests that these foreign substances in the body may cause many modern diseases. Not only can additives affect the foods to which they are added, and therefore the nutritional value of those foods, they can also be harmful in cumulative quantities.

By incorporating wholefoods in your diet, the cumulative dangers of additives are avoided or lessened, and, because true wholefoods have not had anything removed during processing, most if not all of their nutritional value is retained.

Types of wholefood diet

A wholefood diet is not necessarily vegetarian, and could include meat, poultry and fish reared without the aid of chemicals. Organic butchers exist who will supply meat that they claim has been reared naturally and killed in a humane manner. Some people on a wholefood diet will not eat meat or poultry, but will eat fish with an otherwise vegetarian diet.

Vegetarian (Lacto vegetarian)

The recipes in this book (and those served at the Neal's Yard Bakery Restaurant) are based on vegetarian wholefoods. Meat, poultry and fish are excluded; dairy products, eggs and honey are included.

Vegan

A vegan diet is totally vegetarian, and no animal products are consumed. This means that dairy products such as cheese, milk and yogurt are excluded, as are eggs and honey. Vegan recipes in this book are indicated by the symbol ⓥ.

Gluten-free

Gluten is a sticky protein contained in the starchy part of some grains. In recent years medical research has indicated that some allergies may be attributable to gluten consumption. In these cases a gluten-free diet is recommended. Grains and flours which do not contain gluten are maize, rice, millet, buckwheat, chickpea and soya. Gluten-free recipes in this book are indicated by the symbol ⒼⒻ.

A balanced diet

A correct balance of proteins, fats, carbohydrates, fibres, vitamins and minerals is essential for a healthy diet. As a general rule, you should try to eat at least twice as much carbohydrate as protein, keep your sugar and fat intake to a minimum (particularly saturated fats, see p. 45) and cut down on salt. Fibre is also essential for the healthy functioning of the digestive system, although it is not actually digested and absorbed. This means eating mainly cereals, beans, vegetables and fruit, and cutting down on animal fats, sugar and salt.

NUTRIENTS	FUNCTION IN BODY	EFFECT OF DEFICIENCY
Proteins	Essential for formation, growth and repair of all body cells, and for the functioning of the enzymes, hormones and antibodies which regulate and control our bodies. Proteins are made up of amino acids. There are about 20 amino acids, 8 of which are present in protein-containing foods. The rest are synthesized by the body from these 8. Foods which contain all of the 8 essential amino acids are called complete proteins; foods which contain only a few are called incomplete proteins.	Usually coupled with starvation. The body wastes away and metabolic processes decrease.
Fats	These are needed for energy and to form layers of protective tissue in the body. The fat-soluble vitamins A, D, E and K are stored in this fatty tissue. Fats can be saturated or unsaturated, the former containing cholesterol (see p. 45).	Excess is more common than deficiency. Too much fat, particularly saturated, can lead to obesity and heart disease.
Carbohydrates	The body's major source of energy, made up of sugars, starch and fibre. They are also needed to metabolize proteins for body tissue repair, and to run the central nervous system. Unrefined carbohydrates (e.g. grains) are nutritious, but refined carbohydrates (e.g. white sugar) offer only 'empty' calories.	Listlessness, fatigue and nausea. Excess refined carbohydrates are stored as fat in the body, and can lead to tooth decay, high blood pressure, heart disease and diabetes.
Fibre	Not a nutrient, but essential for the elimination of waste material and toxins in the body. Fibre adds bulk to food, and exercises the jaw muscles.	Has been linked to chronic and debilitating diseases of the digestive tract and, possibly, the circulatory system.
Vitamins	Usually needed in minute quantities, but nonetheless essential for healthy functioning of the body. Water-soluble vitamins (the B group and C) need to be taken regularly as they cannot be stored in the body for long; fat-soluble vitamins (A, D, E and K) last rather longer.	
A *(retinol)*	Helps in cell differentiation. Also needed for healthy skin and mucous membranes, and for good night vision.	Softening of bones and teeth, dry skin and night blindness.
B *group*	The major function of all the B vitamins is to break down food into simple sugar molecules for energy and to form new red blood cells. They are also important for the functioning of the brain, nervous and circulatory systems and for healthy hair, skin, eyes and liver. B vitamins work best in conjunction with each other.	
B$_1$ *(thiamin)*	Breaks down carbohydrates for energy. Assists the functioning of brain, nerves and muscles.	Constipation and abdominal pains, and, in extreme cases, beri-beri.
B$_2$ *(riboflavin)*	Breaks down fats, carbohydrates and proteins for energy. Easily destroyed by light.	Mouth and throat infections and eye fatigue. Common in non-milk drinkers.
B$_3$ *(niacin)*	Breaks down fats, carbohydrates and proteins for energy.	Disgestive disorders, sore, swollen tongue and failure to grow in children.
B$_6$ *(pyridoxine)*	Breaks down proteins into amino acids for the formation of red blood cells and hormones.	Anaemia, nervous disorders and fatigue.
B$_{12}$ *(cobalamin)*	Essential for forming red blood cells and for synthesizing RNA and DNA. Also essential for healthy nerves. Vitamin B$_{12}$ can be found in dairy products but is rare in vegetable foodstuffs, so vegans should take a supplement.	Rare but can result in serious anaemia.

NUTRIENTS	FUNCTION IN BODY	EFFECT OF DEFICIENCY
Folic acid	Also a B vitamin. Used in formation of RNA and DNA, and in breakdown of proteins into amino acids. Important in early pregnancy.	Poor growth, gastro-intestinal problems and anaemia.
C *(ascorbic acid)*	Essential for formation of antibodies and for healing and aiding recovery. Helps form collagen, needed for the body's connective tissue. Also needed for absorbing iron and for producing haemoglobin and adrenalin.	Bleeding gums, poor teeth, low resistance to disease and slow healing.
D *(calciferol)*	Needed to absorb and regulate calcium and phosphorus, and for strong bones, teeth and gums. Can be absorbed from sunlight as well as food.	Softening of the bones and rickets.
E *(tocopherol)*	Protects vitamin A and unsaturated fatty acids in the body from harmful oxidation. Assists in healing.	Rare, but can lead to muscular wasting, and abnormal fat deposits and red blood cells.
K *(phytomenadione)*	Essential for blood clotting.	Rare, but can lead to internal and external bleeding.
Minerals	These are necessary for cell growth and repair and regulation of the body. Macro-minerals (calcium, phosphorus, magnesium, sodium, potassium and chloride) are needed in quantities of 100 mg or more a day, and micro-minerals, or trace elements (iron, iodine and zinc) are needed in quantities of only a few mg or less a day. A balance of minerals is very important, as they often work in conjunction with each other. For instance, sodium and potassium work together, as do calcium, phosphorus and magnesium. Taking single mineral supplements can upset this balance, so it is best to obtain them from a varied diet of wholefoods.	
Calcium	Essential for forming bones and teeth, and for maintenance of muscular contractions, nerve impulses and blood clotting. It should be balanced with phosphorus and magnesium.	Muscular problems, fragile bones and tooth decay. Can also lead to insomnia and nervous exhaustion.
Chloride	Needed with sodium and potassium for regulation of body fluid. Helps in formation of gastric juices in stomach for digestion of proteins.	Can lead to imbalance of sodium in body.
Iodine	Needed to form two hormones in the thyroid gland which regulate energy metabolism and protein synthesis.	Can lead to goitre, a swelling of the neck, and also obesity and listlessness.
Iron	Essential for forming haemoglobin in red blood cells, which transport oxygen from the lungs to all cells in the body. Should be balanced with a trace of copper and vitamin C for correct functioning.	Deficiency is common, and can lead to anaemia and fatigue.
Magnesium	Important, with calcium and phosphorus, for the functioning of the skeletal and nervous system.	Muscular weakness and delerium.
Phosphorus	Works with calcium for healthy bones and teeth, and also assists in the body's release of energy. Should be balanced with calcium and magnesium.	Excess is more common.
Potassium	Closely linked to sodium in regulation of body fluids, particularly in the muscle cells and blood	Can lead to impaired neuro-muscular functioning and even heart attacks.
Sodium	Regulates the body's fluid balance and monitors the passage of nutrients into, and waste out of, the cells. Must be balanced with potassium.	Excess is more common, causing fluid retention and high blood pressure.
Zinc	Important for growth and repair of tissues, protein synthesis and the body's defence system. Should be balanced with iron and copper.	Fatigue, low resistance to infection and stunted sexual maturity.

Planning a wholefood vegetarian diet

All of the body's nutritional requirements can be met in a wholefood vegetarian diet. The basic food values of each type of wholefood are described below, and there is a simple chart to show the best proportions of these foods to take as part of your general intake. Detailed nutritional charts are given in the information section of this book, showing the recommended daily allowances of the major nutrients and the corresponding quantities contained in the various wholefoods.

Grains, beans, nuts and seeds

Grains and beans are the most important part of a wholefood vegetarian diet as they are rich in protein, carbohydrates, vitamins (especially the B group), minerals and fibre. When sprouted, they are a particularly good source of vitamins, especially C. It is a mistake to see grains and beans as just stodgy carbohydrates. Carbohydrates are necessary for the processing of other foods and will only be fattening if the body's overall calorific intake is too high. Nuts and seeds do have a high calorific value, being rich in fats and oils, but they are also full of proteins, vitamins and minerals.

Grains, beans, nuts and seeds are the best sources of protein in the plant kingdom. The important point to remember is that their proteins complement each other. Meat, poultry and fish supply us with what is sometimes called complete or first class protein. This means they contain all the amino acids which the body needs to synthesize protein in the body. Grains, beans, nuts and seeds provide incomplete or second class protein, which contains just some of these amino acids. However, the various amino acids present in these plant wholefoods can be combined so that they add up to a complete protein. For instance, the combination of grains and pulses, grains and nuts, grains and seeds, or milk with any of these, will give a complete protein. Soya beans are in fact complete proteins and need no other food in this respect.

Vegetables

Vegetables form an important part of a wholefood vegetarian diet because of the many vitamins, minerals and essential fibre they provide. They are generally low in calories. Dark green, leafy vegetables are the most nutritious, and are particularly important for those not eating dairy products because of their calcium and vitamin B_2 (riboflavin) content.

Take care not to overcook vegetables, especially those high in the water-soluble vitamins B and C. Steaming or light stir-frying is probably the best method of cooking, but because heat, water and even oxygen destroys many of the vitamins, be sure to include some raw vegetables in your diet.

Fruit

Fruit is high in some vitamins, minerals, carbohydrates (in the form of glucose and fructose, or fruit sugar) and fibre. It can have a high calorific value, especially dried fruit, but is low in fats. Most fruits are high in vitamin C, especially citrus fruit. Yellow- and orange-skinned fruits are also often high in vitamin A. All fruits contain dietary fibre in the cell walls and skins, dried fruit containing most of all.

Fruit's natural sweetness makes it an ideal snack food for children, but because some fruit is acidic and high in fibre it can cause upset stomachs and should be eaten in moderation.

Seaweeds

Seaweeds form a useful part of a wholefood vegetarian diet as they are high in protein, vitamins and minerals, particularly calcium, potassium, sodium, iodine and iron. They contain the elusive vitamin B_{12}, seldom found in plant substances and essential in small quantities. Seaweed is therefore of particular importance if you are following a vegan diet.

Dairy produce and non-dairy alternatives

In nutritional terms, one of the most important nutrients that dairy products and eggs can offer a vegetarian is vitamin B_{12}, mainly found in meat products. The protein found in dairy products and eggs is of animal origin, and therefore complete. They also contain vitamin B_2 and calcium.

Eggs, particularly the yolks, are a very nourishing food. However, they are high in cholesterol and for that reason should be eaten in moderation. All dairy products contain saturated fats and cholesterol to some degree, which is why your consumption should be limited. Many non-dairy substitutes are available, such as vegetable margarine and soya milk, which are of nutritional value and free of saturated fat.

Naturally processed products

Naturally processed products are included in a wholefood diet because they are obtained from wholefoods in a natural way without the use of chemicals, retaining most if not all of the nutritional value. Soya bean products such as tofu, tempeh and miso have processed the soya bean into a form much easier to use and cook, and are exceptionally high in protein, iron, calcium and B vitamins as well as being low in fats and cholesterol. Yeast extracts are also a valuable supplement to the diet. Oils, if cold-pressed, are high in nutrients and unsaturated fats; sweeteners such as honey, if unrefined, are useful nutritional alternatives to refined sugar. There is no 'recommended amount' of naturally processed products as they vary so much in their nutritional content, but a selection will provide valuable protein, vitamins and minerals.

The recommended balance

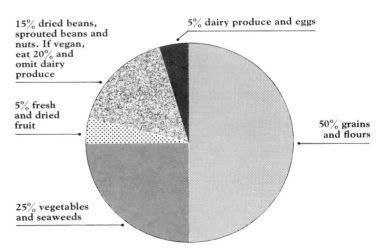

15% dried beans, sprouted beans and nuts. If vegan, eat 20% and omit dairy produce

5% dairy produce and eggs

5% fresh and dried fruit

50% grains and flours

25% vegetables and seaweeds

If you follow these general guidelines for a balanced diet and include an interesting variety of the available wholefoods, you will discover a nutritious, delicious and often exciting way of eating which will have long-reaching benefits. Do remember, however, that if you are planning a major change of diet it is best to change gradually. Do not alter your way of eating overnight, as your system will doubtless object.

The first part of this book is a complete guide to the different kinds of wholefoods, including basic preparation and cooking instructions. Page references to actual recipes are given, as specific examples of the delicious ways in which the wholefoods can be used. The second part of the book contains over 200 attractive and nutritious recipes made with wholefoods, many from the Neal's Yard Bakery Restaurant.

GRAINS

BARLEY
Pot barley ☐
Pearl barley
Barley flakes ☐
BUCKWHEAT
Whole raw buckwheat ☐
Roasted buckwheat ☐
Buckwheat spaghetti
CORN OR MAIZE
Sweetcorn ☐
Popcorn ☐
Polenta ☐

MILLET
Whole millet ☐
Millet flakes ☐
OATS
Oat groats ☐
Pinhead oatmeal ☐
Jumbo rolled oats ☐
Regular rolled oats
Oat bran and germ
RICE
Brown rice ☐
White rice

Rice flakes ☐
Wild rice ☐
RYE
Whole rye grain ☐
Cracked rye
Rye flakes ☐
SAGO AND TAPIOCA
SOYA
Soya flakes
Soya grits
Soya bran

WHEAT (Common wheat)
Whole wheat ☐
Cracked wheat ☐
Bulgar or bulgar wheat
Wheat flakes ☐
Malted wheat
Wheat bran
Wheat germ
WHEAT (Durum wheat)
Semolina
Pasta
Couscous

☐ Pictured opposite page 16

The grains described in this section include cereal and non-cereal grains. Cereals are cultivated members of the grass family: they are, in descending order of world grain production, common wheat and durum wheat, rice, maize, millet and sorghum, barley, oats and rye. Today's cereal crops are by far the most important plant food available, and provide the staple diet for the majority of the world's population. They are abundant in the carbohydrates which our bodies convert into energy, and when used unrefined they are also a rich source of protein, fibre and essential minerals and vitamins. The non-cereals buckwheat, sago, tapioca and soya have also been included in this section because of their similar usage.

Grain products

All cereal grains can be cooked and eaten whole, but most are processed before being prepared as food. This section will describe the various processed products which are available. Individual grains and their products are listed on pages 12-15.

The diagram below shows the different parts of a typical cereal grain. It is a seed, and has three main parts. The *bran* is the outer protective layer; the *endosperm* is the white starchy part which forms the bulk of the grain, providing a storehouse of food for the seed when it starts to grow. The *germ* is the wheat embryo, the point from which new growth starts. By weight, about 85 per cent of the grain is endosperm, 12 per cent is bran and 3 per cent is germ. Different grain products use all or part of the grain; those which use the unrefined grain without removing any part have the greatest food value.

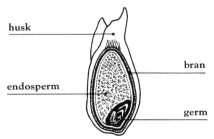

husk

bran

endosperm

germ

Whole grains

Most cereal grains have an indigestible *husk* or hull around them, which must be removed before they can be processed further for use as human food. The only grains which do not have a husk are wheat, rye and maize; these are known as naked or free-threshing grains.

Whole cereal grains are an extremely useful food as, being unrefined, they retain all the nutritional value of the bran and germ. They are delicious cooked and eaten whole, either as a dish on their own or in stews and salads.

Flakes

Flakes are made by flattening whole grains between rollers, making them easier to cook and more easily digestible when eaten raw, for instance in muesli. In addition, flakes are often lightly precooked, either by toasting or steaming.

In most cases, nothing is removed in the flaking process, so the flakes retain the full food value of the whole grain. However, be careful not to confuse genuine cereal flakes with some commercial brands of breakfast cereal, which are often highly processed and refined products with little nutritional value.

Cracked grains/grits

These are cut or broken pieces of cereal grain. As with flakes, they are more easily cooked than whole grains and are often used in porridge, stews and breads. Perhaps the most widely known products in this category are bulgar and couscous, both of which are precooked, though this is not the case with all cracked grains. Some cracked grain products are genuine wholefoods, others are partially refined.

Meals and flours

Meals and flours represent the next stage of processing. Details of milling processes and the different kinds of flours available are given in the chapter on Flours (see p. 16).

Bran and germ

Bran and germ are discarded by-products in the manufacture of white flour. For years they have been used to make animal feed, but more recently they have been promoted as health foods. Wheat bran and germ are the most commonly available, but oat bran and germ, and rice bran and germ (known as rice polishings) can also be found.

Bran and germ do contain valuable elements of the grain, but their health-giving properties should not be over-estimated. They are not in themselves wholefoods, and are of less value when taken in this form than when eaten as part of the whole grain or as part of food made from unrefined wholemeal flour.

Malted grains

Cereal grains, in particular barley and wheat, are grown not only for use as food but also for malting. In the malting process, grains are first steeped in water to stimulate germination, when the grain's carbohydrates are converted into sugars to boost new growth. Just before the first shoot appears, when the sugar level (maltose) is at its highest, the process is stopped by kiln-drying. Malted grains are usually then milled and mixed with water to make a sweet mash, which is fermented for beer and spirit production or used for preparing malt extract.

Malted wheat grains are available in some wholefood shops. They make a sweet and nutty addition to granary-style bread or can be used on muesli as a healthy alternative to sugar.

Storage

Heat, moisture and light are three of the primary causes of deterioration in any foodstuff. Cereal grains are no exception, and are best stored in a cool dry larder or cellar or on kitchen shelves positioned as far away as possible from your stove or oven, and away from direct light if you can.

The action of oxygen is the fourth major cause of deterioration. Whole grains stored in the right conditions can remain usable for many years, and should certainly stay fresh for a year or two on a kitchen shelf. But loss of flavour and nutritional value begins as soon as the grain is broken open during milling, so store flakes, cracked grains and flours in airtight containers. Grain products should be used within 3-6 months.

Note: Each grain is listed alphabetically, and describes the forms in which it is available in order of refinement, from the whole unprocessed grain to the more highly processed product. The flours milled from each grain are dealt with separately in the chapter on Flours (see p. 16). In the basic cooking methods, cup measurements have been included for convenience. One cup is equivalent to 225 ml (8 fl oz).

GRAINS AND THEIR PRODUCTS Per 100 g (4 oz)	Water	Protein	Fat	Carbohydrate	Fibre	Vitamin A	Vitamin B$_1$	Vitamin B$_2$	Vitamin B$_3$	Vitamin B$_6$	Vitamin B$_{12}$	Vitamin C	Vitamin D	Vitamin E	Folic acid	Iron	Calcium	Magnesium	Sodium	Potassium	Phosphorus	Zinc
	g	g	g	g	g	µg	mg	mg	mg	mg	µg	mg	µg	mg	µg	mg	mg	mg	mg	mg	mg	mg
Recommended daily allowance	N	80M 60W	N	N	25-30	750	1.5	1.5	18	1.5	3	30	2.5	8	200	12	500	250	2500	2500	500	15
Barley – whole (pot)	**14**	10.5	2.1	69.3	4	0	0.31	0.1	7.8	0.25	0	0	0	N	50	6	50	91	4	562	N	2.3
– pearl	11	7.9	1.7	83.6	6.5	0	0.05	0.12	2.5	0.22	0	0	0	0.2	20	0.7	10	20	3	120	210	2
Buckwheat – whole	11	11.7	2.4	72.9	9.9	0	0.6	N	4.4	N	0	0	N	N	N	3.9	114	N	N	448	282	N
– spaghetti	**14**	10.8	1.8	73	0.4	0	0.2	0.08	1.2	N	0	0	N	N	N	5	30	N	**700**	N	210	N
Corn – popcorn	N	0.36	0.1	2	0.04	N	N	Tr	Tr	Tr	0	0	N	N	N	0.08	0.4	N	N	N	68	N
Millet – whole	12	9.9	2.9	72.9	3.2	0	0.73	0.38	2.3	N	0	0	N	N	N	6.8	20	162	N	430	311	N
Oats – whole	13	13	5.4	66.1	10.6	0	0.3	0.1	1.5	N	0	0	N	N	N	4.6	55	N	10	N	320	N
– rolled	8	14.2	7.4	68.2	1.2	0	0.6	0.14	1	0.1	0	0	N	N	N	4.5	53	N	2	352	405	N
Rice – brown	12	7.5	1.9	77.4	4.2	0	0.59	0.07	5.3	0.5	0	0	0	N	49	1.4	10	112	3	250	221	1.8
– basmati	11	7.4	0.5	79.8	N	0	N	N	N	N	0	0	0	N	N	1.3	19	N	N	N	N	N
– white	12	6.5	1	86.8	2.4	0	0.08	0.03	1.5	0.3	0	0	0	0.3	29	0.5	4	13	6	110	100	1.3
– flakes	13	6.6	1.2	77.5	N	0	0.21	0.05	4	0.44	0	0	0	N	8	20	N	N	N	N	N	N
– wild	N	12	0.6	60	0.8	0	0.36	0.5	4.9	N	0	0	N	N	N	3.4	15	N	5.5	175	270	N
Rye – whole	11	9.4	1	77.9	0.4	0	0.15	0.07	0.6	N	0	0	N	N	N	1.1	22	N	1	156	185	N
Sago	13	0.2	0.2	94	N	0	Tr	Tr	Tr	Tr	0	0	0	Tr	Tr	1.2	10	3	3	5	29	N
Tapioca	12	0.4	0.1	**95**	N	0	Tr	Tr	Tr	Tr	0	0	0	Tr	Tr	0.3	8	2	4	20	30	N
Soya – grits	N	26	14	25	3.7	**60**	0.8	0.23	1.7	0.6	0	0	N	N	N	6.5	**172**	N	4	**1300**	425	N
Wheat (common) – whole	13	14	2.2	69.1	2.3	0	0.59	0.12	4.3	0.4	0	0	N	N	N	3.1	36	N	3	370	383	N
– cracked	N	8	1.6	55	1.9	0	0.33	0.08	2.7	N	0	0	N	N	N	2.5	33	N	1	N	310	N
– flakes	N	4.9	1	38.2	1.11	0	0.18	0.59	2.05	N	0	0	N	N	N	1	18.2	N	1.17	188	170	N
– bulgar	N	10	N	65	1.5	0	0.24	0.12	3.8	0.19	0	0	N	N	N	3.1	25	N	N	N	290	N
– bran	8	14	5.5	26.8	**44**	0	0.89	0.36	**29.6**	**1.38**	0	0	0	**1.6**	**130**	**12.9**	110	**520**	28	1160	1200	**16.2**
– germ	N	**26.5**	**17.8**	76	4	0	**1.45**	**0.61**	5.8	0.93	0	0	N	*	62	10	118	300	4	1000	**1840**	N
Wheat (durum) – semolina	**14**	10.7	1.8	77.5	N	0	0.1	0.02	0.7	0.15	0	0	0	Tr	25	1	18	32	12	170	110	N
– pasta	11	11.7	6.2	76.1	5.7	0	0.37	0.04	4.8	N	0	0	0	N	18	1.5	23	47	2	230	N	1.5

KEY

All wholefoods are uncooked unless stated otherwise. Some wholefoods may not be included in the chart, as there is currently no nutritional data available. **g**: grams   **mg**: milligrams   **µg**: micrograms   **N**: no available data   **Tr**: trace   **M**: adult men   **W**: adult women.   The recommended daily allowances are averages and vary depending on age, occupation and metabolism.   Figures in bold type indicate the wholefood with the highest level of nutrient.   **✱** Exact figure unknown but thought to be very high.

Barley

Barley originated in the East. It has a short growing season and is suitable for cultivation in a wider range of climatic areas than other cereals. In ancient times barley was more important than wheat as a human food, but today it is grown mainly for animal feed and for malting. It is high in vitamin B$_3$.

Pot barley

Barley grains grow encased in a tough husk, which must be removed before the grain can be used as human food. Pot barley has been scoured to remove this husk, but it does retain some of the bran. Cooked on its own it makes a pleasant change from rice, potatoes or pasta. Alternatively, add to stews, soups or broths.

Basic cooking method (Serves 3-4)

225 g (8 oz) or 1 cup pot barley
675 ml (24 fl oz) or 3 cups water

Wash the grains and put in a saucepan with the water. Bring to the boil, cover and simmer for about 45 minutes until the barley is tender and all the liquid is absorbed. Add a little more water if necessary, or boil off excess liquid by removing the lid of the pan for the last few minutes of cooking.

If you are adding uncooked pot barley to other ingredients, remember that it will need at least 45 minutes of steady cooking but that after 60 minutes it will start to turn mushy, and will absorb three times its volume of liquid.

Recipe: Barley, Fruit & Vegetable Pollo (see p. 99).

Pearl barley

The more refined pearl barley is pot barley which has been polished, like white rice, to remove all the bran. Its nutritional value is therefore diminished. Pearl barley is usually added to soups.

Barley flakes

Barley flakes are made by flattening grains from which the husks have been removed. They are usually lightly toasted, and can either be eaten raw in a muesli or cooked to make a barley porridge.

Recipe: Basic Muesli (see p. 69).

Buckwheat

Despite its name, buckwheat is not a true cereal but a member of the plant family which also includes rhubarb, sorrel and the common dock. Probably originating from China, its major producing areas are the USA, Canada, France and parts of eastern Europe.

Whole raw buckwheat

Whole hulled grains of buckwheat are a dark greenish-pink colour. The basic dish of boiled buckwheat, sometimes called *kasha*, is made from roasted grains. The unroasted grains can be used, but they are best cooked with other ingredients, as in a casserole. Buckwheat has a strong, woody flavour, and needs to be complemented by other strong flavours.

Basic cooking method (Serves 3-4)

200 g (7 oz) or 1 cup whole raw buckwheat
75 ml (3 fl oz) or 5 tbsp melted butter or oil
570 ml (1 pt) or 2½ cups water

To roast the buckwheat, sauté it in the butter or oil in a saucepan over a moderate heat. Keep turning until the grains turn an even brown. Add the water to the roasted buckwheat, bring to the boil, turn down the heat, cover the pan and simmer for 15-20 minutes. Remove the lid for the last few minutes of cooking to boil off any excess liquid. The grains should have swollen and burst.

Recipe: Unroasted Buckwheat Casserole (see p. 117).

Roasted buckwheat (Kasha)

Grains of roasted buckwheat have the same distinctive shape as the raw ones, but are a darker, reddish-brown colour. To cook them, omit the roasting stage of the cooking method above and simply boil the grains as directed in about three times their own volume of water.

Recipe: Buckwheat & Coconut Salad (see p. 90).

Buckwheat spaghetti (Soba)

Not all buckwheat spaghetti is made entirely from buckwheat flour. Often it is made from a mixture of wheat and buckwheat, so if you want gluten-free noodles, check that you are getting 100% buckwheat spaghetti. The noodles are a dark grey colour, and although they are cooked in the same way as ordinary pasta, they have a stronger flavour.

Recipe: Buckwheat Spaghetti with Mushrooms, Dill & Sour Cream (see p. 102).

Corn or maize (Mealie)

The maize plant is the largest of the cereals, often reaching a height of over 3 metres (10 feet). Originating in Mexico, it is now an important crop in tropical and sub-tropical areas throughout the world.

The grains of corn grow in tightly packed rows on an ear or 'cob', each plant producing one or two ripe ears 15-20 centimetres (6-8 inches) long. There are many varieties of maize, but the main types are dent corn, which is dried and ground into meal, popcorn, fresh sweetcorn and those grown for animal feed. The commonest types produce white or yellow grains, but there are also red, purple and even black-seeded varieties.

Sweetcorn (Corn on the cob)

This is the whole ear or cob of maize, to be cooked and eaten as soon as it is ripe. In season, fresh sweetcorn makes a delicious meal. For basic preparation and cooking, see page 31.

Popcorn

Popping corn comes from hard-grained varieties of maize. Partially dried, the moisture that remains in the grains expands and 'pops' them when they are heated.

Basic cooking method (Makes 4 cups)

90 g (3½ oz) or ½ cup popping corn
15 ml (1 tbsp) oil

It is best to pop corn in a heavy-bottomed saucepan with a lid. Lightly brush the bottom of the pan with oil and heat it almost to burning point before adding a layer of corn, one grain thick. Cover with the lid and shake the pan over a high heat until it is all popped.

Polenta

Polenta is similar to cornmeal (see p. 18), but it usually has a fine, granular texture more like semolina than ordinary flour. Polenta is an Italian word, and in parts of Italy the dish made from it (also called polenta) is as common as pasta. Like pasta, polenta can be served hot with just about any sauce. Alternatively, it can be served as fried or grilled strips.

Basic cooking method (Serves 4)

1.1 (2 pts) or 5 cups water
5 ml (1 tsp) salt
150 g (5 oz) or 1 cup polenta

Put the water in a saucepan, add the salt and bring to a rolling boil. Gradually shake in the polenta, stirring constantly with a whisk. When all the polenta has been added, reduce the heat to the lowest possible setting and simmer very gently for about 45 minutes, stirring regularly so that it does not stick.

Either eat as a hot, very thick porridge, or allow to cool and set before cutting into strips which can then be grilled or fried.

Recipe: Polenta Pudding with Seasonal Fruit (see p. 128).

Millet

Native to Asia, millet is probably the least familiar of the cereal grains to the West. Tropical millets, of which sorghum is one, are cultivated in the arid tropics, tolerating poor soils and drought conditions which no other crop could survive. Most varieties have exceptional keeping qualities, making them a valuable reserve against times of famine in many parts of Africa, India and Pakistan.

The most widely cultivated of the temperate millets is common millet. It is high in iron and B vitamins and is gluten-free.

Whole millet

Millet has the smallest grains of any of the cereals. They grow enclosed in outer husks, which must be removed before the grains can be eaten. Hulled millet grains are tiny, round and hard and are usually pale yellow.

Cooked millet has a clean, delicate flavour and light texture that make it particularly appetizing in hot weather. It should not be combined with strongly flavoured foods as its flavour can easily be overwhelmed. Serve hot with steamed or stir-fried vegetables or allow to cool and use in salads.

Basic cooking method (Serves 4)

a knob of butter
200 g (7 oz) or 1 cup whole millet grains
675 ml (24 fl oz) or 3 cups water

Melt the butter in a saucepan, add the millet and stir over a moderate heat for 2-3 minutes until some of the grains begin to crack open. Use just enough butter to coat the grains lightly. Add the water, bring to the boil and then turn the heat right down, cover the pan and simmer without stirring for 40-45 minutes. The grains should burst open and fluff out, and all the water should be absorbed. Add a little extra water if the pan goes dry before the millet is cooked, or remove the lid for the last few minutes to boil off any excess liquid.

Millet may also be baked in the oven as a sweet pudding. Cook it exactly like Rice Pudding (see p. 130), except that millet may need slightly more liquid.

Recipe: Millet Casserole (see p. 108).

Millet flakes

Flaked millet, the whole hulled grain flattened between rollers, can be cooked into a porridge or eaten raw as part of a gluten-free muesli.

Recipe: Gluten-free Muesli (see p. 70).

Oats

Oats, native to central Europe, are an important cereal of the temperate zones. They are distinguishable from wheat and barley by their open, spreading seed head. The grains are easily digestible with a rich, creamy flavour.

In the USA, the word 'oatmeal' is often used to mean the cooked breakfast cereal known in the UK as porridge. 'Oatmeal' is used in the UK to denote raw oats milled to various degrees of coarseness, as distinct from rolled oats or oat flakes, which are flattened between rollers.

Oat groats

Oat groats are the whole oat grains, with only the husks removed. They are usually pale yellow in colour, long and thin with a smooth, shiny surface. Like other cereal grains they may be boiled and eaten whole, but they are more commonly used after being processed into one of the forms described below.

Pinhead oatmeal (Steel-cut oats)

Pinhead oatmeal is made by chopping up whole oat groats, each grain being cut into three or four pieces. When cooked it produces a coarser porridge than rolled oats, taking longer to cook but having a rather fuller flavour which many people prefer.

Recipe: Pinhead Porridge (see p. 71).

Jumbo rolled oats (Oat flakes)

Most rolled oats are partially cooked in steam before being flattened between rollers, greatly reducing the eventual cooking time needed. Jumbo rolled oats are made from oat groats and make a fairly coarse porridge.

Jumbo rolled oats can be eaten raw in muesli, or toasted with oil and honey or malt extract to make the crunchy breakfast cereal known as 'granola' (see pp. 68-69). They are also widely used in biscuits, flapjacks and crumbles.
Recipe: Basic Porridge (see p. 70).
Regular rolled oats (Oat flakes)
Regular rolled oats are made by flattening the cut pieces of oat grain known as pinhead oatmeal (see previous page). They consist therefore of smaller, finer pieces than jumbo rolled oats, and cook more quickly, giving a smoother porridge. Like jumbo oats, they have usually been partially cooked in steam before going through the rollers.

Commercial brands of instant porridge oats, which may have been precooked for longer and rolled more thinly to reduce cooking time to a minimum, tend to be a good deal more expensive than the rolled oats available in wholefood shops.

Regular rolled oats can be used in parkin and flapjack, and as a decorative topping on the crust of brown bread.
Recipe: Oat & Raisin Biscuits (see p. 143).
Oat bran and germ
The bran and germ of the oat grain is a fine brown powder which can be made into a quick and nourishing gruel or thin porridge and then flavoured with a little puréed fruit or vegetables. This gruel is suitable for babies from about 9 months on. Oat bran and germ can also be sprinkled over savoury dishes.

Rice

Rice is one of the world's two most important food crops, the other being wheat. Rice originated in Asia and is now grown throughout the humid tropical and sub-tropical regions. India and China are the largest producers, though rice is also widely grown in the USA and Italy.

Rice is a good source of starch, although it contains less protein than other cereal grains. There are many varieties of rice, but they fall into the basic categories of short grain and long grain. Short grain rice has a softer, stickier texture and is often used in Japanese and Chinese cooking. Long grain rice has dry, separate grains and is often used in Indian cooking. The choice is really a matter of personal preference. Long grain rice usually takes longer to cook.

The practice of refining the grains of rice by polishing or 'pearling' them removes the bran and germ to leave a smooth white grain. This has led to diseases such as beri-beri in areas where people have had little other than white rice to eat. Unpolished brown rice is widely available, and some wholefood shops also stock rice that has been organically grown.
Brown rice
Simple boiled brown rice makes a delicious accompaniment to almost any savoury dish. Rice is often cooked badly; but if you use the following method the rice will be tender but firm with a delicate flavour that does not need to be helped by a lot of salt.

Rice can be served hot with any savoury dish. Nutritionally, it makes a particularly good combination with lentils, beans or peas.

Basic cooking method (Serves 3-4)
225 g (8 oz) or 1 cup brown rice
450 ml (16 fl oz) or 2 cups water
a little salt
Wash the rice and put it with the water in a saucepan. Bring to the boil over a moderate heat. When the water starts to boil, reduce the heat so that it is barely simmering and then leave the pan as tightly covered as possible to cook. Do *not* stir the rice, as stirring breaks up the grains and releases a starchy substance which will gather at the bottom of the pan, stick and burn.

40 minutes after it has come to the boil, all the liquid should have been absorbed and the rice should be almost cooked. If not, add more water or boil off the excess as necessary. Remove the pan from the heat and allow to stand, covered, for at least 5 minutes before serving. The rice will continue to cook during this time.

It is better to wait until the rice is cooked before seasoning it with salt. You can flavour rice during cooking with herbs, or colour it with saffron. A similar yellow colour can be achieved with turmeric, but this gives the rice a rather muddy taste. Alternatively, add a few whole coriander seeds during cooking.

The instructions given here are for short grain brown rice. Long grain will take about 5-10 minutes longer to cook, and may require a little more water.
Recipe: Rice Pudding (see p. 130).
White rice
White rice lacks the flavour and texture of brown rice, as well as much of the nutritional value. If you do wish to use it, try to find a good quality rice that has not been over-polished, such as Basmati. Remember that the more 'instant' a commercial brand of rice claims to be, the less flavour and goodness it is likely to have, and that it may even have been bleached.
Rice flakes
Rice flakes are made from either brown or white rice and are usually toasted before being flattened between rollers. They may be cooked to make a rice porridge or used as part of a gluten-free muesli.
Recipe: Gluten-free Muesli (see p. 70).
Wild rice
This wild grass, not in fact a true rice at all, is native to the Great Lakes area of North America where it was traditionally gathered by the American Indians. The difficulty of harvesting wild rice makes it very expensive, but it is thought to be rich in vitamins and particularly rich in proteins. It has a subtle, slightly 'nutty' flavour.

Rye

Rye is a hardy cereal, tolerating cold climates and poor soils. Native to Southwest Asia, it is now an important food crop in northern and eastern Europe and in some areas of Russia. It is also grown in the USA and Canada, where it is used mainly in the production of rye whisky. Rye is the only cereal other than wheat that contains enough gluten to be suitable for making leavened bread, although it is usually mixed with wheat flour. It is particularly high in B vitamins, potassium and magnesium.

Whole rye grain
Rye grains are thin and long, with a greenish-grey colour and a distinctive, slightly bitter flavour.

Cooked rye grains make a good addition to a thick vegetable soup or stew, combining particularly well with sweet root vegetables such as carrots or parsnips. Rye is also fairly easy to sprout (see p. 23).
Basic cooking method (Serves 4)
225 g (8 oz) or 1 cup whole rye grains
675 ml (24 fl oz) or 3 cups water
Wash the rye thoroughly before adding it to the water in a saucepan. Bring to the boil, reduce the heat, cover the pan and simmer for about 45 minutes. The grains should have started to burst. Drain through a sieve.
Recipe: Rye Grain & Vegetable Broth (see p. 78).
Cracked rye (Kibbled rye)
Cracked rye, produced in the same way as cracked wheat, is used mainly in the making of heavy, coarse rye breads popular in northern and eastern Europe.
Recipe: Soak a spoonful overnight and add to Basic Wholewheat Bread (see p. 149).
Rye flakes
Rye flakes are whole rye grains that have been flattened and lightly toasted. They will add a pleasant tangy flavour to a muesli.
Recipe: Granola 1 (see p. 68).

Sago and tapioca

Sago and tapioca are not derived from cereals, but are used in a similar way to many cereal products. Sago is a granular product, prepared from the starchy pith of the sago palm. Tapioca, similar in appearance to sago although usually consisting of smaller granules, is prepared from the starch of the cassava root. Both products may be used to make the sweet puddings which bear their names. Nutritionally, their value is strictly limited as they consist exclusively of carbohydrate.
Recipe: Apricot & Orange Sago Cream (see p. 121).

Soya

Soya is not a cereal crop but a pulse, a member of the family that includes all the beans, lentils and peas. The soya products listed in this section are included because of their similar usage to many cereal products. Whole soya beans and other soya products such as miso, tamari and tofu are dealt with elsewhere (see pp. 50 and 51 respectively).
Soya flakes
Soya flakes are made by toasting and then flattening whole soya beans. They can be cooked into a porridge or baked in biscuits and crumbles.
Soya grits
Soya grits are crushed and cooked soya beans. They can be used in any dish to replace whole soya beans, for example in pasties, pies and bean loaves, and will take far less time to cook.
Recipe: Soya & Oat Porridge (see p. 71).
Soya bran
This is the coarse outer layer of the soya bean, milled into small flakes. Like wheat bran, it may be sprinkled on breakfast cereal or added

WHEAT FLOUR	METHOD OF MILLING	EXTRACTION RATE	REMOVED	ADDED	DESCRIPTION AND USES
Wholewheat or wholemeal wheat flour	Stoneground	100%	Nothing	Nothing	Best food value and best flavour, especially if stoneground and freshly milled. Wholewheat bread, cakes, pastries, etc.
	Roller mill	95-100%	Bran and some germ removed as part of the milling process	Some of the germ and all but the largest particles of the bran re-added	
Wheatmeal or brown flour	Stoneground	80-90%	Some bran and germ	Nothing	Lighter than wholewheat in colour, texture and taste. Bread, cakes, pastries, etc.
	Roller mill	80-90%	All bran and germ	Usually only bran re-added. Chemical additives may also be present	
Malt-blend or granary-style flour	Stoneground	80-90%	Some bran and germ	Whole and milled malted grains	Makes sweet, crunchy granary-style bread, either alone or mixed with wholewheat flour
	Roller mill	70-75%	All bran and germ	Whole and milled malted grains, plus bleaching agents and improvers	
Strong white flour	Roller mill	70-75%	All bran and germ	Usually the full range of chemical additives, though unbleached flour can be found	Lightest of all, but with least flavour and least food value. White bread, cakes, pastries, etc.

Flour strength

The 'strength' of a flour is a measure of its gluten content. Gluten is a form of protein, a sticky substance of great elasticity contained in the starchy part of the grain. Wheat contains the most gluten, rye rather less. Maize, rice, millet and the non-cereals buckwheat, chickpea, soya, potato, sago and tapioca are all entirely gluten-free.

When flour is mixed with water and yeast in breadmaking, the gluten in the flour forms 'strands' which trap the bubbles of carbon dioxide given off by the fermenting yeast. This gives an aerated, elastic dough which rises well and means that the loaf will hold together when sliced.

Strong flours contain 10-14 per cent gluten; soft flours contain 7-10 per cent gluten. Only wheat and rye flour contain enough gluten to make yeasted bread. Of the wheat flours, white flour is stronger than wholewheat flour because it has had all the bran and germ (which contain no gluten) removed.

The stronger wheats are valued by commercial millers and bakers for their high gluten content, which gives lighter, higher loaves, but the softer types are widely acknowledged to have the best flavour. The stronger wheats come mainly from the USA and Canada and the softer types come mainly from Europe, including the UK, and Australia.

Strong flours are generally used for bread and for puff and flaky pastries. Soft flours are good for sauces, cakes, shortcrust pastry and biscuits, giving them a soft, melt-in-the-mouth texture. The gluten in a flour can be affected by the handling it is given and also by other ingredients. Heavy kneading and working of a dough will actually make the gluten more elastic, and therefore stronger, as will adding salt or an acidic ingredient such as lemon juice. Gentle handling of a mixture will help keep the gluten content soft, as will the addition of sugar or fat. This is why many cakes and sweet or fruit breads do not rise as much as bread made from strong wheat flour.

Storage

As with grains, heat, moisture and light are the main causes of deterioration in flour. Use airtight containers and store away from direct heat or light. A cool, dry larder or cellar is ideal.

Stoneground wholemeal flour is best used as freshly milled as possible. If you can, buy only the quantity you need for the next month or two, although it should keep for longer. There are a few small mills, including the Neal's Yard Flour Mill in London, where it is possible to buy really fresh flour. Alternatively, you may wish to consider buying a domestic hand or electric stonegrinding mill, so that you can grind your own.

FLOURS Per 100 g (4 oz)	Water	Protein	Fat	Carbohydrate	Fibre	Vitamin A	Vitamin B₁	Vitamin B₂	Vitamin B₃	Vitamin B₆	Vitamin B₁₂	Vitamin C	Vitamin D	Vitamin E	Folic acid	Iron	Calcium	Magnesium	Sodium	Potassium	Phosphorus	Zinc
	g	g	g	g	g	µg	mg	mg	mg	mg	µg	mg	µg	mg	µg	mg	mg	mg	mg	mg	mg	mg
Recommended daily allowance	N	80M 60W	N	N	25-30	750	1.5	1.5	18	1.5	3	30	2.5	8	200	12	500	250	2500	2500	500	15
Buckwheat flour	N	4.8	1	28.1	1	0	0.22	0.06	1.8	0.22	0	0	N	N	N	1.8	N	N	N	N	120	N
Cornmeal	12	9.3	3.3	71.5	N	**25**	0.3	0.08	1.8	N	0	3	N	N	N	4.2	17	N	1	284	N	N
Millet flour	13	5.8	1.7	75.4	N	0	0.68	0.19	2.8	N	0	0	N	N	N	N	40	N	21	365	N	N
Oatmeal	9	12.4	**8.7**	72.8	7	0	0.5	0.1	1	0.12	0	0	0	0.8	60	4.1	55	110	33	370	380	**3**
Potato flour	N	8.8	0.88	**88**	1.7	Tr	0.45	0.15	3.7	Tr	0	**20.6**	N	N	N	**18.8**	36	N	37	1706	194	N
Rice flour	12	6.4	0.8	80.4	N	0	0.1	0.05	2.1	N	0	0	0	0	N	1.9	24	N	5	241	N	N
Rye flour	**15**	8.2	2	75.9	N	0	0.4	0.22	1	0.35	0	0	0	0.8	78	2.7	32	92	1	410	360	2.8
Soya flour	7	**36.8**	7.2	28.2	**11.9**	N	**0.75**	**0.36**	2.4	**0.57**	0	0	0	N	N	6.9	210	**240**	1	**1660**	**640**	N
Wheat flours – brown 85%	14	12.8	2	68.8	7.5	0	0.42	0.06	4.2	0.3	0	0	0	Tr	51	3.6	150	110	4	280	270	2.4
– plain white	13	9.8	1.2	80.1	3.4	0	0.33	0.02	2	0.15	0	0	0	Tr	22	2.4	150	20	2	140	110	0.7
– self-raising	13	9.3	1.2	77.5	3.7	0	0.28	0.02	1.5	0.15	0	0	0	Tr	19	2.6	**350**	42	**350**	170	510	0.6
– strong white	**15**	11.3	1.2	74.8	3	0	0.31	0.03	2	0.15	0	0	0	Tr	31	2.2	140	36	3	130	130	0.9
– wholewheat 100%	14	13.2	2	65.8	9.6	0	0.46	0.08	**5.6**	0.5	0	0	0	1	57	4	35	140	3	360	340	**3**

KEY

All wholefoods are uncooked unless stated otherwise. Some wholefoods may not be included in the chart, as there is currently no nutritional data available. **g**: grams **mg**: milligrams **µg**: micrograms **N**: no available data **Tr**: trace **M**: adult men **W**: adult women. The recommended daily allowances are averages and vary depending on age, occupation and metabolism. Figures in bold type indicate the wholefood with the highest level of nutrient.

Barley flour
(Barley meal)

Barley flour is milled from pot barley. Because some of the bran is removed along with the husk it has a rather pale colour. Barley has a very low gluten content, making it unsuitable for use in leavened doughs unless combined with wheat flour, but it can be used in biscuits and cakes or to make a delicious unleavened barley bread.

Recipe: Dervish Barley Bread (see p. 152).

Buckwheat flour

Buckwheat flour, milled from whole raw buckwheat, is grey in colour, darker even than wholemeal rye flour. Buckwheat contains no gluten, so the flour is not suitable on its own for making yeasted bread. Delicious buckwheat pancakes can be made, however, using either buckwheat flour on its own or a mixture of buckwheat flour and wheat flour.

Buckwheat flour is particularly useful to those on gluten-free diets. Undiluted, its flavour is likely to be too strong for most people, but a little will add a pleasant bite to cakes and biscuits made with other flours.

Recipe: Buckwheat Pancakes with Tomato Sauce (see p. 101).

Chickpea flour
(Gram/Besun flour)

Gram is the Indian word for any pulse, whether lentils, peas or beans. Gram flour is most commonly milled from whole chickpeas. It is widely used in Indian cookery, made into samosas and bhajis and mixed with wholewheat flour to make chapatis. It is also used for thickening sauces, to which it gives a pleasant, nutty flavour. Like all the pulses, chickpeas contain no gluten.

Recipe: Onion Bhajis with Yogurt Sauce (see p. 86).

Cornmeal
(Maize/Mealie meal)

Cornmeal is available in various degrees of coarseness and is usually a strong yellow colour. This is 100% wholemeal corn, preferably stoneground. Do not confuse it with the much paler meal sometimes available, from which the germ has been removed and which therefore has little food value and a very thin flavour, or with the highly refined corn starch sold as a thickening agent.

Corn contains no gluten at all, so cornmeal is not suitable for making yeasted bread unless combined with wheat flour. But it may be used on its own or mixed with other flours to make an enormous range of soda breads, soups, muffins, cakes, pancakes and dumplings. It may also be cooked as porridge, and is a very pleasant alternative to oat porridge. The method is shown below.

Serve hot, like oat porridge, with milk or cream. When cold, it may be cut into slices, fried in a little butter and served with honey or jam for a delicious 'next day' breakfast.

Basic cooking method (Serves 4)
150 g (5 oz) or 1 cup cornmeal
675 ml (24 fl oz) or 3 cups cold water
a little salt

Mix the cornmeal with about a third of the cold water. Put the rest of the water in a saucepan, add a little salt and bring to the boil. Stir in the mixture of meal and water, using a whisk to prevent lumps forming. Stir continuously over a moderate heat until a thick porridge consistency is reached. Remove the pan from the heat, cover and leave to stand for 5 minutes before serving.

As with oat porridge, any left over can be cooled and stored overnight in the refrigerator, where it will set firm.

Recipe: Use instead of chickpea flour in Tomato Soup (see p. 79).

Malt-blend or granary-style flour

Granary is, in fact, the brand name of one manufacturer's malted blend, but it seems to be widely used to describe any malt-blend flour. These flours are based on either white or wheatmeal flour, with an addition of malted wheat grains and ground malted wheat grains, also called malted flour. Crushed rye grains are also sometimes added.

The malt-blends based on white flour are likely to contain some chemical bleaching agents and improvers. Those based on stoneground wheatmeal flour are usually free from chemical additives.

Malt-blend flours are fairly pale in colour, with a scattering of dark malted grains. They are strong flours, intended for breadmaking, the malted grains giving the bread a distinctive, sweet, nutty flavour and crunchy texture. If you want to tone down the sweet, crunchy effect, you can mix malt-blend and ordinary wholewheat flour half-and-half.

Recipe: Granary-style Bread (see p. 153).

Masa harina

This is Mexican cornmeal (maize flour) which has been treated with lime, and is used to make tortillas. A tortilla dough is made from masa harina, water and salt. Balls of the dough are flattened into rounds and then fried in a hot, ungreased frying pan.

Maslin

Maslin means mixed, and usually refers to a mixture of rye and wheat. In the past, rye and wheat were often sown together as a mixed crop, and the resulting mixture of grains was milled and then baked as maslin bread, which was the common English bread for hundreds of years.

Millet flour

Millet contains no gluten, so millet flour is not suitable on its own for making yeasted bread. Because its delicate flavour is easily swamped, it is best not mixed with other flours, but it can be used instead of oatmeal or cornmeal to make muffins and pancakes. It can also be cooked like semolina into an easy pudding.
Recipe: Rhubarb & Banana Crumble (see p. 129).

Oatmeal (fine)

This fine oat flour is the main ingredient of traditional Scottish bannocks and oatcakes, cooked on a griddle above an open flame. It has a very low gluten content, so its use in the baking of leavened bread is limited, but a small proportion of fine oatmeal (up to a quarter) added to wholewheat flour gives a rich, moist bread with a good flavour and excellent nutritional value. A half-and-half mixture of fine oatmeal and wholewheat flour makes delicious sweet muffins and wonderful pancakes. (For pancakes, allow the mixed batter to stand for at least 1 hour before using.)
Recipe: Dervish Barley Bread (see p. 152).

Oatmeal (medium)

Medium oatmeal is a coarse oat flour, milled from hulled oat groats. It can be used in biscuits, scones and crumble toppings, or added to soups or wholewheat bread and cakes for extra texture and a rich, creamy oat flavour.
Recipe: Creamed Cauliflower Soup (see p. 73).

Potato flour or potato starch
(Farina)

Potato flour is not in any sense a wholefood, but it deserves mention because of its value, especially in gluten-free diets, as a thickener. It can be mixed with an ordinary wheat flour to make potato bread or potato scones, although a far better flavour and food value can be achieved by using freshly cooked and mashed whole potatoes instead.
Recipe: Cheesecake (see p. 122).

Rice flour

Refined rice flour is used in commercial catering as a non-stick dusting for breads and pastries and as a thickening agent. However, 100% wholemeal rice flour milled from whole brown rice is far better value as a food. Rice is totally gluten-free, so wholemeal rice flour cannot be used to make an ordinary yeasted loaf, but it can be used to make a variety of gluten-free cakes, biscuits and pancakes. It can also be cooked in a pan with milk or water, like wholemeal semolina (see p. 15).

Rye flour

Rye flour may be either 100% wholemeal or white. White rye flour, from which most or all of the bran has been removed, has of course less flavour and a lower food value. Wholemeal rye flour is darker than wholemeal flour, with a distinctive grey colour. Its strong flavour makes it most suitable for bread, though in central Europe it is also used for biscuits and gingerbread, as well as for the well-known Scandinavian crispbreads.

Rye contains less gluten than wheat, so rye bread always tends to be heavier than an equivalent wheat bread. The greater the proportion of rye flour used, the denser the bread is likely to be. For this reason, most rye bread contains at least half wheat flour. If you do use only wholemeal rye flour, do not expect your bread to be very much darker than wholewheat bread. The European *schwarzbrod* or black rye bread contains molasses, coffee, chocolate or other colourings, and is in fact often made from white rye flour.
Recipe: Rye Bread (see p. 154).

Soya flour

Soya flour is made by partially cooking soya beans and grinding them into a creamy yellow-coloured flour. It is available in three forms: full-fat, medium-fat and fat-free. Rich in protein like all soya products, it can be used to enrich whole wheat bread and cakes, giving them a full, creamy flavour.

As with all the pulses, soya beans contain no gluten, so soya flour may be used for gluten-free cakes. For yeasted breads, it should be used in combination with wheat. Soya flour can also be used in cakes, puddings, pastries and biscuits. Mixed to a cream with water it makes a good substitute for egg glaze.
Recipe: Apple, Soya & Almond Pudding (see p. 120).

Strong white flour

White flour is not stoneground. The bran and germ have been removed not by sieving but by the steel roller milling process, described on page 16. Most white flour has been bleached, so try to find a supplier of unbleached strong white flour if you can. Slightly creamy in colour, unbleached flour will produce a less anaemic bread than white flour, with a good yellow-gold crust.

The plain 'household' flours available in any grocery or supermarket are not intended for breadmaking. It is better to buy a strong white flour which not only makes good white bread but which can also be used as a general-purpose flour for pastry and sponges, and for thickening gravies and sauces. Adding a small proportion of strong white flour to wholewheat flour in breadmaking increases the strength of the dough, as the strong white flour releases its gluten quickly.
Recipe: Basic White Bread (see p. 150).

Wheatmeal or 'brown' flour

Wheatmeal is wheat flour with an extraction rate between that of wholewheat and that of white flour, normally 80-90% (see chart on p. 17). Recent legislation in the UK has prohibited the use of the term 'wheatmeal' and requires flours of this type to be called simply 'brown'.

Wheatmeal is paler in colour than wholewheat flour, but still quite a bit darker than white flour. For many people it is a happy medium as it makes lighter bread and cakes than wholewheat flour, but has a better flavour and a higher nutritional content than white flour.

100% Wholewheat or wholemeal wheat flour

Wholewheat flour is simply milled wheat grains, with nothing removed. It is a light golden brown, and close inspection should reveal the dark particles of bran and the yellow flecks of germ which give it its colour. It comes in various grades, from fine to coarse. At Neal's Yard Bakery, a fairly coarse wholewheat flour is used to make all the bread, pitta breads and pizzas, and a finer wholewheat flour, also stoneground, is used for all the cakes, sponges, scones, biscuits, pastries and croissants. There are, in fact, very few baked goods that cannot be made successfully using wholewheat flour. Wholewheat breads and cakes are not, of course, as light as those made with white flour, but nor are they as pallid or bland in appearance and taste.
Recipe: Basic Wholewheat Bread (see p.149).

DRIED BEANS, PEAS & LENTILS

Aduki beans ☐   Cannellini beans ☐   Lentils ☐   Soya beans ☐
Black-eyed beans ☐   Chickpeas ☐   Marrowfat peas ☐   Split peas ☐
Black kidney beans ☐ Flageolet beans ☐   Mung beans ☐
Broad beans   Ful medames ☐   Pinto beans ☐
Butter beans ☐   Haricot beans   Red kidney beans ☐

☐ Pictured opposite page 17

Beans, peas and lentils are pulses, the seeds of pod-bearing leguminous plants. Some are eaten fresh, such as green peas, green beans and runner beans; most are eaten dried.

For thousands of years fresh seeds, peas and beans have been dried and stored. Many poorer cultures still rely on dried pulses for their survival, especially during times of drought and crop failure. Beans have sometimes been regarded as a poor man's food, but in these days of growing food shortages and increased nutritional awareness their true value is recognised.

The growing cycle for most beans is about three months. The majority prefer a warm, temperate climate though hardier strains do grow successfully in colder northern areas. Because of their durable nature, dried beans, peas and lentils are not subjected to additives, a rare phenomenon in this day and age. But do rinse and sort them through before you soak and cook them, because it is common to find small twigs, pods and stones that have not been removed.

Nutritional value

Dried beans, peas and lentils are highly nutritious, containing protein, vitamins, minerals and fibre. They are particularly high in vitamins B_1 and B_2, iron and potassium, and also contain very little fat. Dried pulses form a vital part of a wholefood vegetarian diet.

The protein which pulses contain is incomplete, that is, it contains only a certain number of the amino acids needed to make up a complete protein (see p. 8). To make up a complete protein, beans can be combined with either or all of the following: grains, nuts, seeds or milk. An exception is the soya bean, which contains all of the essential amino acids and is therefore a complete protein.

Storage

Once cooked and cooled, beans may be kept for several days in an airtight container in the refrigerator, or frozen (see p. 65). Beans can last for years and still be capable of germinating in the right conditions, as has been proved with legumes excavated from Inca temples and the tombs of the pyramids. However, as with most foods, the fresher they are the better. In general, you should not store beans for more than a year. Buy them in small quantities and store in clean, dry airtight jars. Store away from sunlight, and do not keep in glass jars unless you are going to use them up very quickly.

Soaking

Most beans need soaking and cooking before eating, the exact times varying according to type and age. Beans triple in size when soaked and cooked, so be sure to place them in a sufficiently large bowl or saucepan. Rinse them well and remove any stones or debris. Cover with three times their volume of water and leave to stand for the suggested soaking time (see the chart opposite). Do not soak for more than 12 hours as the beans may begin to ferment. Lentils and split peas do not need soaking.

Alternatively, to speed up the soaking process, put the beans in a saucepan covered with three times their volume of cold water, bring to the boil and cook for 5 minutes. Remove from the heat and leave to stand for at least 1 hour before cooking.

Cooking

When you have soaked the beans, transfer to a saucepan with their liquid (which will contain vitamins and minerals from the beans) and top up with fresh cold water if necessary to cover. Do not add salt during cooking as it will toughen the skins. Cover with a lid and boil gently until cooked. Remove one or two, let cool a little and then taste.

All beans can be cooked this way except kidney beans and soya beans. Black and red kidney beans sometimes contain a toxic substance on the outer skin which can be removed by vigorous boiling for the first 15 minutes of the cooking time. Soya beans contain a substance called trypsin-inhibitor, which prevents the body from absorbing protein, so they should be boiled vigorously for the first hour. If you are using a pressure cooker, fast boiling will happen automatically.

You can save time by cooking extra beans and refrigerating them once they have cooled. They will keep happily there for 3-4 days in an airtight container. Chickpeas and soya beans should be rinsed daily, however.

Soaking and cooking chart

DRIED BEANS, PEAS AND LENTILS	SOAKING TIME	COOKING TIME	PRESSURE-COOKING TIME
Aduki beans	3-4 hours	1 hour	15 minutes
Black-eyed beans	8-12 hours	1 hour	15 minutes
Black kidney beans	8-12 hours	1½ hours, boiling vigorously for the first 15 minutes	20 minutes
Broad beans	8-12 hours	1½ hours	20 minutes
Butter beans	8-12 hours	1½ hours	20 minutes
Cannellini beans	8-12 hours	1½ hours	20 minutes
Chickpeas	8-12 hours	3 hours	40 minutes
Flageolet beans	8-12 hours	1½ hours	20 minutes
Ful medames	8-12 hours	2 hours	30 minutes
Haricot beans	8-12 hours	1½ hours	20 minutes
Lentils: large / small	none / none	30 minutes / 20 minutes	10 minutes / 10 minutes
Marrowfat peas	8-12 hours	1 hour	15 minutes
Mung beans	4-8 hours	45 minutes	10 minutes
Pinto beans	8-12 hours	1½ hours	20 minutes
Red kidney beans	8-12 hours	1½ hours, boiling vigorously for the first 15 minutes	20 minutes
Soya beans	8-12 hours	4 hours, boiling vigorously for the first hour	50 minutes
Split peas: green / yellow	none / none	30 minutes / 30 minutes	10 minutes / 10 minutes

DRIED BEANS, PEAS & LENTILS Per 100 g (4 oz)	Water	Protein	Fat	Carbohydrate	Fibre	Vitamin A	Vitamin B₁	Vitamin B₂	Vitamin B₃	Vitamin B₆	Vitamin B₁₂	Vitamin C	Vitamin D	Vitamin E	Folic acid	Iron	Calcium	Magnesium	Sodium	Potassium	Phosphorus	Zinc
	g	g	g	g	g	µg	mg	mg	mg	mg	µg	mg	µg	mg	µg	mg	mg	mg	mg	mg	mg	mg
Recommended daily allowance	N	**80M 60W**	N	N	25-30	750	1.5	1.5	18	1.5	3	30	2.5	8	200	12	500	250	2500	2500	500	15
Aduki beans	**16**	21.5	1.6	58.4	4.3	6	0.5	0.1	2.5	N	0	0	N	N	N	4.8	75	N	7	N	350	N
Black-eyed beans	12	22.7	1.6	56.8	N	10	0.59	0.22	**7.7**	0.48	0	1	0	N	**439**	6.5	110	53	6	688	360	N
Broad beans	14	25	1.2	51.8	6	65	0.45	0.19	6	N	0	0	0	N	N	4.2	104	N	8	1123	360	N
Butter beans	12	19.1	1.1	49.8	21.6	Tr	0.45	0.13	2.5	0.58	0	0	0	N	110	5.9	85	164	**62**	**1700**	320	2.8
Chickpeas	10	20.2	5.7	50	15	190	0.5	0.15	1.5	N	0	**3**	0	N	180	6.4	140	160	40	800	300	N
Haricot beans	11	21.4	1.6	45.5	**25.4**	Tr	0.45	0.13	0.56	2.5	0	0	0	N	N	6.7	180	180	43	1160	310	2.8
Kidney beans	11	22.1	1.7	45	25	Tr	0.54	0.18	2	0.5	0	Tr	0	N	140	6.7	140	180	40	1160	410	2.8
Lentils	12	23.8	1	53.2	11.7	60	0.5	0.2	2	0.6	0	Tr	0	N	35	7.6	39	77	36	670	240	3.1
Marrowfat peas	13	21.6	1.3	50	16.7	**250**	0.6	0.3	3	0.13	0	Tr	0	Tr	33	4.7	61	116	38	990	300	3.5
Mung beans	12	22	1	35.6	22	24	0.45	0.2	2	0.5	0	Tr	0	N	140	8	100	170	28	850	330	N
Pinto beans	8	22.9	1.2	**63.7**	4.3	N	0.84	0.21	2.2	0.5	0	N	0	N	N	6.4	135	N	10	984	457	N
Soya beans	10	**34.1**	**17.7**	28.6	N	24	**1.1**	**0.31**	2.2	**0.88**	0	N	0	N	100	**8.4**	**226**	**265**	5	1677	**554**	N
Split peas	12	22.1	1	56.6	11.9	150	0.7	0.2	3.2	0.13	0	Tr	0	Tr	33	5.4	33	130	38	910	270	**4**

KEY
All wholefoods are uncooked unless stated otherwise. Some wholefoods may not be included in the chart, as there is currently no nutritional data available.
g: grams **mg**: milligrams **µg**: micrograms **N**: no available data **Tr**: trace **M**: adult men **W**: adult women.   The recommended daily allowances are averages and vary depending on age, occupation and metabolism.   Figures in bold type indicate the wholefood with the highest level of nutrient.

Aduki beans
(Adzuki/Azuki/Feijoa beans)
These are small dark red or brown beans with a characteristic sweet, nutty flavour and a smooth, creamy texture.

Aduki beans originated in China and are much favoured in Japan where they are known as the 'King of beans'. They have been used medicinally for many years in China and Japan to treat kidney disorders. Aduki beans are now grown in many Southeast Asian countries but chiefly in China and Thailand.

Aduki beans can be used in soups, pâtés, savoury and sweet dishes. They may also be sprouted (see p. 23).
Recipe: Aduki Bean Soup (see p. 72).

Black-eyed beans
(Cowpeas/Black-eyed peas)
These small cream-coloured beans with black and yellow 'eyes' probably originated in Africa, where they can still be found. They reached America via the slave trade in the seventeenth century and were adopted by the Southern farmers. They are now principally grown in California.

Black-eyed beans have a smooth, creamy flavour, and are high in folic acid. They are quick to prepare and blend well with other flavours, and they are delicious in pâtés, casseroles and soups. Black-eyed beans may also be sprouted (see p. 23).
Recipe: Beanburgers (see p. 99).

Black kidney beans
(Black beans/Frijoles negros)
These large black-skinned, kidney-shaped beans are part of the huge common bean family which originated in South America. Columbus introduced the family to Europe in the sixteenth century and many varieties evolved. Black kidney beans are now principally grown in Thailand and China, and are extremely popular in America and the Caribbean. (Interestingly, Chinese 'black bean sauce' is usually made from fermented, salted soya beans and not from black beans.)

Tender and sweet-tasting, black kidney beans can be used in any recipe requiring red kidney beans, and they are delicious in soups, salads, curries and other savoury dishes. See the special cooking instructions on page 20.
Recipe: Black Bean Chilli (see p. 100).

Broad beans
(Fava/Windsor/Horse beans)
These large, pale brown beans are indigenous to Europe, and were very popular in England during the Middle Ages. They are most often eaten as a fresh vegetable, though dried broad beans are extremely popular in southern Europe. The main producers are Spain and Greece. Nutritionally, broad beans contain some protein and are quite high in potassium.
Recipe: Vegetable Pâté (see p. 87).

Butter beans
(Lima/Madagascar beans)
These large creamy-white or pale green beans originated in South America and travelled to Central and North America, Africa and the Far East. A main grower is now Madagascar. They are called butter beans because of their pale, creamy colour.

Butter beans are particularly high in sodium and potassium. They have a soft, floury texture and a smooth, succulent flavour and are delicious in salads, pâtés, soups and almost any savoury dish. Lima beans are a slightly smaller, sweeter variety of butter bean. They retain their shape well when cooked.
Recipe: Butter Bean Salad (see p. 90).

Cannellini beans
(Fazolia beans)
Cannellini are small, white kidney-shaped beans and are in fact part of the large common bean family. They are very popular in Argentina where they were first cultivated, but now they are widely grown and exported from Italy. They have a firm, fluffy texture, even after cooking, and a good savoury flavour. Try them in soups, salads and savoury dishes.
Recipe: Minestrone (see p. 77).

Chickpeas
(Garbanzos/Bengal gram/Chana dal)
These small golden brown, hazelnut-shaped beans originated in western Asia and travelled through India and the Middle East to the Mediterranean. There are several varieties, but of the two main types the Middle Eastern chickpea is slightly smaller and darker than the Mediterranean chickpea.

In India chickpeas are called *gram*, and a coarse flour is milled from them to make chapatis, breads and bhajis. In the Middle East they are used to make hummus and falafal.

Chickpeas are high in fats, vitamin A, vitamin C and folic acid, and their distinctive, nutty flavour is delicious in salads, casseroles and other savoury dishes. They may also be sprouted (see p. 23).
Recipe: Hummus (see p. 83).

Flageolet beans
(Green haricot beans)
These pale green, slender beans have a rich, delicate flavour. Part of the common bean family, they are principally grown in France and Italy, where they were first cultivated.

Flageolet beans are eaten fresh as well as dried, and are delicious in salads and savoury dishes. They can be sprouted (see p. 23).

Ful medames
(Egyptian/Field/Foul beans)
These are small, round brown beans which need a lot of cooking. Part of the broad bean family, they were first cultivated in the Middle East. They are very popular in the Middle East and Egypt, where they are now principally grown for export.

Ful medames are very good in soups, casseroles, salads and other savoury dishes.

Haricot beans
(Navy/Boston/Northern/
Pearl haricot beans)
These small, white beans are in fact a variety of common bean and are principally grown in America. They are the main ingredient in tinned baked beans. White haricot beans, or large white beans as they are sometimes known, are a larger, creamy-white variety.

Haricot beans are particularly high in fibre. They are light and tasty and can be used in pâtés, soups and other savoury dishes.
Recipe: Homestyle Baked Beans (see p. 107).

Lentils
(Dhal/Dal)
These small beans originated in Southeast Asia and spread to Europe via India and the Middle East, where they are still very popular.

There are several varieties of lentil, the most common being the small, red lentil (sometimes sold split), the larger green or continental lentil and the Indian brown lentil, which is a red lentil from which the outer casing has not been removed. Other types which are sometimes available include the yellow lentil, and the Puy lentil from France.

Lentils are particularly high in vitamin B_6. They do not require any soaking and cook quickly. Lentils will cook to a soft, grainy-textured purée, although green and Puy lentils will retain some of their shape. You can use lentils as purées or in soups, bakes, burgers and curries. They can also be sprouted very successfully (see p. 23).
Recipe: Fresh Coriander Dhal (see p. 105).

Marrowfat peas
(Whole green/Blue peas)
Marrowfat peas are large, grey-green in colour and have a floury texture. They belong to the same family as the garden or common pea. All peas were similar in appearance and taste to the marrowfat pea until the sixteenth century, when the sweet green pea we are familiar with today was developed, now the most common variety of fresh pea (see p. 30). They contain more vitamin A than any other dried bean.

Marrowfat peas are mainly grown in northern Europe. They are the main ingredient in 'mushy peas', a traditional dish in the North of England. Dried marrowfat peas need long soaking and cooking and are delicious in soups and other savoury dishes.
Recipe: Vegetable Pâté (see p. 87).

Mung beans
(Green/Golden gram)
These tiny olive-green beans originated in India but they grew quickly in popularity in the Far East and are now common in most countries from China to southern Indonesia. They are now principally grown in Australia, Thailand and China.

Mung beans are available whole, split and skinned. They are often eaten sprouted and are then known as bean sprouts or bean shoots. You can sprout your own (see p. 23).

Mung beans are high in iron and have a good flavour and creamy texture. They can be used in soups, casseroles and mixed grain dishes.
Recipe: Mung Bean Casserole (see p. 109).

Pinto beans
(Pink beans)
These medium-sized, speckled brown beans are part of the common bean family and are indigenous to Mexico. They are now grown mainly in the USA. Pinto beans are very high in carbohydrate and also contain a fair amount of vitamin B_1 and phosphorus.

In Mexico pinto beans are mainly used in chilli dishes or cooked and re-fried. They turn pink when cooked and can be used in salads, soups, pâtés and other savoury dishes. They lose their colour when cooked but not their distinctive flavour.
Recipe: Pinto, Courgette & Mushroom Bake (see p. 109).

Red kidney beans
(Mexican/Chilli beans)
These are large, shiny, red kidney-shaped beans with a rich floury texture. There are a number of varieties with colours ranging from maroon to pinky-red. Red kidney beans are a member of the common bean family. They originated in Central America and are now grown principally in East Africa and America.

Red kidney beans are very high in fibre and also contain magnesium. They are delicious in soups, casseroles and chilli dishes, and are the main ingredient in the traditional Mexican dish *chilli con carne*. For specific cooking instructions, see page 20.
Recipe: Red Bean Salad (see p. 93).

Soya beans
(Soybeans)
These small, round beans originated in China and have been cultivated there for many thousands of years. They are now principally grown in North America and Canada. Soya beans are usually yellow or black but green and red varieties are also grown.

Nutritionally, soya beans contain higher proportions of protein, fats, B vitamins and minerals than any other bean. They contain complete or first class protein, similar to that found in animal foodstuffs (see p. 8). Soya beans also have a high proportion of unsaturated fatty acids, which contain linoleic acid and lecithin. Both these substances help lower the level of cholesterol in the blood, therefore reducing the risk of hardening and thickening of the arteries and associated heart disease.

Soya beans do take a very long time to soak and cook (for special cooking instructions, see p. 20). It is possible to buy soya grits which need no soaking and cook in about 30 minutes (see p. 14 for details). When cooked, whole soya beans have a firm, nutty flavour and are delicious in salads, risottos, pâtés and other savoury dishes. They can also be sprouted (see p. 23).

By-products of the soya bean are described later in this book. They are soya flour (see p. 19), soya milk (see p. 47), soya oil (see p. 49), miso (see p. 50) and tamari and shoyu, or soya sauces (see p. 51).
Recipe: Soya Bean Salad (see p. 93).

Split peas
Split peas are a variety of common pea which have a natural tendency to split when dried and hulled. They may also be steamed and polished. Yellow split peas are grown commercially in Britain and green split peas in Belgium. They are both slightly sweeter than the whole, marrowfat pea.

Split peas need no soaking and cook quickly, but they do not retain their shape when cooked. They make excellent purées and can be used in soups, savoury bakes and pâtés. Split peas are used to make pease pudding, a traditional dish in the North of England.
Recipe: Fresh Coriander Dhal (see p. 105).

SPROUTED GRAINS, BEANS & SEEDS

First accounts of sprouting came from China many thousands of years ago, and the Aztecs and certain North American Indian tribes were also familiar with sprouted grains, beans and seeds. Although sprouted barley was used in Roman times to obtain malt for making beer, and sprouted beans were used by Captain Cook and the crew of the *Endeavour* in the eighteenth century to prevent scurvy, Europe has been slower to discover their nutritional and medicinal properties, and it is only in recent years that keen interest has developed.

Sprouted grains, seeds and beans are highly nutritious, and can be easily sprouted at home. Commercially produced sprouts are also available from most wholefood shops.

Nutritional value

Sprouted grains, beans and seeds are some of the most complete foods available to us, being rich in protein, fats, carbohydrates, fibre, vitamins, minerals and trace elements. They are generally eaten a few days after germination has taken place. At germination, a frenzy of activity occurs inside the previously dormant seed, breaking down the proteins, carbohydrates and oils into far less complex and more digestible amino acids, sugars and fatty acids. Minerals combine with enzymes to become easily assimilated by the body. Vitamins already present in the dormant seed increase dramatically in quantity and vitamin C, not present in unsprouted grains, seeds and beans, is synthesized. The vitamins found in most sprouted grains, beans and seeds are vitamins A, B_1, B_2, B_6, C, D and E.

Soya bean sprouts are the most nutritious of all, as they also contain vitamins U and K. Another exceptional sprout is alfalfa, which contains vitamin B_{12}. This essential vitamin is only found in three other plant substances, namely comfrey, seaweeds and fermented soya bean products.

What can be sprouted

Most grains, beans and seeds may be sprouted. They must be whole and neither hulled, split, cracked nor roasted. In other words, pearl barley, split peas, cracked wheat or roasted buckwheat will not sprout. It is possible to find whole, untreated grains, beans and seeds in most wholefood shops and granaries. Do not buy grains or seeds intended for pets, agricultural use or horticultural use as they may have been chemically treated.

Not all whole cereal grains can be sprouted. Wheat, rye and maize grains can be sprouted successfully (in fact, wheat grains are one of the easiest and most rewarding to sprout) but other cereal grains grow encased in an indigestible husk (see p. 11). The removal of this husk generally damages the grains too much for them to be viable for sprouting.

Using sprouts

Sprouted grains, beans and seeds are usually eaten raw in salads and sandwiches, but they can also be used in soups, stir-fries, casseroles and other savoury dishes, and can be added to breads. Wheat sprouts are particularly delicious, and fenugreek sprouts have a slightly spicy flavour. Aduki sprouts have a nutty taste that is good in salads, and alfalfa sprouts make a tasty and nutritious sandwich filling.

Sprouting grains, beans and seeds

If you have a sprouter, follow the manufacturer's instructions. Alternatively, you can use a jam jar:
1 Measure the quantity of seeds you will need. 15 ml (1 tbsp) of dried seeds is about right for a 900 g (2 lb) jam jar. The seeds may expand to eight times their original size, so be sure to have enough room for adequate air circulation and swelling. Pick over the seeds to remove any that are damaged or pieces of grit.
2 Soak the seeds for the suggested time (see chart below) in at least three times their volume of cool water, preferably filtered.
3 Drain the seeds. The soaking liquid will contain minerals, sugars and amino acids and can be reserved for soups or sauces. Put the seeds into the jam jar and stand in a warm, ventilated place out of direct sunlight (an airing cupboard is ideal).
4 All sprouting seeds need rinsing between two and five times a day (see chart below). This removes the toxic wastes produced by the multiplying cells. If the seeds are not rinsed, they will rot. After rinsing be sure to drain well, as excess water will also cause the seeds to deteriorate.
5 Within 2-6 days the sprouts will be ready for harvesting. All sprouts should be eaten within a week of germination. After this time photosynthesis begins to take place and the nutritional value of the sprouts diminishes.

Sprouting mucilaginous seeds

Mustard, cress and radish are mucilaginous seeds. They are unsuitable for sprouting in jars and are best grown as follows:
1 Place a thick layer of absorbent cloth or blotting paper on a saucer and sprinkle the seeds on top.
2 Instead of rinsing, just sprinkle water on to the seeds four or five times per day and keep the paper moist at all times. Do not allow it to dry out or become waterlogged.
3 Harvest when the sprouts are ready (see chart below).

Sprouting chart

GRAINS, SEEDS AND GRAINS	SOAKING TIME	RINSING FREQUENCY PER DAY*	HARVESTING TIME
Aduki beans	12 hours	3	3-6 days
Alfalfa seeds	6 hours	3	3-6 days
Barley grains	12 hours	3	3-4 days
Black-eyed beans	12 hours	3	3-4 days
Buckwheat grains	12 hours	3	4-5 days
Chickpeas	12 hours	4	5-6 days
Cress seeds	none	5	4-5 days
Dried peas	12 hours	3	3-5 days
Fenugreek seeds	12 hours	3	4-5 days
Flageolet beans	12 hours	3	4-5 days
Haricot beans	12 hours	3	4-5 days
Lentils	8 hours	3	2-5 days
Millet grains	12 hours	3	2-3 days
Mung beans	12 hours	3	2-6 days
Mustard seeds	none	4	4-5 days
Pumpkin seeds	12 hours	3	2-4 days
Radish seeds	none	5	4-5 days
Rice	12 hours	3	2-3 days
Rye grains	12 hours	3	3-5 days
Sesame seeds	8 hours	3	3-4 days
Soya beans	10 hours	4	2-6 days
Sunflower seeds	12 hours	3	2-6 days
Wheat grains	12 hours	3	2-4 days

*Note: Sprouting seeds should ideally be rinsed at least three times a day, but if this is impossible once in the morning and once in the evening will be sufficient.

FRESH VEGETABLES

Artichokes, globe ☐
Asparagus ☐
Aubergines ☐
Avocados ☐
Beetroots
Broad beans
Broccoli ☐
Brussels sprouts
Cabbages
Carrots
Cauliflowers
Celeriac ☐

Celery
Chard
Chicory ☐
Courgettes ☐
Cucumbers
Endive ☐
Fennel ☐
French beans
Jerusalem artichokes ☐
Kohlrabi ☐
Leeks
Lettuces

Marrows, pumpkins and
  squashes ☐
Mushrooms
Okra ☐
Olives ☐
Onions
Parsnips
Peas
Peppers ☐
Potatoes
Radicchio ☐
Radishes ☐

Runner beans
Salsify/Scorzonera ☐
Seakale
Spinach
Swedes
Sweetcorn
Sweet potatoes ☐
Tomatoes
Turnips
Watercress
Yams

☐ Pictured opposite page 32

An essential part of the human diet since prehistoric times, the serious cultivation of vegetables began as the early hunter-gatherers gradually relinquished their nomadic lifestyles. Initially farmed in China, the Middle East and South America, many varieties of vegetables were brought to Europe as a result of conquest and exploration. Today the production of vegetables for domestic consumption is a major industry in many countries and there is a wide range of both local and imported produce to choose from.

Vegetables play an important role in a wholefood diet. Served raw or cooked, they offer a rich variety of attractive colours, textures and flavours to add interest to your diet. They are made up primarily of water (at least 80 per cent of content in many cases); the rest is carbohydrate, protein and fat. They are also a valuable source of fibre, and contain a range of vitamins and minerals. The leafy vegetables tend to be particularly nutritious and you should include at least one serving in your daily diet.

Sources
Ideally, vegetables should be organically grown (see p. 7) and eaten straight from your own garden. If this is not possible, you should try to buy organically grown vegetables. These are increasingly available with the growth of public awareness of the danger of chemically grown foods, and can even be found in many supermarkets.

Locally grown produce is also recommended. You should familiarize yourself with the growing seasons of vegetables and make the most of them when they are cheap and plentiful.

Additives
Unless you grow your own or can buy organically grown vegetables (see p. 7), it is probable that many of the vegetables you buy or the soil in which they are grown will have been treated with some sort of chemical spray or pesticide. Since many vegetables are imported it is possible that preservatives or mould inhibitors have been used. The simplest answer is to peel them, but since the most nutritious part of many vegetables is just beneath the skin, this would be a terrible waste. However, a good wash or scrub with a vegetable brush will remove excess chemicals, without removing essential nutrients.

Choosing vegetables
The best quality, freshest vegetables will have the finest flavour and are the most nutritionally sound. When choosing vegetables at your greengrocer or local market, do not be dissuaded from holding them and checking them as necessary to ensure you get good quality produce.

1 Choose firm, undamaged vegetables.
2 Avoid limp, faded or withered vegetables.
3 Avoid vegetables with bruising, soft spots or frostbite.
4 Do not buy more than you need, especially of salad vegetables. These will keep in the refrigerator but are usually best if bought and consumed on the day of purchase.
5 Do not be persuaded always to buy the cheapest: this is often false economy as you may have to throw some away.
6 Do not always assume the bigger the better. Very often the smaller the vegetable, the sweeter and tastier it will be.
7 Make the most of vegetables with a short seasonal availability, such as globe artichokes, asparagus, peas and beans.

Storage
Most vegetables will keep for a few days in a cool, airy place. An old-fashioned larder with open ventilation to the outside is ideal for this, or the vegetable compartment of a refrigerator. Wire or plastic vegetable racks are also suitable but make sure that you position them in a cool place and not next to the cooker or any other machine which gives off heat. As a general rule, vegetables to be stored should not be washed, sliced or packed too closely together.

In general, if your lifestyle and budget allow, leave the greengrocer to worry about storage. Shopping daily or every couple of days means less to struggle home with and hopefully the freshest, best quality vegetables of the day.

If growing your own, pick as required or freeze (see p. 63).

Cooking methods
Ideally, the majority of vegetables require a minimum of cooking if their character, taste and freshness are to be maintained. To prepare, wash well or scrub with a vegetable scrubber and trim or top and tail as required.
Baking
This simple method of cooking vegetables needs little personal attention and leaves the top of the stove free for other food.

Prepare the vegetables by dicing, chopping or slicing as desired. Place in a lidded ovenproof dish, brush with melted butter or oil, season to taste and bake in a preheated oven, 200°C (400°F/Gas 6) until tender.

This method is suitable for root vegetables and can also be used for soft vegetables such as courgettes, marrows and mushrooms. Root vegetables will take about 1-1½ hours to cook and soft vegetables 15-30 minutes, depending on size.

Boiling

Boiling vegetables has become less popular because of the loss of valuable nutrients into the water and the tendency to over-cook. However, it is still a useful cooking method and the vegetable liquid can be used to make stocks and sauces.

First prepare the vegetables by trimming, dicing, chopping or slicing as required. Bring a saucepan of water to the boil and add a little salt if desired. Add the vegetables to the water. Do not use too much water: the vegetables just need to be covered. Cover the pan, return to the boil and simmer until tender.

Most vegetables can be boiled. They are best left whole so that fewer of the nutrients can leak into the water.

Braising

First, prepare the vegetables by dicing, chopping or slicing as desired. Blanch the vegetables by plunging into boiling water for 2-3 minutes. Drain, heat a little vegetable oil or butter in a heavy-bottomed saucepan and lightly brown the vegetables.

Now add 150 ml ($\frac{1}{4}$ pt) of vegetable stock or water to each 450 g (1 lb) of prepared vegetables. Cover with a tightly fitting lid and simmer gently until cooked. Remove the vegetables. The liquid can be reduced to make a sauce by rapid boiling, or by thickening with arrowroot or kuzu (see p. 50).

Alternatively, put the browned vegetables into a lidded oven-proof dish with a little hot liquid and cook in a preheated 180°C (350°F/Gas 4) oven for 15-20 minutes or until tender.

Braising is particularly suitable for root vegetables, but can also be used for fennel, leeks, celery, endive and red cabbage.

Deep-frying

Make sure you choose a vegetable oil with a high smoke point for deep-frying, such as groundnut, sesame or soya oil.

First chop, slice or prepare the vegetables as desired and pat dry to prevent the oil spitting. Heat the oil in a deep, heavy-bottomed saucepan, preferably fitted with a wire net with which to raise or lower the food. Heat to approximately 190°C (375°F/Gas 5). To check whether the oil is hot enough, drop in a cube of bread and watch if it browns within 40 seconds.

Lower the prepared vegetables into the hot oil. Fry until tender and crisp and then drain well on kitchen paper.

Deep-frying is suitable for potato chips, onion rings and vegetables coated with batter (Japanese tempura-style).

Pressure-cooking

Vegetables cook extremely quickly in a pressure cooker. Prepare the vegetables or leave whole as desired and follow the manufacturer's instructions for cooking times.

Use this method for older, tougher vegetables rather than tender young ones as these can easily overcook.

Shallow-frying or sautéeing

For shallow-frying or sautéeing, first prepare the vegetables by dicing, chopping or slicing. Dry on kitchen paper.

Heat a little vegetable oil or butter in a heavy-bottomed frying pan and add the vegetables. Cook over a high heat for 1-2 minutes, then reduce the heat and cook until tender.

Shallow-frying is suitable for soft vegetables such as courgettes, tomatoes and aubergines, and also for root vegetables.

Steaming

There are a variety of petal steamers available designed to fit inside a lidded saucepan. A colander or sieve will do as well, so long as the saucepan lid fits snugly into the top and the steam from the boiling water does not escape round the sides.

Vegetables may be left whole if small enough, or they can be diced, chopped or sliced as desired. Cover the bottom of the saucepan with 5-7 ml (2-3 in) of water and bring to the boil. Add the vegetables in the steamer, cover and steam until tender. Steaming takes a few minutes longer than boiling.

All vegetables may be steamed.

Stir-frying

The tradition of stir-frying or quick-frying comes from the East. A wok (special pan) is best suited for the purpose. Its shallow, rounded shape allows you to use very little oil, yet still have a large surface area to cook in. Be sure to use vegetable oil with a high smoke point such as groundnut, sesame or soya oil.

Dice, chop or slice the vegetables into small pieces. Pat dry. Heat the oil in the wok, and add the vegetables, beginning with the vegetable which needs the longest cooking time. Stir continuously. As soon as the pieces of vegetable are well covered in oil and the flavour is sealed in, push them gently to the sides of the wok and add the next vegetable. In this way you end up with lightly cooked, crisp and nutritious vegetables.

All vegetables can be cooked this way, so long as they are cut into small pieces.

FRESH VEGETABLES Per 100 g (4 oz)	Water	Protein	Fat	Carbohydrate	Fibre	Vitamin A	Vitamin B₁	Vitamin B₂	Vitamin B₃	Vitamin B₆	Vitamin B₁₂	Vitamin C	Vitamin D	Vitamin E	Folic acid	Iron	Calcium	Magnesium	Sodium	Potassium	Phosphorus	Zinc
	g	g	g	g	g	µg	mg	mg	mg	mg	µg	mg	µg	mg	µg	mg	mg	mg	mg	mg	mg	mg
Recommended daily allowance	N	80M 60W	N	N	25-30	750	1.5	1.5	18	1.5	3	30	2.5	8	200	12	500	250	2500	2500	500	15
Artichokes, globe (cooked)	84	1.1	Tr	2.7	0	90	0.07	0.03	0.09	0.07	0	8	0	0	30	0.5	44	27	15	330	40	0
Asparagus	92	3.4	Tr	1.1	1.5	500	0.1	0.08	0.8	0.04	0	20	0	2.5	30	0.9	26	10	2	240	85	0.3
Aubergines	93	0.7	Tr	3.1	2.5	Tr	0.05	0.03	0.8	0.08	0	5	0	0	20	0.4	10	10	3	240	12	0
Avocados	69	4.2	**22.2**	1.8	2	100	0.1	0.1	1	**0.42**	0	15	N	**3.2**	66	1.5	15	29	2	400	31	N
Beetroots	87	1.3	Tr	6	3.1	Tr	0.03	0.05	0.1	0.05	0	6	0	0	90	0.4	25	15	84	300	32	0.4
Broad beans	84	4.1	0.6	7.1	4.2	250	0.1	0.04	3	0	0	15	0	Tr	0	1	21	28	20	230	99	0
Broccoli and calabrese	89	3.3	Tr	2.5	3.6	2500	0.1	0.3	1	0.21	0	110	0	1.3	130	1.5	100	18	12	340	67	0.6
Brussels sprouts	88	4	Tr	2.7	4.2	400	0.1	0.15	0.7	0.28	0	90	0	1	110	0.7	32	19	4	380	65	0.5
Cabbages – Chinese	90	0.9	0.1	2	0.4	110	0.04	0.03	0.5	N	0	19	0	N	N	0.5	32	N	17	190	30	N
– green	90	3.3	Tr	3.3	3.1	300	0.06	0.05	0.3	0.16	0	60	0	0.2	90	0.9	75	20	23	260	68	0.3
– red	90	1.7	Tr	3.5	3.4	20	1.06	0.05	0.3	0.21	0	55	0	0.2	90	0.6	53	17	32	300	32	0.3
– white	90	1.9	Tr	3.8	2.7	Tr	0.06	0.05	0.3	0.16	0	55	0	0.2	26	0.4	44	13	7	280	36	0.3
Carrots	90	0.7	Tr	5.4	2.9	**12000**	0.06	0.05	0.6	0.15	0	6	0	0.5	15	0.6	48	12	95	220	21	0.4

FRESH VEGETABLES Per 100 g (4 oz)	Water	Protein	Fat	Carbohydrate	Fibre	Vitamin A	Vitamin B₁	Vitamin B₂	Vitamin B₃	Vitamin B₆	Vitamin B₁₂	Vitamin C	Vitamin D	Vitamin E	Folic acid	Iron	Calcium	Magnesium	Sodium	Potassium	Phosphorus	Zinc
	g	g	g	g	g	µg	mg	mg	mg	mg	µg	mg	µg	mg	µg	mg	mg	mg	mg	mg	mg	mg
Recommended daily allowance	N	80M 60W	N	N	25-30	750	1.5	1.5	18	1.5	3	30	2.5	8	200	12	500	250	2500	2500	500	15
Cauliflowers	93	1.9	Tr	1.5	2.1	30	0.1	0.1	0.6	0.2	0	0.6	0	0.2	39	0.5	21	14	8	350	45	0.3
Celeriac (cooked)	90	1.6	Tr	2	4.9	0	0.04	0.04	0.5	0.1	0	0.5	0	0	0	0.8	47	12	28	400	71	0
Celery	94	0.9	Tr	1.3	1.8	Tr	0.03	0.03	0.3	0.1	0	0.3	0	0.2	12	0.6	52	10	140	280	32	0.1
Chard	N	3.2	0.4	6	1.2	**9400**	0.07	0.19	0.7	N	0	28	0	N	N	3.2	130	N	150	560	42	N
Chicory	**96**	0.8	Tr	1.5	0		0.05	0.05	0.5	0.05	0	0.5	0	0	52	0.7	18	13	7	180	21	0.2
Courgettes	N	0.8	Tr	2.5	0.4	210	0.03	0.06	0.6	0.05	0	25	0	N	N	0.3	18	N	0.5	130	19	N
Cucumbers	**96**	0.6	Tr	1.8	0.4	Tr	0.04	0.04	0.2	0.04	0	0.2	0	Tr	16	0.3	23	9	13	140	24	0.1
Endive	93	1.8	Tr	1	2.2	2000	0.06	0.1	0.4	0	0	0.4	0	0	**330**	2.8	44	10	10	380	67	0
French beans (cooked)	**96**	0.8	Tr	1.1	3.2	400	0.04	0.07	0.3	0.06	0	5	0	0.2	28	0.6	39	10	3	100	15	0.3
Jerusalem artichokes (cooked)	80	1.6	Tr	3.2	0	30	0.1	Tr	0	0	0	2	0	0.2	0	0.5	54	N	10	430	68	0.1
Kohlrabi	N	2.8	0.2	9	1.6	30	0.1	0.05	0.3	N	0	71	0	N	0	0.5	54	N	10	430	68	N
Leeks	86	1.9	Tr	6	3.1	40	0.05	0.05	0.6	0.25	0	18	0	0.8	0	1.1	63	10	9	310	43	0.1
Lettuces	**96**	1	0.4	1.2	1.5	1000	0.07	0.08	0.3	0.07	0	15	0	0.5	34	0.9	23	8	9	240	27	0.2
Marrows	**96**	0.6	Tr	3.7	1.8	30	Tr	0.04	0.3	0.06	0	5	0	Tr	13	1	17	12	1	210	20	0.2
Mushrooms	92	1.8	0.6	0	2.5	0	0.1	**0.4**	**4**	0.1	0	3	0	Tr	23	1	3	13	9	470	**140**	0.1
Okra	90	2	Tr	2.3	3.2	90	0.1	0.1	1	0.08	0	25	0	0	0	1	70	**60**	7	190	60	0
Olives (in brine)	77	0.9	11	Tr	4.4	180	Tr	Tr	0.1	Tr	0	N	0	N	N	1	61	22	**2250**	91	N	N
Onions	93	0.9	Tr	5.2	1.3	0	0.03	0.05	0.2	0.1	0	10	0	Tr	16	0.3	31	8	10	140	30	0.1
Parsley	79	5.2	Tr	Tr	**9.1**	7000	0.15	0.3	1	0.2	0	150	0	1.8	0	**8**	330	52	33	**1080**	130	0.9
Parsnips	83	1.7	Tr	11.3	4	Tr	0.1	0.08	1	0.1	0	15	0	1	67	0.6	55	22	17	340	69	0.1
Peas – fresh	79	**5.8**	0.4	10.6	5.2	300	**0.32**	0.15	2.5	0.16	0	25	0	Tr	N	1.9	15	30	1	340	100	0.7
– frozen	79	**5.8**	0.4	7.2	7.8	300	**0.32**	0.1	2.1	0.1	0	17	0	Tr	78	1.5	33	27	3	190	90	0.9
Peppers – green	94	0.9	0.4	2.2	0.9	200	Tr	0.03	0.7	0.17	0	100	0	0.8	11	0.4	9	11	2	210	25	0.2
– red	94	1	0.2		1.3	3300	0.06	0.06	0.4	N	0	**204**	N	N	N	0.4	10	N	N	N	22	N
Potatoes	76	2.1	0.1	20.8	2.1	Tr	0.11	0.04	1.2	0.25	0	15	0	0.1	14	0.5	8	24	7	170	40	0.3
Pumpkins	93	0.6	Tr	3.4	0.5	1500	0.04	0.04	0.4	0.06	0	5	0	Tr	13	0.4	39	8	1	310	19	0.2
Radicchio	**96**	1.6	Tr	Tr	0.8	1840	0.08	0.08	Tr	0.08	0	16	N	N	N	0.08	64	N	8	256	24	N
Radishes	93	1	Tr	2.8	1	Tr	0.04	0.02	0.2	0.1	0	25	0	0	24	1.9	44	11	59	240	27	0.1
Runner beans	89	2.3	0.2	3.9	2.9	400	0.05	0.1	0.9	0.07	0	20	0	0.2	60	0.8	27	27	2	280	47	0.4
Salsify (cooked)	81	1.9	Tr	2.8	N	Tr	0.03	N	N	N	0	4	0	N	N	1.2	60	14	8	180	53	N
Seakale (cooked)	**96**	1.4	Tr	0.6	1.2	N	0.06	N	N	N	0	18	0	N	N	0.6	48	11	4	50	34	N
Spinach (cooked)	85	5.1	0.5	1.4	6.3	6000	0.07	0.15	0.4	0.18	0	25	0	2	140	4	**600**	59	120	490	93	0.4
Spring onions	92	1.6	0.4	4.8	N	890	0.1	0.11	0.5	N	0	29	0	N	N	1.2	43	N	4	178	N	N
Swedes	91	1.1	Tr	4.3	2.7	Tr	0.06	0.04	1.2	0.2	0	25	0	0	27	0.4	56	11	52	140	19	N
Sweetcorn (on the cob)	65	4.1	2.4	23.7	3.7	240	0.15	0.08	1.8	0.19	0	12	0	0.8	52	1.1	4	47	1	300	130	**1.2**
Sweet potatoes	70	1.2	0.6	21.5	2.5	4000	0.1	0.06	0.8	0.22	0	25	0	4	52	0.7	22	13	19	320	47	N
Tomatoes	93	0.9	Tr	28	1.5	600	0.06	0.04	0.7	0.11	0	20	0	1.2	28	0.4	13	11	3	290	21	0.2
Turnips	93	0.8	0.3	3.8	2.8	0	0.04	0.05	0.6	0.11	0	25	0	0	20	0.4	59	7	58	240	28	N
Watercress	91	2.9	Tr	0.7	3.3	3000	0.1	0.1	0.6	0.13	0	60	0	1	200	1.6	220	17	60	310	52	0.2
Yams	73	2	0.2	**32.4**	4.1	12	0.1	0.03	N	0	0	10	0	N	N	0.3	10	40	N	500	40	0.4

KEY
All wholefoods are uncooked unless stated otherwise. Some wholefoods may not be included in the chart, as there is currently no nutritional data available.
g: grams **mg:** milligrams **µg:** micrograms **N:** no available data **Tr:** trace **M:** adult men **W:** adult women. The recommended daily allowances are averages and vary depending on age, occupation and metabolism. Figures in bold type indicate the wholefood with the highest level of nutrient.

Artichokes, globe

Globe artichokes are from a thistle-like plant similar to the *cardoon*, which is indigenous to North Africa. Artichokes are now grown in both Europe and America.

Their delicate flavour and unusual appearance make them a delightful addition to any meal. Choose ones with tightly closed leaves and no sign of browning.

Preparation and cooking
Remove the tough outer leaves. Cut off the thick stems close to the base so that the artichokes will stand up by themselves. Rinse them well and leave upside down to drain. Half fill a large pan with salted water and bring to the boil. Add the artichokes and simmer gently for 30-40 minutes or until one of the outer leaves pulls away easily. Drain.

If you require the hearts, remove the leaves and carefully pull off all the hairy 'choke' with your fingers or with a knife. This can be done before or after basic cooking.

Serving suggestion: Warm with melted butter or a hollandaise sauce, or cold with Mayonnaise (see p. 96).

Asparagus

Asparagus is thought to have originated in the Middle East and found its way to Europe in the late Middle Ages. The most common varieties are green and white.

Asparagus should be eaten as fresh as possible. Look for tight, well formed heads and avoid those with very thin or very thick stems, or those which are wrinkled and woody.

They are usually eaten as a starter, but can also be added to soups, soufflés or quiches. Their delicate flavour can be lost if they are added to highly seasoned or spicy food.

Preparation and cooking

Trim the ends, wash well and tie in bundles of about 8 stalks. Put the bundles, tips up, into a deep saucepan and add sufficient boiling water to cover the stalks but not the tips. These should be covered with foil. Simmer gently for about 10 minutes or until tender. The fresher the asparagus, the less the cooking time required. Eat hot or cold.

Serving suggestion: Warm with melted butter or hollandaise sauce, or cold with Mayonnaise (see p. 96) or French dressing.

Recipe: Use instead of broccoli in Red Pepper & Broccoli Quiche (see p. 111).

Aubergines
(Eggplant)

This spectacular purple or white vegetable is probably native to India and travelled via the Middle East to the Mediterranean. It is important in the local cuisines of both regions, and there are many recipes for its use.

When buying, look for firm and shiny skins. Their size makes no difference to flavour.

Aubergines are often stuffed and baked or sautéed, or used in ratatouille.

Preparation and cooking

Young fresh aubergines need only to be washed and the stalks and leaves removed before being sliced and cooked. Older aubergines can taste slightly bitter and contain a great deal of water, but this can be remedied by slicing thickly, sprinkling with salt and leaving to drain or 'bleed' for 30 minutes in a colander. Rinse and pat dry before cooking.

Sauté aubergine slices in a little butter or oil over a high heat until lightly browned, about 5 minutes on each side.

Serving suggestion: Seasoned with fresh mint.

Recipe: Stuffed Aubergines with Tomato Sauce (see p. 115).

Avocados
(Alligator pears)

Botanically classed as a fruit, avocados are generally used as vegetables. They can be rough and purple-black or smooth and green: the small black variety generally taste best. Choose avocados which yield all over to gentle pressure.

Avocados are usually eaten raw with a vinaigrette dressing but they are also delicious sliced, puréed or cooked in savoury dishes.

Preparation and cooking

Cut in half lengthwise and remove the large stone. Peel and slice thinly if required. If preparing in advance, a little lemon juice sprinkled over will prevent discolouration.

If you are going to use avocado in a cooked dish, add at the very end of cooking and simply warm through before serving.

Serving suggestion: Halved with French dressing in the centre.

Recipe: Egg & Avocado Mayonnaise Dip (see p. 82).

Beetroots
(Beets)

Beetroots are native to the Mediterranean, and are now grown in Europe and America. Both raw and ready-cooked beetroots can be bought. Ready-cooked beetroots have often been boiled in a mixture of water and acetic acid and have a strong vinegary taste. Where possible, buy ones that have been cooked in plain water or boil yourself (see below). Being a root vegetable, they store better when raw. Buy firm, small beetroots if you can.

Raw beetroot can be grated in salads. Cooked beetroot is delicious served hot on its own, with a sauce or in soups.

Preparation and cooking

Cut off the roots and tops and wash well, taking care not to tear the skin, or the colour and flavour will be lost during cooking. Place in a pan of cold, salted water and bring to the boil. Simmer for 40-60 minutes or until tender. Cool a little. Remove the skin, leave whole or slice or dice as required.

Serving suggestion: Cold and chopped with fresh mint in a salad.

Recipe: Potato & Beetroot Soup (see p. 78).

Broad beans
(Fava/Windsor/Horse beans)

Broad beans originated in the Middle East and have been eaten there and in Europe for thousands of years. They are best eaten young and tender and you should look for small, plump pods. Immature broad bean pods can also be cooked whole, like mange tout (see peas, p. 30).

Broad beans can be used raw or cooked in salads, as a side vegetable, puréed or in savoury dishes. They can be eaten dried (see p. 21).

Preparation and cooking

To use raw in salads, split the pods and remove the beans, or just trim if eating whole.

To cook, boil in a little salted water for 10-12 minutes (less for young pods) or until tender. Or, steam for 15-20 minutes.

Serving suggestion: Steamed and tossed in sour cream with fresh parsley, chives or dill.

Recipe: Creamy Broad Bean Soup (see p. 75).

Broccoli

Broccoli is a variety of cauliflower, and has been grown in Europe for nearly 3,000 years. There are several varieties: white, green, and purple; hearting (rather like a cauliflower) or sprouting. Calabrese is a green sprouting variety. Look for strong stalks and heads for the sprouting varieties and closely packed heads for the hearting varieties.

Broccoli can be served as a side vegetable or added to soups, quiches and savoury dishes.

Preparation and cooking

For sprouting broccoli, be sure to cook the leaves and stems as well as the heads. Trim off any tough or fibrous ends from the stalks and wash well. Halve the stalks and heads lengthwise if they are large. Steam for 6-10 minutes. For hearting broccoli, cook as for cauliflower (see p. 28).

Serving suggestion: With fresh parsley.

Recipe: Red Pepper & Broccoli Quiche (see p. 111).

Brussels sprouts

Brussels sprouts are another sturdy European vegetable, well suited to cold climates and frosty nights. Look for small, compact sprouts and avoid those with yellowing leaves.

Preparation and cooking

Wash thoroughly, trim the stalk end and peel away the outer leaves. Make a small incision in the base of each sprout and then simmer gently in boiling, salted water for 5-6 minutes or steam for 6-10 minutes. Drain well. Alternatively, sauté until tender.

Serving suggestion: Tossed in melted butter with fresh marjoram.

Recipe: Chestnut Roast (see p. 104).

Cabbages

Cabbages have long been grown in Europe, and there are a number of varieties.

Red and white cabbages are round and firmly packed. They are delicious shredded finely in salads, or cooked for a few minutes only so as to retain their crispness.

Savoy cabbage is a beautiful green cabbage with loose wrinkled leaves, whereas the roundhead or common cabbage has smoother leaves. Both can be eaten raw or cooked.

Chinese cabbage (sometimes called **pe-tsai**) is similar to cos lettuce in appearance, tall and elegant with its own distinctive flavour. Another type of Chinese cabbage is **pak-choi**, with broad white stalks and dark green leaves. Both can be eaten raw or stir-fried.

Preparation and cooking

Remove any damaged leaves, cut the cabbage down the centre and remove the hard core. For salads, wash if necessary and shred finely.

To cook, shred or cut into wedges and put in a large saucepan with a few inches of boiling salted water. Cook for 2-4 minutes with a tightly fitting lid. Remove from the heat and drain well in a colander. Shredded cabbage can also be steamed for 4-6 minutes.

Serving suggestion: Shredded and stir-fried in soya oil and shoyu (see p. 51).

Recipe: Curried Coleslaw (see p. 90).

Carrots

These sweet and easily digestible root vegetables are native to Europe, now cultivated worldwide. They are very nutritious, and their sweet flavour and bright orange colour make them an attractive vegetable for young children.

In early spring and summer, baby carrots are sold with their leafy tops which can also be eaten. Main crop carrots are usually larger and coarser. Buy firm, bright carrots.

Preparation and cooking

For early crop or baby carrots, remove the tops and wash well. For salads, young raw carrots can be grated, eaten whole or cut into bite sized pieces. To cook, steam for about 10-15 minutes until tender but crisp.

Main crop carrots may need a good scrubbing and should be sliced, diced or chopped into similar sized pieces before being boiled for 10-15 minutes or steamed for 20 minutes.

Serving suggestion: Tossed in melted butter and sprinkled with fresh basil.

Recipe: Savoury Kombu & Carrots (see p. 112).

Cauliflowers

Cauliflowers are thought to have originated in the Middle East and they reached Europe by the thirteenth century.

Look for cauliflowers with firm heads and crisp green leaves. Eat raw or cooked.

Preparation and cooking

For salads, wash as necessary, trim off the stem and leaves, and break into small florets.

To cook whole, first cut off the base of the stem so that the cauliflower will stand on its own. Trim off any old or broken leaves. Put in a lidded saucepan with about 7·5 cm (3 in) of boiling salted water. Boil vigorously for 10-15 minutes or until tender but still firm.

Alternatively. cut into small pieces and steam for 4-8 minutes.

Serving suggestion: Cooked with coriander.
Recipe: Cauliflower & Carrots with Spicy Hazelnut Sauce (see p. 103).

Celeriac
(Celery root/Celery rave)

Celeriac has its origins in the Mediterranean regions of Europe. It looks rather like a turnip and has a taste similar to celery. It can be eaten raw in salads, steamed, boiled or puréed.

Preparation and cooking

For salads, peel off the outer skin if it looks tough and cut into small pieces or grate.

To cook, cut into small pieces and boil for 10-15 minutes or steam until soft, about 15-20 minutes. Celeriac can also be braised for 15-20 minutes or stir-fried.

Serving suggestion: Use cooked and puréed in place of mashed potatoes in savoury dishes.

Celery

Celery is native to Europe but is also grown in America. It is low in calories and has negligible nutritional value. However, its crisp lively flavour makes it a delicious addition to salads and it is often used in Chinese dishes, soups or casseroles. Look for crisp, smallish celery.

Preparation and cooking

To eat raw, wash well and trim off the root and leaf ends. You can reserve the leafy tops for decoration or as a flavouring.

To braise celery, first wash well, remove the leafy tops and cut into medium-sized lengths. If braising on top of the stove, cook gently for about 10 minutes. If braising in an oven cook for 10-12 minutes. You can also boil celery for 8-10 minutes or steam for 12-15 minutes.

Serving suggestion: With fresh herbs.
Recipe: Sprouty Salad (see p. 94).

Chard
(Swiss chard/Seakale beet)

This vegetable comes from central and eastern Europe. Other varieties include rhubarb chard and spinach beet, which taste like spinach. Chard has dark green wrinkled leaves which surround strong white stalks. It is highly nutritious, although, as with spinach (see p. 31), you need to buy a large amount as it decreases in size when you cook it.

Preparation and cooking

Wash the leaves well and trim the stalks. If the stems are very thick, cut out and chop into smallish pieces. Steam for 8-10 minutes.

Serving suggestion: Tossed in butter.
Recipe: Stir-fry Swiss Chard & Mushrooms (see p. 115).

Chicory
(American or French endive/ Belgian witloof)

Chicory probably originated in western Asia. It is grown commercially under layers of straw in order to produce the broad, tightly packed white leaves. It has a slightly bitter taste and is popular in salads.

Preparation and cooking

For use in salads, wash, trim off the base and either slice or peel off each leaf separately.

To bake, trim the root end and either leave whole or cut lengthwise down the centre. Chicory can also be braised, or boiled whole in a very little salted boiling water with a knob of butter for about 20 minutes or until tender.

Serving suggestion: Sprinkled with paprika.
Recipe: Mushroom, Apricot & Chicory Salad (see p. 92).

Courgettes
(Zucchini/Italian squash)

Courgettes are a miniature variety of marrow, picked and eaten in an immature state. They are dark green in colour and can be long and cylindrical or round in shape. Choose small courgettes as these have less tough skins.

Courgettes can be eaten raw in salads, sautéed, steamed or stuffed.

Preparation and cooking

For use in salads, trim the ends, wash well and either grate or slice finely. Do not peel.

To sauté or steam courgettes, first wash and leave whole or slice thinly. Sauté sliced courgettes in a little butter for 5-8 minutes, or steam for 4-6 minutes until just tender.

To stuff courgettes, cut in half lengthwise, remove the pips and fill with your choice of stuffing. Put in an oiled baking tray and cook at the centre of a 180°C (350°F/Gas 4) oven for about 20 minutes or longer, depending on size.

Serving suggestion: With fresh thyme.
Recipe: Swede & Orange Pie (see p. 116).

Cucumbers

Cucumbers originated in India, travelled to Europe and were popular with the Greeks and Romans. The cucumber is the fruit of the plant, picked and eaten in an immature state. There are a number of varieties, ranging from the small ridged cucumber to the long, smooth type. Choose small, smooth cucumbers as these will be most tender.

Preparation and cooking

For salads, simply wash and slice or cut into the size you desire. There is no need to peel them unless their skins are very tough. If they are bitter, salt and 'bleed' as for aubergines (see p. 27). Be careful to rinse off the salt before using.

To steam, cut into small pieces and cook for about 3 minutes. To sauté, cook in oil or butter for 3-5 minutes.

Serving suggestion: With fresh thyme.
Recipe: Lettuce, Cucumber & Miso Soup (see p. 76).

Endive
(American chicory)

The beautiful, green curly leaved endive is a member of the chicory family, native to southern Asia or Egypt.

The most popular varieties are the batavian or escarole endive and the curly or mop-head endive. Endive is generally used in salads but can also be sautéed and eaten hot or added to soups and savoury dishes. It has a slightly bitter flavour.

Preparation and cooking

For salads, wash well and shred raw or blanched. To blanch, plunge into boiling water for 2-3 minutes. Drain and cool before using.

To cook, sauté in a little oil or butter for about 3-5 minutes. Endive can also be braised.

Serving suggestion: Raw with vinaigrette.
Recipe: Use instead of lettuce in Green Salad with Dill Dressing (see p. 91).

Fennel
(Florence fennel)

This bulbous, pale green and white vegetable with its slight anise flavour originated in Europe, probably in or around Greece.

Choose white or pale green bulbs as dark green fennel may be bitter. Fennel can be eaten raw in salads or braised.

Preparation and cooking

Cut off the tough fibrous stalks and trim the base. If using raw, slice or chop thinly. If preparing in advance, keep in water with a little lemon juice to prevent browning.

To bake fennel, cut into thin slices, put in an oiled or buttered lidded ovenproof dish and cook gently in a 180°C (350°F/Gas 4) oven for about 30 minutes or until just tender. Fennel can also be boiled for 10-12 minutes or steamed for about 10-15 minutes. Be careful not to overcook.

Serving suggestion: With fresh parsley.
Recipe: Fennel & Tomato Salad (see p. 91).

French beans

Originally from Central America, these beans, as their name suggests, were probably brought to Europe for cultivation by French explorers in the seventeenth century. They are a variety of green bean.

The sweet-flavoured beans should be bright green, firm and crisp. They are best eaten as a side vegetable, but can also be added to soups, savouries and quiches, or cold in salads.

Preparation and cooking

Wash well in cold water and top and tail with a sharp knife. Cut into small slices. To cook, boil for 5-10 minutes or steam for 10-15 minutes or until tender. Drain. If serving cold in salads, rinse in cold water.

Serving suggestion: Warm with a knob of butter and a little grated nutmeg or lemon juice, or cold with vinaigrette.
Recipe: Gado-gado (see p. 106).

Jerusalem artichokes

Jerusalem artichokes were introduced to Europe from North America early in the seventeenth century. They are related to the globe artichoke and the sunflower.

They have a distinctive, twisted tuberous appearance, and crisp, sweet flesh which is delicious whether eaten raw or cooked. Choose firm artichokes which are as smooth as possible.

Preparation and cooking

To eat raw, remove any hard nodules, wash well and cut into similar sized pieces.

Cook in boiling, salted water for 15 minutes until tender or steam for about 20 minutes. (A little lemon juice in the cooking water will prevent the artichokes from browning.) They can also be shallow-fried for 10-15 minutes, turning often to prevent sticking. If you need to peel, do so after cooking.

Serving suggestion: With cream and nutmeg.
Recipe: Artichokes & Tomatoes with Basil (see p. 97).

Kohlrabi

This strange-looking vegetable is a member of the cabbage family. It probably originated in Europe and has increased in popularity in recent years. It is high in vitamin C.

Kohlrabi is not the actual root of the plant but a bulbous part of the stem from which the leaves grow out. It can be purple or green, and is best when young, crisp and tender.

Kohlrabi can be eaten raw in salads, cooked as a side vegetable or added to savoury dishes. It has a delicate flavour reminiscent of turnips.

Preparation and cooking

Cut off the twiggy stems protruding from the vegetable and wash well. To eat raw, grate or cut into small pieces for salads.

To cook, chop and steam for about 15 minutes until tender, or boil in salted boiling water for 10-15 minutes. Kohlrabi can also be braised and sautéed.

Serving suggestion: With butter and chives.
Recipe: Fresh Vegetable Curry (see p. 106).

Leeks

Leeks are native to Europe and are thick-stemmed cream-coloured vegetables with a mild, onion-like flavour. Choose leeks which are small and firm, with crisp tops.

Leeks are often served with a white sauce, but are also delicious in soups, stews and other savoury dishes.

Preparation and cooking

Leeks can be very dirty and need thorough washing and cleaning. Trim the root and any tough green parts. Slit down the middle and leave whole or cut into small rings and steam for 5-10 minutes depending on size. It is best not to boil leeks as they lose their flavour and tend to fall apart easily. Leeks can also be braised for about 10-12 minutes.

Serving suggestion: With a white or cheese sauce (see p. 109).
Recipe: Leeks Vinaigrette (see p. 84).

Lettuces

Lettuces have been cultivated for many thousands of years. Probably originating in the Mediterranean region, they were popular with the Greeks, the Romans and the Chinese and can be found worldwide.

There are three main varieties of lettuce: the cabbage (or butterhead) lettuce, the cos (or romaine) lettuce and the crisphead lettuce. Cabbage lettuces are round with firm hearts and are fairly loosely packed. Cos lettuces have long leaves and are crisper and sweeter than the other varieties. Crisphead lettuces have tightly packed, solid heads. Iceberg is a popular variety of crisphead lettuce.

Lettuces are generally interchangeable, although the crisp, firm-hearted varieties tend to have more flavour. Lettuces are most commonly used in salads but can also be eaten as a hot vegetable or in chilled soups.

Preparation and cooking

For salads, wash the leaves well in cold water and either leave whole or chop or tear into smaller pieces as desired.

To eat as a hot vegetable, prepare as above and then stir-fry in a little oil or butter for a few seconds only until soft and warmed through. Do not overcook.

Serving suggestion: Raw and chilled with vinaigrette dressing.
Recipe: Lettuce, Cucumber & Miso Soup (see p. 76).

Marrows, pumpkins and squashes

This large vegetable family probably originated in Central and South America and quickly spread to North America and Canada. During the late sixteenth and seventeenth centuries, visitors to the New World returned to Europe with marrows and pumpkins. Of the many varieties now grown, the most common are the striped and plain marrows, the Naples squash and the American pumpkin.

All marrows and pumpkins have a delicate, watery flavour. They can be eaten as a light side vegetable, stuffed or even, in the case of the American pumpkin, used in sweet dishes such as pumpkin pie.

Preparation and cooking

If the marrow, pumpkin or squash is young enough, the skin can be cooked and eaten. If it is too old, peel first. Halve or slice into rings as required and scoop out the seeds.

Steam or sauté in small pieces for about 5-10 minutes or until just tender.

To stuff a marrow, pumpkin or squash, cut in half lengthwise and remove the pith and seeds, leaving about 2.5 cm (1 in) of flesh. Fill with your choice of stuffing and bake in a 180°C (350°F/Gas 4) oven for about 30 minutes until cooked.

Serving suggestion: With fresh mixed herbs and a little butter.

Mushrooms

Wild mushrooms have been prolific in Asia and Europe for many centuries, but it was not until the end of the seventeenth century that cultivated mushrooms appeared in Europe.

Mushrooms are edible fungi. They contain small quantities of valuable nutrients and their subtle flavour and distinctive texture make them a delightful addition to almost any savoury dish.

Commercial button mushrooms are related to the larger, flat field mushrooms. The latter are tastier but the button mushrooms are easier to use for salads and garnish. Choose from fresh specimens and eat on the day of purchase if possible. They can be eaten raw or lightly cooked.

Preparation and cooking

Most mushrooms need only to be wiped gently to remove any dirt from their skins. They need not be peeled but you should trim the root. If they need to be washed, drain well to prevent from becoming soggy. If eating raw, slice if desired.

Mushrooms can be lightly sautéed, baked or added to casseroles or soups. They need very little cooking, so add towards the end of a savoury dish or sauté over a fairly high heat for a few minutes only to seal in the juices. Steam mushrooms for 5-10 minutes or poach in a little salted water for 3-5 minutes.

Serving suggestion: Steamed or baked with crushed garlic and melted butter.
Recipe: Stuffed Baked Mushrooms (see p. 86).

Okra
(Lady's fingers/Gumbo)

Okra originated in Africa, and are widely used in African, Middle Eastern and Oriental cookery. They are the immature seed pods of the plant and are often used in soups, casseroles or spicy dishes. The pods should be green and firm.

Preparation and cooking

Trim the ends and wash well. Cut into pieces or leave whole as required. To reduce their 'slimy' texture, cut in small pieces, sprinkle with salt, leave for 20 minutes to drain in a colander and then rinse off. Sauté for 5-10 minutes (depending on size) or steam gently for 10-15 minutes until tender.

Serving suggestion: Steamed and chilled with vinaigrette.
Recipe: Summer Okra Casserole (see p. 116).

Olives

Olives are the fruit of a tree native to the Mediterranean. There are a number of varieties, but basically they are either black or green. Black olives are fully ripened; green olives are immature. Olives are very rich in oil, and are used for olive oil (see p. 49).

Olives are available whole, pitted or stuffed with almonds, red pepper or pimientos. They are usually sold in oil or brine.

Preparation and cooking

Olives are usually eaten raw as a savoury cocktail snack but they can be added to many savoury dishes, either whole (pitted) or chopped as required.

Use olives in pizzas, pasta sauces, spicy casseroles and savoury tomato dishes. They can also be puréed and added to dips, sauces and even bread.

Recipe: Wholewheat Pizza (see p. 119).

Onions

Onions originated in Central Asia and spread both eastwards and westwards to all the major continents. Different varieties are now grown all over the world.

There are many types of onion. They can be white, yellow or red, small or large, round or slender. Some onions can be eaten raw, such as spring onions (scallions) or shallots, and all can be used in most savoury dishes.

Preparation and cooking

Peel, trim and slice, chop or cut as desired. Whole onions can be boiled for 15-30 minutes, depending on size. Whole or sliced onions can be steamed for 40 or 15 minutes respectively. Sauté sliced onions in a little oil or butter for 5-10 minutes until soft and golden.

For baking, place the unpeeled whole onions on a baking tray and cook in a 150°C (300°F/Gas 2) oven for 1½-2 hours.

Serving suggestion: With a herb butter.
Recipe: Onion Bhajis with Yogurt Sauce (see p. 86).

Parsnips

Parsnips are native to eastern Europe. They have a sweet and slightly floury taste, and are delicious raw, cooked or puréed. Choose firm, young roots with no soft brown parts.

Preparation and cooking

Cut off the leafy tops and trim the root. Do not peel unless the skin seems very hard. Leave whole, quarter or slice. Steam sliced parsnips for 10-15 minutes until soft, or boil vigorously for 15-20 minutes and mash or purée. Parsnips can be sautéed for 10-15 minutes, or blanched and baked in a 200°C (400°F/Gas 6) oven for 45-60 minutes.

Serving suggestion: With butter and nutmeg.
Recipe: Sesame Roast Parsnips (see p. 114).

Peas

Peas are native to the Middle East. During the sixteenth or seventeenth centuries the sweet green shelling peas we are familiar with today were developed.

Most peas today are frozen or tinned and fresh peas are quite a rarity. Home-grown garden peas are best of all, so pick them when they are small and sweet (petit pois) as they can become rather tough and floury if left too long. Mange tout (snow peas or sugar peas) are another variety. These immature peas are eaten with their pods and are crisp and sweet.

Fresh peas can be puréed, added to soups, casseroles, salads and other savoury dishes.

Preparation and cooking

First shell the peas, discarding any that are discoloured or damaged: about 450 g (1 lb) of podded peas gives about 225 g (8 oz) of shelled peas. Wash and put in a saucepan with the minimum amount of salted boiling water. Boil for 2-10 minutes, depending on the size and freshness of the peas. Drain well. Peas can also be steamed and take about 3-8 minutes.

For mange tout, first top and tail, then stir-fry in a small amount of butter or oil for a minute or so and serve immediately.

Serving suggestion: Tossed in a little butter with fresh mint.
Recipe: Pineapple Salad (see p. 92).

Peppers

Peppers are indigenous to South America and the West Indies, but they travelled to Europe in the sixteenth century and are now grown extensively in the southern Mediterranean.

There are many types of pepper, varying in shape, taste and colour. They can be red, green or yellow, square or heart-shaped and mild or pungent in taste. The larger, sweet-tasting varieties (bell peppers, pimientos and pepperons) are delicious raw in salads or cooked in savoury dishes. For the smaller, extremely hot chilli peppers, see page 57.

Buy firm, glossy peppers. Red, green and yellow are more or less the same, although the red peppers tend to be sweeter.

Preparation and cooking

Slice off the stem end and remove the seeds and stalk. Leave whole or slice as required.

To cook, steam whole peppers for 10-15 minutes, or slice and sauté or stir-fry in a little oil or butter for 5-10 minutes.

To stuff peppers, prepare as above and fill with your choice of stuffing. Bake for about ¾-1 hour in a 150°C (300°F/Gas 2) oven.

Serving suggestion: With a little marjoram.
Recipe: Ratatouille (see p. 110).

Potatoes

Indigenous to South America, potatoes arrived in Europe in the seventeenth century. Many varieties of potato are available.

When buying potatoes in bulk, store in a cool place away from the light, to prevent them from turning green or sprouting. New potatoes should be eaten fresh and not stored. Potatoes should be firm and blemish-free.

Preparation and cooking

To cook new potatoes, first wash well, taking care not to damage the skins. Boil in lightly salted water for as short a time as possible, about 10 minutes. For older, main crop potatoes, cook in one of the following ways:

Boiled potatoes. Scrub well. If large, halve or quarter. Put into a saucepan of cold water and bring to the boil. Add salt and simmer gently until cooked, about 15-20 minutes. Drain well, season and add a knob of butter.

Steamed potatoes. Scrub thoroughly, cut the potatoes into similar sized pieces and steam until cooked, about 25-30 minutes.

Roast potatoes. Wash and cut into similar sized pieces. Do not peel or the valuable nutrients just under the skins will be lost. Put in a saucepan, pour boiling water over and simmer for 10 minutes. Drain and pat dry. Heat some vegetable oil in a roasting pan in a 200°C (400°F/Gas 6) oven until hot. Take the pan out of the oven, carefully add the potatoes and baste them evenly. Return to the top shelf of the oven and roast for about 45-55 minutes or until golden brown, turning the potatoes over once or twice, and basting occasionally.

Jacket potatoes. This is one of the most nutritious and delicious ways to eat potatoes. Preheat the oven to 220°C (425°F/Gas 7). Wash, dry and prick the skins to prevent splitting. Bake in the centre of the oven for 1-1½ hours.

Serving suggestion: With grated cheese.
Recipe: Gado-gado (see p. 106).

Radicchio
(Radicchio rosso)

Radicchio is another form of chicory. Its exciting red colour makes it a welcome addition to any salad. Prepare and use for chicory (see p. 28).

Radishes

Radishes are relatives of the cabbage family and are native to southern Asia. They are thought to be one of the oldest cultivated vegetables in the world. They grow well in almost any climate and their crisp texture, bright pink-red colour and peppery flavour make them a pleasant addition to any salad. White, yellow and black radishes can also be found. Look for firm, blemish-free specimens. Radish seeds may be sprouted (see p. 23).

Preparation and cooking

Top and tail radishes and wash well. Cut into rings or small pieces if desired. Radishes are usually eaten raw, but can be steamed for 5-10 minutes, according to size. They can also be sliced and stir-fried.

Serving suggestion: With butter and chives.
Recipe: Red Bean Salad (see p. 93).

Runner beans

Runner beans are a variety of green bean. They originated in Central America and were probably introduced to Europe during the seventeenth century. They should be eaten as young and fresh as possible. When buying, choose crisp, bright beans.

Preparation and cooking

Wash and top and tail the beans, and pull away the stringy edges if necessary. They can be left whole but are usually sliced diagonally. This can be done with a bean slicer, if available. Cook in boiling water for about 5 minutes or steam for about 10 minutes. Drain well.

Serving suggestion: With butter and sage.
Recipe: Use instead of okra in Summer Okra Casserole (see p. 116).

Salsify/Scorzonera

Salsify originated in Europe and still grows wild in southern Europe and southern Asia. It has long, white, bitter-tasting roots, and is very similar to the fibrous roots of wild chicory. It is also known as oyster plant.

Scorzonera is related to salsify, and has a similar appearance but is black-skinned and has more tiny root fibres growing out of the main fibre. It is sometimes known as black salsify or viper's grass.

Both can be used for soups, salads, as a cooked vegetable or added to savoury dishes.

Preparation and cooking

Cut off the tiny roots from the main fibre. Top and tail and wash very well. For salads, grate and sprinkle with a little lemon juice if desired.

Cook in boiling salted water for about 20 minutes or until tender. Salsify can also be steamed (about 30 minutes) or sautéed in a little butter or oil for about 20-25 minutes until tender.

Serving suggestion: With a little cumin.

Seakale

Indigenous to western Europe, seakale has long, thick white stalks and small, dark green, wrinkled leaves. It is actually a herb of the mustard family, but is eaten as a vegetable.

Seakale has a pleasant, nutty flavour and can be used raw, steamed or sautéed.

Preparation and cooking

Wash well and cut into pieces.

To cook, sauté or steam for 3-5 minutes only, so that it remains crisp. Overcooking seakale can make it rather tough and the flavour is diminished.

Serving suggestion: Sautéed in a little butter or oil with garlic.

Recipe: Use to replace the chard in Stir-fry Swiss Chard & Mushrooms (see p. 115).

Spinach

Spinach is thought to have originated in Persia, and had been brought by the Moors to Europe by the tenth century. It is one of the most nutritious vegetables, being rich in iron, calcium and magnesium.

Young spinach can be eaten raw in salads and older spinach cooked as a vegetable or served in soups, quiches and other savoury dishes. Look for firm, green leaves. Spinach shrinks considerably when cooked, to about a third or a quarter of the original volume.

Preparation and cooking

For salads, first wash extremely well. Remove coarse stalks as necessary. Chop or tear into smallish pieces.

To cook, first trim any tough stalks and then wash and rinse well. Put straight into a large saucepan with a little salt but no added water and cook gently until the leaves are soft, about 8-10 minutes. Drain well.

Serving suggestion: With a little nutmeg.

Recipe: Nori & Spinach Rolls (see p. 85).

Swedes
(Rutabaga)

Swedes originated in northern Europe, where they were a major food before the advent of the potato, and grow best in cold climates.

Normally the round yellow-orange root is the part that is used, although the green leafy tops are more nutritious.

Look for small, unblemished specimens. Swedes can be boiled and mashed, served on top of pies or bakes, or added to soups and savoury dishes.

Preparation and cooking

Scrub well but do not peel unless the skin is particularly tough or damaged. Cut into even pieces or slices and boil for 15-20 minutes or steam for 20-25 minutes or until tender. Drain well before serving.

Serving suggestion: Mashed with a little butter and grated nutmeg.

Recipe: Swede & Orange Pie (see p. 116).

Sweetcorn
(Corn/Maize/Indian corn)

Sweetcorn has been cultivated in parts of southern America for many thousands of years. The plants travelled to central and northern America and then to Europe in the sixteenth century.

Buy or pick sweetcorn as fresh as possible. Look for shiny, cream-coloured cobs surrounded by green leaves with black tassels at the top. The corn can be eaten whole, on the cob, or as kernels. Add hot or cold kernels to savoury dishes.

Preparation and cooking

For corn on the cob, remove the outer leaves and silky fibres and trim the stalk. Boil in plenty of salted water for 10 minutes or until tender. If the recipe calls for corn off the cob, cook as above and then scrape the cob thoroughly downwards with a sharp knife, so that all the corn comes off. Cut close to the cob so that the nutritious germ is not lost.

Serving suggestion: With melted butter, salt and lots of black pepper.

Recipe: Sweetcorn & Mushroom Salad (see p. 95).

Sweet potatoes
(American yams)

The exact origin of the sweet potato is uncertain. Columbus brought them to Europe from America, but they were already cultivated in parts of Asia at this time. They feature in many Creole and South American dishes.

Despite the name, sweet potatoes are not related to the potato but have similarities both in looks and usage. Beneath the yellow or pink-brown skin the starchy interior can be pale yellow or bright orange. Use as an alternative to mashed potatoes, or cook in casseroles, bakes and sweet dishes.

Preparation and cooking

To bake, choose sweet potatoes of a similar size or cut into similar sized pieces. Wrap in silver foil if you wish. Put on a baking tray and cook in a 220°C (425°F/Gas 7) oven for about 1½ hours or until cooked.

To boil or steam sweet potatoes, wash well but do not peel unless the skin is very tough. Cut into small pieces and either boil in salted boiling water for 15-20 minutes or steam for 20-25 minutes or until very soft. To make a purée, put in a blender with a little butter or oil and seasoning and blend until smooth.

Serving suggestion: Puréed with a little ginger or nutmeg.

Recipe: Caribbean Stew (see p. 102).

Tomatoes

Tomatoes originated in South America and were introduced to southern Europe in the sixteenth century. They are in fact botanically classed as fruit but are used in savoury dishes.

There are many varieties to choose from, with differing shapes and sizes. Choose firm, blemish-free specimens, which should not be too dark in colour.

Although tomatoes are not especially nutritious, their bright colour stimulates the appetite and their pleasant flavour blends well with many other vegetables. They can be eaten raw or cooked in soups, purées, sauces and other savoury dishes.

Preparation and cooking

For salads, wash and leave whole, halve, quarter or slice into rings as required.

For use in hot dishes, tomatoes are often first skinned by pouring boiling water over them and leaving for about 15 minutes. The skins should then peel away easily.

Tomatoes can be halved and grilled for 3-4 minutes or baked whole. To bake, cut 2 slits crosswise in the top to prevent bursting and bake for 10 minutes in a 180°C (350°F/Gas 4) preheated oven.

Serving suggestion: With fresh basil.

Recipe: Buckwheat Pancakes with Tomato Sauce (see p. 101).

Turnips

Turnips are an ancient northern European vegetable, and were a major food before the arrival of the potato from South America.

The edible part is the swollen root, normally round and white with a little pink or green colouring around the base. They have a crisp, bitter flavour. As with swedes, the greens or flowered turnip tops are far more nutritious than the roots and can be cooked as a leaf vegetable. The roots should have blemish-free skins.

Turnips can be eaten raw but are usually cooked in curries, savoury dishes and soups. Young baby turnips are particularly tender and best for eating raw.

Preparation and cooking

Cut off the root and leafy tops and wash well. For salads, chop or grate as required.

Cook baby turnips whole in boiling salted water for 10-15 minutes. For main crop turnips, cut into similar sized pieces and boil for 10-15 minutes or steam for about 15-20 minutes or until tender. To cook the green tops, cut off any fibrous stalks, wash well, break into pieces and steam for 5-10 minutes until tender. Add a splash of lemon juice during cooking if desired.

Serving suggestion: Boiled and puréed as an alternative to mashed potato.

Recipe: Use instead of parsnip in Fresh Vegetable Curry (see p. 106).

Watercress

Watercress is a member of the mustard family and has grown wild in Europe for thousands of years. It is extremely high in fibre and vitamin C. Watercress can be used raw in salads, as a garnish, or cooked in soups and savoury dishes. Avoid wilting, discoloured specimens.

Preparation and cooking

For salads or garnishes, simply cut off the roots, wash well and chop or tear into bite-sized pieces.

To cook, prepare as above and sauté gently for 3-5 minutes.

Serving suggestion: With orange vinaigrette.

Recipe: Cream of Watercress Soup (see p. 74).

Yams

Yams are native to the Orient, and are now also grown in the tropical regions of America. A large tuberous root, yams have a thick outer bark which must be peeled off before cooking. They should not be confused with the American yam, which is in fact another name for sweet potato.

Peel and then prepare and use as for potatoes (see opposite page).

FRESH FRUIT

Apples ☐
Apricots
Bananas ☐
Blackberries
Blueberries
Boysenberries
Cherries ☐
Clementines ☐
Cranberries ☐
Currants
Damsons
Dates ☐

Figs
Gooseberries
Granadillas ☐
Grapefruit ☐
Grapes ☐
Greengages
Guavas ☐
Kiwifruit ☐
Kumquats
Lemons ☐
Limes ☐
Loganberries

Lychees
Mangoes ☐
Mangosteens
Melons ☐
Mulberries
Nectarines
Oranges ☐
Papayas ☐
Peaches ☐
Pears ☐
Persimmons
Pineapples ☐

Plums
Pomegranates ☐
Rambutans
Raspberries
Rhubarb
Satsumas
Strawberries
Tangerines
Ugli

☐ Pictured opposite page 33

There is evidence of the cultivation of fruit as long as 8,000 years ago; centuries of exploration, conquest and trade have ensured the development of indigenous produce and the introduction of non-native fruit in many parts of the world. Today, many varieties of fruit are available, local and imported.

As with vegetables, fresh fruits are an important component of a wholefood diet. They offer an attractive choice of colours, flavours and textures and are nutritionally important. Most fruits are valuable sources of vitamin C and carbohydrate in the form of natural sugars (fructose). They also contain dietary fibre as well as other vitamins and minerals (see the nutritional chart on page 33). Best eaten raw, fruit can also be cooked in a variety of ways. Use as a snack, as a substitute for puddings, with grains or yogurt for breakfast, in salads, cakes, pies or flans, or extract the juices for a healthy drink (see p. 61).

Sources
Try to use local organically grown produce (see p. 7) rather than imported fruit wherever possible and make maximum use of the fruit in season.

Additives
Unless you grow your own fruit or have a good organic supplier, it is likely that most of the fruit you buy will have been treated with pesticides. In general, a thorough scrub and/or wash should be sufficient to remove additives. Apples and pears in particular have firm skins which can withstand many sprays without the underlying flesh being affected. However, with babies and young children, it may be wise to peel fruit skins.

Citrus fruit for export is also treated with anti-fungal and anti-bacterial preservatives, as well as glazing and sealing agents, which can cause allergic reactions and irritations. Always wash in warm soapy water and rinse well, especially when the recipe calls for the rind or zest of a fruit.

Choosing fruit
Look for a healthy colour and avoid withered, damaged or discoloured specimens. When choosing firm fruit check for bruising and soft spots. Stone fruit should be firm but yielding. For berry and other soft fruit, avoid punnets stained with juice and check that the underneath fruit is not crushed or mouldy.

Storage
Soft fruit deteriorates rapidly and is best purchased on the day required or stored overnight in the refrigerator. Apples, the harder varieties of pears and citrus fruit can be bought in larger quantities and will last for some time in a cool, dry, well-ventilated place. Tropical fruit is best consumed within a few days of ripening: a slightly unripe mango, melon or papaya will ripen in a few days if put in a warm place. Most fruit can be frozen (see p. 65).

Cooking methods
In general, fruit is at its best when eaten raw. However, rhubarb, damsons, cooking apples, and damaged, over-ripe or unripe fruit (particularly gooseberries, plums and apricots) benefit from being cooked.

Stewing or poaching
Slice or chop the fruit as required. Heat a little water (filtered if possible) in a heavy-bottomed saucepan and sweeten if liked. Flavour with lemon rind, cinnamon or a little ground nutmeg. Add the fruit to the boiling water and simmer gently until tender. Small pieces of fruit will cook very quickly (about 4 minutes) but allow longer for whole fruit. Test with a skewer or sharp knife to see if they are cooked.

This method is suitable for apples, pears, gooseberries, cherries, blackberries, plums, damsons, apricots, peaches, nectarines and rhubarb. You can also poach dried fruit, after initial soaking.

Puréeing
Stew or poach the fruit (see above) and cool. Drain off most of the liquid, remove any stones or large pips and liquidize the fruit in a blender. Alternatively, push the fruit through a metal sieve with a wooden spoon. Sweeten as required, either with sugar or a natural sweetener such as honey.

This method is suitable for all fruit which can be stewed or poached (see above). However, ripe soft fruit such as strawberries and raspberries can be puréed raw. Just press through a sieve or liquidize in a blender.

Baking
This method is suitable for firm fruit such as cooking apples, some varieties of pears, peaches and nectarines.

For apples and pears, remove the core and fill with dried fruit, flavoured with cinnamon or ground cloves. Slit the skin in a ring about half-way down with a sharp knife, to prevent bursting. Place in a shallow baking dish and bake at 200°C (400°F/Gas 6) until tender. This will take 30-50 minutes. Serve hot or cold.

For peaches and nectarines, remove the stone and cut into halves. The indentations can be filled with a sweet stuffing of your choice, if desired. Bake as above for 20-30 minutes or until tender.

Fresh Vegetables (See p. 24)

Squash (see p. 29) is used in the same way as marrow.

Courgettes (see p. 28) can be eaten raw in salads or cooked in a number of ways.

Peppers (see p. 30) can be white, green, red or yellow in colour.

Hokkaido is an orangy-red variety of squash (see p. 29).

Okra (see p. 29) are the immature seed pods of a plant, eaten whole.

Radicchio (see p. 30) is a salad vegetable with a sharp, fresh taste.

Fennel (see p. 28) has a slightly aniseed flavour.

Olives (see p. 29) can be green or black, depending on their age when picked.

Avocados (see p. 27) can be green, as here, or purply-black in colour.

Aubergines (see p. 27) are rich and smoky.

Curly or **mop-head endive** (see p. 28) has a sharp taste, good in salads.

Chicory (see p. 28) has a slightly bitter taste, and can be eaten raw or cooked.

Globe artichokes (see p. 26) are popular as a starter.

Asparagus (see p. 26) has a delicate, subtle flavour.

Broccoli (see p. 27) can be sprouting and green, as here, or hearting and purple.

Radishes (see p. 30) are usually red in colour, but black can also be found.

Sweet potatoes (see p. 31) are orange-fleshed.

Celeriac (see p. 28) has a flavour similar to celery.

Kohlrabi (see p. 29) can vary in shape and be purple or green.

Jerusalem artichokes (see p. 29) have crisp, sweet flesh with a slightly nut-like flavour.

Scorzonera (see p. 30) is a type of salsify and has a similar bitter flavour.

Watermelons (see p. 36) can be ridged or smooth.

Ogen melon (see p. 36) has pale green, sweet flesh.

Pomegranates (see p. 37) contain delicious red pips.

Dates (see p. 34) are rich, sticky and nutritious.

Pineapples (see p. 37) have golden-yellow flesh, sweet and yet slightly sharp.

Grapes (see p. 35) can be black or green, and have a lovely delicate flavour.

Granadillas (see p. 35) are full of juicy, tangy seeds.

Kiwifruit (see p. 35) have a slightly tart flavour.

Guavas (see p. 35) are soft-fleshed and very aromatic.

Papayas (see p. 36) have pinky-orange, juicy flesh and a distinctive aroma.

Mangoes (see p. 36) have a lovely scent and soft, almost slippery flesh.

Bananas (see p. 34) are a nutritious, filling fruit.

Lemons (see p. 35) are used for their sharp, acidic taste and fresh aroma.

Limes (see p. 36) are used in the same way as lemons.

Cherries (see p. 34) can be red, black or even yellow.

Peaches (see p. 36) have velvety skin, which varies in colour, and soft flesh.

There are many varieties of **pear** (see p. 36). The two shown here are dessert pears: **Packham** (top), a soft, sweet pear, and the harder **Conference** (bottom).

Grapefruit (see p. 35) can vary in colour and in sweetness.

The **sweet orange** (see p. 36).

Clementines (see p. 34) are sweet-tasting citrus fruit.

Cranberries (see p. 34) are acid, so are not eaten raw.

Bramley cooking apple (see p. 33).

Three **apples** (see p. 33): **Cox's Orange Pippin, Red Delicious** and **Granny Smith.**

FRESH FRUIT Per 100 g (4 oz)	Water	Protein	Fat	Carbohydrate	Fibre	Vitamin A	Vitamin B₁	Vitamin B₂	Vitamin B₃	Vitamin B₆	Vitamin B₁₂	Vitamin C	Vitamin D	Vitamin E	Folic acid	Iron	Calcium	Magnesium	Sodium	Potassium	Phosphorus	Zinc
	g	g	g	g	g	µg	mg	mg	mg	mg	µg	mg	µg	mg	µg	mg	mg	mg	mg	mg	mg	mg
Recommended daily allowance	N	80M 60W	N	N	25-30	750	1.5	1.5	18	1.5	3	30	2.5	8	200	12	500	250	2500	2500	500	15
Apples – cooking	86	0.3	Tr	9.6	2.4	30	0.04	0.02	0.1	0.03	0	15	0	0.2	5	0.3	4	3	2	120	16	0.1
– eating	65	0.2	Tr	9.2	1.5	23	0.03	0.02	0.1	0.02	0	2	0	0.2	4	0.2	3	4	2	92	6	0.1
Apricots	87	0.6	Tr	6.7	2.1	1500	0.04	0.05	0.6	0.07	0	7	0	N	5	0.4	17	12	Tr	320	21	0.1
Bananas – eating	71	1.1	0.3	19.2	3.4	200	0.04	0.07	0.6	**0.51**	0	10	0	0.2	22	0.4	7	**42**	1	350	28	0.2
– cooking (plantains)	67	1	0.2	28.3	5.8	60	0.05	0.05	0.7	0.5	0	20	0	N	16	0.5	7	33	1	350	35	0.1
Blackberries	82	1.3	Tr	6.4	7.3	100	0.03	0.04	0.4	0.05	0	20	0	**3.5**	N	0.9	63	30	4	210	24	N
Blueberries	85	0.6	Tr	14.3	N	130	0.02	0.02	0.4	0.06	0	22	0	N	6	0.7	10	2	1	65	9	0.1
Cherries	82	0.6	Tr	11.9	1.7	120	0.05	0.07	0.3	0.05	0	5	0	0.1	8	0.4	16	10	3	280	17	0.1
Cranberries	87	0.4	Tr	3.5	1.1	20	0.03	0.02	0.1	0.04	0	12	0	N	2	1.1	15	8	2	120	11	N
Currants – black	77	0.9	Tr	6.6	8.7	200	0.03	0.06	0.3	0.08	0	200	0	1	N	1.3	60	17	3	370	43	N
– red	83	1.1	Tr	4.4	8.2	70	0.04	0.06	0.1	0.05	0	40	0	0.1	N	1.2	36	13	2	280	30	N
– white	83	1.3	Tr	5.6	6.8	Tr	0.04	0.06	0.1	0.05	0	40	0	0.1	N	0.9	22	13	2	290	28	N
Damsons	76	0.5	Tr	9.6	4.1	220	0.1	0.03	0.3	0.05	0	3	0	0.7	3	0.4	24	11	2	290	16	0.1
Dates	23	2.2	0.5	**72.9**	8.7	50	0.09	**0.1**	2.2	N	0	0	0	N	N	**3**	59	N	1	**648**	63	N
Figs	85	1.4	Tr	9.5	2.5	500	0.06	0.05	0.4	0.11	0	2	0	N	N	0.4	34	20	2	270	32	0.3
Gooseberries	90	1.1	Tr	3.4	3.2	180	0.04	0.03	0.3	0.02	0	40	0	0.4	N	0.3	28	7	2	210	34	0.1
Granadillas	73	**2.8**	Tr	6.2	**15.9**	10	Tr	**0.1**	1.9	N	0	20	0	N	N	1.1	16	39	**28**	350	N	N
Grapes	76	0.6	Tr	15.3	0.9	Tr	0.04	0.02	0.3	0.1	0	4	0	N	6	0.3	18	6	2	240	21	0.1
Grapefruit	91	0.6	Tr	5.3	0.6	Tr	0.05	0.02	0.2	0.03	0	40	0	0.3	12	0.3	17	10	1	230	16	0.1
Greengages	78	0.8	Tr	11.8	2.6	N	0.05	0.03	0.4	0.05	0	3	0	0.8	3	0.4	17	8	1	310	23	0.1
Guavas	83	0.8	0.6	9.4	N	168	0.05	0.05	1.2	N	0	**242**	0	N	N	0.9	23	13	4	289	N	N
Kumquats	81	0.9	0.1	17.1	3.7	600	0.08	**0.1**	N	N	0	36	0	N	N	0.4	63	N	7	236	23	N
Lemons	85	0.8	Tr	3.2	5.2	Tr	0.05	0.04	0.2	0.11	0	80	0	N	N	0.4	**110**	12	6	160	21	0.1
Limes	91	0.5	**2.4**	5.6	N	10	0.03	0.02	0.1	0	0	46	0	0	N	Tr	13	N	2	82	0	N
Loganberries	85	1.1	Tr	3.4	6.2	80	0.02	0.03	0.4	0.06	0	35	0	0.3	N	1.4	35	25	3	260	24	N
Lychees	82	0.9	Tr	16	0.5	Tr	0.04	0.04	0.3	N	0	40	0	N	N	0.5	8	10	3	170	35	N
Mangoes	83	0.5	Tr	15.3	1.5	1200	0.03	0.04	0.3	N	0	30	0	N	N	0.5	10	18	7	190	13	N
Melons – cantaloupe	94	1	Tr	5.3	1	**2000**	0.05	0.03	0.5	0.07	0	25	0	0.1	30	0.8	19	20	14	320	30	0.1
– honeydew	94	0.6	Tr	5	0.9	100	0.05	0.03	0.5	0.07	0	25	0	0.1	30	0.2	14	13	20	220	9	0.1
– watermelon	94	0.4	Tr	5.3	N	20	0.02	0.02	0.2	0.07	0	5	0	0.1	3	0.3	5	11	4	120	8	0.1
Mulberries	85	1.3	Tr	8.1	1.7	Tr	0.05	0.04	0.4	0.05	0	10	0	N	N	1.6	36	15	2	260	48	N
Nectarines	80	0.9	Tr	12.4	2.4	500	0.02	0.05	1	0.02	0	8	0	N	5	0.5	4	13	9	270	24	0.1
Oranges	86	0.8	Tr	8.5	2	50	**0.1**	0.03	0.2	0.06	0	50	0	0.2	**37**	0.3	41	13	3	200	24	0.2
Papayas	87	0.5	0.1	11.3	N	710	0.03	0.05	0.4	N	0	73	0	0	1	0.7	24	8	4	221	0	**0.4**
Peaches	86	0.6	Tr	9.1	1.4	500	0.02	0.05	1	0.02	0	8	0	N	3	0.4	5	8	3	260	19	0.1
Pears	83	0.3	Tr	10.6	2.3	10	0.03	0.03	0.2	0.02	0	3	0	Tr	11	0.2	8	7	2	130	10	0.1
Persimmons	64	0.8	0.4	33.5	1.5	N	N	N	N	N	0	66	0	N	N	2.5	9	N	1	310	26	N
Pineapples	84	0.5	Tr	11.6	1.2	60	0.08	0.02	0.2	0.09	0	25	0	N	11	0.4	12	17	2	250	8	0.1
Plums, dessert	84	0.6	Tr	9.6	2.1	220	0.05	0.03	0.5	0.05	0	3	0	0.7	3	0.4	11	7	2	190	16	Tr
Pomegranates	80	1	0.6	16.6	N	0	0.07	0.01	0.3	0	0	7	0	N	N	0.7	13	12	1	379	0	N
Raspberries	83	0.9	Tr	5.6	7.4	80	0.02	0.03	0.4	0.06	0	25	0	0.3	N	1.2	41	22	3	220	29	N
Rhubarb (cooked)	**95**	0.6	Tr	0.9	2.4	55	Tr	0.03	0.3	0.02	0	8	0	0.2	4	0.4	93	13	2	400	19	N
Strawberries	89	0.6	Tr	6.2	2.2	30	0.02	0.03	0.4	0.06	0	60	0	0.2	20	0.7	22	12	2	160	23	0.1
Tangerines	87	0.9	Tr	8	1.9	100	0.07	0.02	0.2	0.07	0	30	0	N	21	0.3	42	11	2	160	17	0.1

KEY
All wholefoods are uncooked unless stated otherwise. Some wholefoods may not be included in the chart, as there is currently no nutritional data available. **g**: grams **mg**: milligrams **µg**: micrograms **N**: no available data **Tr**: trace **M**: adult men **W**: adult women. The recommended daily allowances are averages and vary depending on age, occupation and metabolism. Figures in bold type indicate the wholefood with the highest level of nutrient.

Apples

Apples originated in the Middle East and are now commercially grown in most countries with a temperate climate. There are over 2,000 varieties, both cooking and dessert.

To eat raw or for use in salads, choose a dessert apple: Cox's Orange Pippin, Laxton's Superb, Red Delicious, Granny Smith, Spartan, Starking or Worcester Pearmain. There may be other local varieties available. For stewing, baking or puréeing, use a cooking apple: Bramley's Seedling, Grenadier or Lord Derby. If flavour and shape are important, as in pies and flans, use a dessert apple rather than a cooking apple.

Apples can be used in soups, salads, savoury dishes, puddings, cakes, pickles, jams, chutneys and for juices. They are also available dried (see p. 39).

Preparation and cooking
Wash the apples and peel if desired. Core and cut into quarters or slices as required. If not using immediately, brush with a little lemon juice to prevent browning. Stew, purée or bake whole.
Recipe: Apple, Soya & Almond Pudding (see p. 120).

Apricots

These gorgeous yellow-orange fruits originated in China and are now widely available. There are several varieties.

Look for apricots with a good colour and no blemishes. If they are ripe, they should yield evenly to pressure. However, most imported apricots are picked unripe before shipping. If you buy unripe apricots, leave on a window ledge or shelf at room temperature for a few days; fully ripe apricots should be refrigerated.

Apricots can be eaten raw or cooked. Use in soups, salads, savoury dishes, puddings, cakes, jams, pickles, chutneys or for fresh juice. Apricots are also available dried (see p. 39).

Preparation and cooking
Wash and remove the skin if desired by pouring boiling water over the fruit and leaving to stand for 10 minutes. The skin should then peel off easily. Cut in half and remove the stone. Leave halved or slice as desired. Brush with a little lemon juice to prevent browning.

To cook, either stew or purée.
Recipe: Mushroom, Apricot & Chicory Salad (see p. 92).

Bananas

Bananas originated in the Tropics. There are many varieties and they are generally available all year round.

There are two main types, for cooking and to eat raw. Eating bananas are usually bright yellow. Look for firm fruit without black patches which indicate bruising. Black speckles do not mean that the fruit is bad but it will probably need to be eaten fairly soon.

Bananas for cooking, or plantains, are larger, usually green in colour and should not be eaten raw. They are used in many Caribbean and African dishes. Bananas are also available dried (see p. 39).

Preparation and cooking
Peel off the outer skin and use as required. Brush with a little lemon juice to prevent browning. If using in a fruit salad, add just before serving. Cooking and eating bananas can also be baked whole or sliced and fried.
Recipe: Baked Bananas with Yogurt Sauce (see p. 121).

Blackberries
(Bramble)

This northern European plant still grows successfully wild, in what remains of the dwindling rural hedgerow. It is also grown commercially in America. Look for plump, glossy, fresh fruit.

Blackberries combine well with apples, as in traditional apple and blackberry pie, but they are also delicious eaten raw or cooked into cakes and pies, fools and soufflés, or made into jams and jellies.

Preparation
Wash the blackberries carefully in a colander. Drain and remove any imperfect fruit. Serve raw with a little sweetener and/or cream or natural yogurt.
Recipe: Use instead of raspberries in Redcurrant & Raspberry Summer Pudding (see p. 129).

Blueberries

Although northern European in origin, blueberries are mainly grown commercially in America. The smaller bilberry can be used in the same way.

Choose firm, undamaged fruit and eat raw or use in puddings, cakes, jams and jellies.

Preparation and cooking
Wash and drain thoroughly in a colander and serve raw with a little sweetener and/or cream or yogurt as desired.

To cook, simmer gently in a little water for 5-10 minutes until tender. They do not contain many pips so do not need to be sieved.
Recipe: Use instead of apricots in Hunza Cream (see p. 125).

Boysenberries

Developed in California, these are similar to large raspberries or loganberries.

Look for firm, undamaged fruit, and eat on the day of purchase or store in a refrigerator. Prepare and use as for raspberries.
Recipe: Fresh Fruit Flan (see p. 125).

Cherries

Middle Eastern in origin, cherries are grown commercially in America and many European countries. There are basically two types of cherry, bitter and sweet. The bitter, dark-skinned cherries such as May Duke or Morello are used mainly for cooking and jam-making. Sweet cherries can vary in colour from pale yellow to deep purple-red. Look for glossy fruit which yield to gentle pressure and eat on day of purchase or store in a refrigerator. Use in salads, puddings, cakes and jams.

Preparation and cooking
Raw cherries should be washed and de-stalked before eating. To cook, boil gently for 5-10 minutes in a little water. Set aside to cool. Remove the stones by cutting into the centre of each cherry with a sharp knife or use a special cherry pitter.
Recipe: Cherry Pie (see p. 123).

Clementines

Clementines are a cross between a sweet orange and a tangerine. They are fairly small, loose-skinned, orange-red fruit. They are very sweet and contain virtually no pips.

Look for firm, heavy fruit without soft or brown spots. As with all citrus fruit, they may be stored at room temperature or in a refrigerator and will usually last for about 10 days. Eat on their own, or in sweet and savoury salads, puddings and cakes.

Preparation
Remove the skins and break the flesh into natural segments. Clementine skins are fairly thin and they do not have much pith. Use the juice and grated rind as flavouring.

Cranberries

Though European in origin, cranberries are mainly grown commercially in America and Finland. They are too tart to eat raw and are usually made into cranberry sauce or jellies. You very seldom find them fresh but many stores do stock deep-frozen cranberries.

Preparation and cooking
Wash fresh cranberries in a colander and drain well and simmer in a little water for 5-10 minutes until tender. For most sauces and jellies, straining or sieving the fruit is necessary. If bought frozen, thaw as directed on the packet and use as desired.
Recipe: Use instead of gooseberries in Gooseberry Fool (see p. 125).

Currants

Currants may be red, black or white. They are very tart and are usually not eaten raw but made into puddings, pies, jams, jellies or juices. Look for plump, evenly coloured fruit.

Preparation and cooking
Currants grow in thick clusters on little stalks. Each currant must be removed from its stalk before cooking. Wash and drain well in a colander, and simmer in a little water until tender or use as desired.
Recipe: Redcurrant & Raspberry Summer Pudding (see p. 129).

Damsons
(Prune plums)

Damsons are a type of sour plum, dark purple in colour. Because of their tart flavour, they are generally used for cooking. Choose fresh looking fruit which yield all over under gentle pressure. Use in puddings, jams and jellies.

Preparation and cooking
Wash thoroughly and simmer gently for 10 minutes in a little water. Remove from heat allow to cool. Halve, remove the stones and then purée or use as desired.
Recipe: Use instead of prunes in Prune & Raspberry Whip (see p. 128).

Dates

The fruit of the date palm, dates are native to the northern Persian Gulf. They are cultivated in Algeria, Tunisia and the USA.

The small oblong fruit are usually golden or dark brown, with a shiny, sticky skin, and a long narrow stone inside the fibrous flesh. Eat raw on their own or in salads, or cooked in puddings. (For dried dates, see p. 39.)

Preparation
Wash fresh dates and remove the stones. Eat raw or use as required.
Recipe: Use instead of apricots in Sprouty Salad (see p. 94).

Figs

Figs are indigenous to Syria, Turkey and India. Fresh figs can be green or purple, and there are over 700 varieties. Look for even-coloured fruit which yield evenly under gentle pressure. Fresh figs are extremely delicate.

A perfectly ripe fresh fig is best eaten and savoured on its own. Slightly unripe figs may be steamed or poached as a pudding or used in cakes, jams, chutneys or pickles.

Figs are also available dried (see p. 39) and are often roasted and made into a caffeine-free coffee substitute (see p. 61).
Preparation and cooking
Fresh figs need only be washed carefully before eating. To cook slightly unripe figs, steam or poach in a little water for 5-10 minutes until tender.
Recipe: Add to Tropical Fruit Salad (see p. 132).

Gooseberries

Gooseberries are in fact a member of the currant family. They have a short summer season, often lasting only a few weeks. Choose firm undamaged fruit. The large, plump yellow varieties are often sweet enough to eat raw, but the smaller green ones need to be cooked. Use raw in fruit salads or cooked in cakes, puddings and tarts, jams and pickles.
Preparation and cooking
Wash the raw fruit well and top and tail with scissors or a sharp knife, before eating. To cook, wash, top and tail and then simmer in a little water for 5-10 minutes until tender. Gooseberries have many pips so strain or sieve, if desired.
Recipe: Gooseberry Fool (see p. 125).

Granadillas
(Passion fruit)

Granadillas are a small knobbly purplish-brown tropical fruit native to Brazil, with a hard shell encasing numerous juicy pips. They have a very strong tangy flavour which is particularly good in fruit salads and drinks.
Look for firm, heavy granadillas with slightly wrinkled skins. Use in puddings, sweet and savoury salads, cakes, juices and jams.
Preparation
Cut the fruit in half with a sharp knife. Scoop out the seeds and juice with a teaspoon, and eat raw or used as required. If you do not like the pips, pass through a sieve or strainer.
Recipe: Tropical Fruit Salad (see p. 132).

Grapefruit

Grapefruit are one of the largest members of the citrus family and originated in the West Indies. They may have white or pink flesh: white grapefruit are good for making juice; the pink-fleshed varieties are generally sweeter and may be eaten like an orange.
Look for even-coloured heavy fruit, which are juicier. Use raw in salads and starters, or cook in cakes, puddings or marmalades. Grapefruit halves can also be grilled or baked.
Preparation
Pink grapefruit may be peeled and eaten like an orange. To prepare a grapefruit, cut in half and cut inside the edge with a grapefruit or sharp knife to free the flesh from the skin. Carefully cut between the segments, freeing the flesh from the dividing membranes.
Recipe: Citrus Cocktail (see p. 81).

Grapes

Grapes probably originated in western Asia. They can be red, black or green and are grown commercially in many parts of the world, both as dessert grapes and for making wine.
Common dessert varieties are the Hothouse and Napoleon Red (red grapes) and the Muscatel, Californian Seedless and South African Walthamcross (white grapes). Seedless varieties are also available.
Look for plump, fresh grapes, which are firmly attached to their stems. Grapes are often dried for raisins, currants and sultanas (see p. 39).
Preparation
Grapes are usually eaten raw. They have a delicate flavour which can become lost in highly-flavoured dishes.
Before eating grapes, wash carefully. If you wish to remove their skins and pips, cover with boiling water for 30 seconds, drain and peel off the skins. Cut the peeled grapes in half and remove the pips.
Recipe: Halve, de-pip and add to Tropical Fruit Salad (see p. 132).

Greengages

Greengages are a northern European plum. They are small and greenish-yellow. Look for even-coloured fruit which yield all over to gentle pressure. Eat greengages as one would a dessert plum, either raw, stewed or puréed or in puddings, cakes and jams. They are one of the sweetest varieties of plum.
Preparation and cooking
To eat raw, wash well. To cook, put in a saucepan, cover with water and simmer gently until tender, about 10-15 minutes. Leave to cool, halve and remove the stones. Use as required, adding a little sweetener if liked.
Recipe: Use instead of apricots in Apricot & Orange Sago Cream (see p. 121).

Guavas

Guavas are grown in most tropical and subtropical countries, and probably originated in Haiti. Round or pear-shaped, they usually have yellow skins with bright red or pink flesh containing numerous pips, similar to a tomato. Look for yellow fruit which yield evenly to gentle pressure.
Guavas are perhaps an acquired taste but make a delicious and unusual addition to fresh fruit salads, and can also be used in puddings, cakes and jams.
Preparation
Wash the guava well and cut into quarters. Peel off the skin and eat the flesh and pips. A little lemon juice sprinkled over will prevent discolouration.
Recipe: Add to Tropical Fruit Salad (see p. 132).

Kiwifruit
(Chinese gooseberries)

Kiwifruit originated in China. The outside of the fruit is brown and hairy and inside is bright green flesh surrounding tiny black edible seeds.
Look for undamaged fruit which yield evenly to gentle pressure.
Nutritionally, kiwifruit are rich in vitamin C. Eat kiwifruit on their own or add sliced to salads, puddings, cakes and jams, or use as an attractive garnish for sweet or savoury salads.
Preparation
Fresh kiwifruit should be peeled with a sharp knife before eating. Slice or cut into quarters for a salad. For use as a garnish, slice crosswise or lengthwise as desired.
Recipe: Tropical Fruit Salad (see p. 132).

Kumquats

These tiny citrus fruits, no bigger than an olive, originated in China. Their popularity has grown in Western countries over the past few years, and they are increasingly available.
Look for small, heavy, bright orange fruit, without marks or blemishes. The whole fruit is eaten including the skin, which is usually sweeter than the flesh inside.
Preparation
Wash thoroughly and remove any stalks. Use whole, halve or slice thinly as desired.
Recipe: Chop and add to the stuffing in Baked Apples (see p. 121).

Lemons

Lemons originated in India and are now grown in subtropical countries all over the world. They are an extremely versatile fruit and can be used in a large range of dishes, both savoury and sweet. Do not forget to make use of the lemon zest or rind as this can add a wonderful tang to certain dishes. Lemon juice will also prevent fruit and vegetables from discolouring once they have been cut into chunks or slices.
Look for even-coloured, heavy fruit without blemishes. Avoid shrivelled or soft fruit.
Lemons are not suitable for eating raw but the juice and rind can be added to soups, savouries, puddings, cakes, jams and pickles. They are also used for garnishes.
Preparation
Cut the lemon in half crosswise and extract the juice with a lemon squeezer or by hand. Lemons are good for garnishing a range of dishes: slice crosswise or cut into wedges or in different directions for a variety of effects. Remove the pips if desired.
To obtain lemon rind, wash and dry the fruit and then grate finely, turning the lemon often to avoid the white pith. Alternatively, quarter the lemon and remove the peel in four pieces. Scrape out the pith and slice finely for shredded rind or chop finely as desired.
Recipe: Tabouleh (see p. 95).

Limes

Limes are the tropical equivalent of lemons. Indian in origin, they grow widely in tropical climates. They are smaller than lemons and are vibrant green, turning to yellow at their peak of ripeness. Look for firm, heavy fruit. Prepare and use as for lemons.
Recipe: Tapioca & Lime Soufflés (see p. 131).

Loganberries

Loganberries look like large, dark raspberries and have a similar flavour. They are a cross between a raspberry and a blackberry. Look for firm undamaged fruit. Prepare and use as for raspberries.
Recipe: Use instead of strawberries in Strawberry Mousse (see p. 130).

Lychees

Chinese in origin, these succulent tropical fruit have a rough, brownish-pink skin and creamy-coloured smooth flesh surrounding a large black pip. The flesh has a subtle, delicate taste and fine aroma.

Look for firm heavy fruit, avoiding those with cracked or damaged shells or with a wrinkled appearance.
Preparation
Peel off the outer shell. Eat the flesh immediately or add to fruit salads. The large pips can first be removed with a sharp knife if desired.
Recipe: Add to Tropical Fruit Salad (see p. 132).

Mangoes

Mangoes are indigenous to India but are now grown extensively in all tropical countries. There are over 1,000 types of mango tree, and the fruit varies greatly in size and colour.

Look for firm, heavy fruit which yield slightly to pressure and are without blemishes or bruises. Mangoes can be enjoyed on their own or used in fruit salads, cakes, drinks, chutneys and jams. Dried mangoes are also available (see p. 39).
Preparation
Mangoes have a large stone in the middle. Cut the fruit lengthwise on one side, as close to the stone as possible. Repeat on the other side of the stone so you have two large slices of flesh which can be peeled off the stone. Scoop the flesh out of the skin with a spoon or cut into smaller pieces as required.
Recipe: Tropical Fruit Salad (see p. 132).

Mangosteens

Mangosteens are Far Eastern fruit and are very seldom found in the West, but should not be missed if available.

The outside of the fruit is a deep purple. Inside the thick, pithy shell is a rich, cream-coloured fruit similar in taste and texture to a lychee. Look for heavy, bright fruit and eat by themselves or in fruit salads.

Preparation
Break or cut open the hard outer casing. Segment and eat the creamy flesh, discarding the pip or pips within. The flesh adheres tightly to the pip(s), so remove as you eat.
Recipe: Add to Tropical Fruit Salad (see p. 132).

Melons

Melons are indigenous to Asia and Africa and there are many different varieties. They have a high water content, low calorific value and a delicate, sweet flavour. Look for firm, heavy fruit without bruises or soft spots and which yield to fingertip pressure around the stem base. Smell the fruit as it may give off a delicate bouquet when ripe.

There are five common melons:
1 Cantaloupe are round with dark green, ribbed skins and orange flesh.
2 Charentais are small and round with yellow-green skin and sweet, orange flesh.
3 Honeydew are oval with bright yellow or dark green skins and greenish-yellow flesh.
4 Ogen are small and round with ribbed striped skins and very sweet yellow or pale green flesh.
5 Watermelons are the largest of the melons and are oval or round with dark green, sometimes striped or mottled skins. The flesh is bright pinky-red and very crisp and sweet, and contains numbers of flat, black pips.

Melons are often eaten as a starter, either on their own or filled with other ingredients. They are also delicious in sweet and savoury salads.
Preparation
Cut the melon in half lengthwise and scoop out the seeds. Cut into wedges if desired. Watermelons have seeds throughout the flesh, so pick them out as best as you can. Because melons contain so much water, cut over a large bowl to catch the juice. Use as required.
Recipe: Melon & Tomato Salad (see p. 91).

Mulberries

Mulberries are the fruit of the mulberry tree. There are many varieties but white and black are the most common. They have a distinctive flavour. Prepare and use as for raspberries.
Recipe: Use instead of raspberries in Prune & Raspberry Whip (see p. 128).

Nectarines

Nectarines are Chinese in origin and not a cross between a peach and a plum as many people suppose. They are in fact a variety of smooth-skinned peach and the name is probably derived from 'nectar', owing to the delicious flavour. The colour can vary from yellow to red.

Prepare and use as for peaches.

Oranges

Oranges are probably the most popular citrus fruit. Far Eastern in origin, they are now grown commercially in many subtropical countries. There are hundreds of varieties, which fall into two main groups: bitter for cooking and sweet for eating.

Look for firm, bright, heavy fruit without soft spots or blemishes.

Eat oranges by themselves or add to savoury and sweet salads, puddings, cakes, jams and marmalades. Orange juice is also delicious on its own or in soups and savouries. Orange zest or rind can be added to many sweet and savoury dishes. Remember to wash the orange well before grating.
Preparation
Wash and dry the orange. Carefully score the orange with a sharp knife into quarters, taking care not to pierce the flesh. Peel off the skin and pith, segment the flesh or slice into rings.
Recipe: Apricot & Orange Sago Cream (see p. 121).

Papayas
(Pawpaws)

Papayas originated in Central America and are now abundant in all tropical countries. They vary in size and colour, the most common being the yellow-skinned varieties. The flesh is bright pink and contains numerous tiny black seeds, with a sharp, peppery flavour.

Look for papayas without soft spots or blemishes and which give evenly under gentle pressure.

Papaya makes a wonderful breakfast alternative to grapefruit or prunes. Use also in sweet or savoury salads and puddings.
Preparation
Cut the papaya in half lengthwise, scoop out the seeds and discard. Eat from the skin or peel and slice as desired.

Peaches

Peaches are probably Chinese in origin, and there are over 2,000 varieties. They have a furry skin and vary from yellow to pinkish-red.

Look for firm heavy fruit without soft spots or blemishes and which give evenly under gentle pressure.

Peaches are enjoyed on their own, or added to salads, cakes, puddings, jams and chutneys. They are also available dried (see p. 39).
Preparation and cooking
Wash and cut in half with a sharp knife. Remove the stone and use the fruit as required. If you wish to peel the peach, pour over boiling water, leave for 30 seconds, drain off the water and the skins should peel off easily. Brush with a little lemon juice to prevent discolouration. Peaches can also be baked.
Recipe: Peach Custard Tart (see p. 126).

Pears

West African in origin, pears are now grown in most temperate countries. There are over 5,000 varieties, which include dessert and cooking pears, and they are generally available all year round.

Look for firm fruit without soft spots or bruising and which yield to gentle pressure at the stalk. Pears can be eaten on their own or used in sweet and savoury salads, puddings, cakes, jams and pickles. They are also available dried (see p. 39).
Preparation
Wash, core and peel as desired. Eat whole or slice lengthwise. Cut pears may be sprinkled with lemon juice to prevent discolouration.
Recipe: Peach & Pear Crumble (see p. 127).

Persimmons
(Kaki fruit/Sharon fruit/Date plums)

Persimmons originated in China and Japan and are now grown in many subtropical countries. They resemble large orange tomatoes and have succulent, sweet orange flesh.

Look for heavy, bright fruit without blemishes or cracks in the skin. The fruit should yield evenly to gentle pressure. When ripe, persimmons are really quite soft. Do not be persuaded to eat unripe as they contain tannic substances which taste horrible.

Persimmons are best enjoyed on their own or in a fruit salad, but they may be added to puddings and cakes or made into jams and chutneys if desired.

Preparation
The stalk of a really ripe persimmon will pull away easily. Having removed the stalk, cut the fruit in half and scoop out the flesh. Alternatively, cut into quarters and carefully peel off the skin.

Recipe: Place slices on top of Polenta Pudding with Seasonal Fruit (see p. 128).

Pineapples

Pineapples are one of the most popular tropical fruits. Indigenous to South America, they can be found in almost every tropical country in the world and are generally available all year round.

Look for firm, heavy fruit without soft spots or blemishes. They should yield gently to fingertip pressure and may have a pleasant aroma when ripe. Another way of testing for ripeness is to carefully pull a leaf out of the crown. If the leaf comes away easily, the pineapple is probably ready to eat.

Pineapples are delicious on their own or in sweet and savoury salads, savoury dishes such as risottos, puddings, cakes and jams.

Preparation
There are many ways to cut a pineapple. One of the simplest is to cut the pineapple crosswise in 2 cm (1 in) slices and then cut off the skin around the edges of each slice. If the core in the middle seems very tough or fibrous, this may also be removed. Take care to remove all the tiny black 'eyes' with the skin because they can cause skin irritation in and around the mouth if eaten.

Pineapples may also be cut into wedges or chunks or you can cut a lid off the crown and scoop out the flesh inside. The shell may then be filled with a mixture of fresh fruit, mousse, sorbet or ice cream, or even chopped vegetables for a savoury salad.

Recipe: Pineapple Salad (see p. 92).

Plums

Plums are European in origin and are commercially grown in many temperate countries. There are many varieties including both dessert and cooking plums. They can be small or large and vary in colour from golden-yellow to green or deep purple.

Look for firm, plump fruit which yield evenly to gentle pressure. Avoid shrivelled or extremely soft plums. Dessert plums can be eaten by themselves or added to fruit salads. Both dessert and cooking plums can be used in puddings, cakes and jams.

Preparation and cooking
Dessert plums should be washed, halved and the stones removed. Peel if desired. Cooking plums may be stewed in a little water until tender, about 10-15 minutes. Leave to cool and then carefully remove the skins and stones. Use as required.

Recipe: Add 100 g (4 oz) plums to Rice Pudding (see p. 130).

Pomegranates

Pomegranates are indigenous to Persia. Their hard, reddish shells reveal hundreds of bright red, juicy seeds when cut open.

Look for firm, even-coloured fruit, the heavier the better, and without blemishes.

Pomegranates are eaten raw. The deep red pips are sucked for their juice and then usually discarded. Pomegranate juice is used as a flavouring, to add to sweet or savoury dishes or drinks.

Preparation
Cut a thin slice off the stem end of the pomegranate, cut the fruit into sections and bend back to reveal the juicy red seeds. If you want to extract the juice, press the seeds through a sieve into a bowl.

Rambutans

This delightful Far Eastern tropical fruit is still quite rare in the West. It has a pinkish-red spiky outer casing and cream-coloured flesh which resembles a lychee in looks and in flavour.

Choose healthy looking fruit, heavy in weight with a good pinky-red tinge. If very green, they will probably not be ripe. Eat on their own or added to fruit salads.

Preparation
Break open the hairy outer shell. Inside the creamy white flesh is a hard pip which can be removed if desired with a sharp knife.

Raspberries

White, red and black varieties are available, although red is the most common. Look for firm, undamaged fruit in clean, unstained punnets with no mould. They are very delicate when fully ripe. Use in cakes, puddings, jams and sauces or simply eat on their own or in fruit salad with cream or smetana (see p. 47).

Preparation and cooking
Wash gently in a colander, picking over the fruit to remove any stalks which may still be attached. To cook, simmer gently in a little water for 5-10 minutes and then sieve or strain if desired.

Recipe: Prune & Raspberry Whip (see p. 128).

Rhubarb

Rhubarb is the stem of a plant probably native to Tibet. It is in fact a vegetable but is always used as a fruit. Outdoor rhubarb has thick, succulent stems, dark red or green in colour. It has a sharp acid flavour. Forced rhubarb is smaller and pinker and usually sweeter.

Rhubarb is always eaten cooked. Use in puddings, cakes, jams and pickles.

Preparation and cooking
Wash the rhubarb, trim and remove any strings. Cut into 2 cm (1 in) pieces. Simmer in a little water until tender, about 10-15 minutes. Add sweetener and use as required.

Another way of cooking rhubarb which does not require additional liquid is to prepare it as above and then to place it in an ovenproof dish or on a baking sheet and cook in a 200°C (400°F/Gas 6) oven for 5 minutes or until tender. Be careful not to let it burn.

Recipe: Rhubarb & Almond Mousse (see p. 129).

Satsumas

Satsumas are a loose-skinned variety of citrus fruit, similar in appearance to a tangerine but seedless, with a sweeter flavour and thicker skin. Look for heavy, undamaged fruit and avoid any which look dry, withered or with soft spots.

Satsumas are delicious eaten by themselves or added to sweet and savoury salads, puddings, cakes and marmalades.

Preparation
Peel off the skin, remove any pith, break into natural segments and use as desired.

Recipe: Use instead of oranges in Watercress & Orange Salad (see p. 96).

Strawberries

Strawberries are probably the most popular summer fruit. American in origin, they are now commercially produced all over the world.

Choose firm, undamaged fruit and eat on the day of purchase or refrigerate. Use in salads, both savoury and sweet, soups, puddings, cakes, jams, jellies and juices.

Preparation and cooking
Wash carefully in a colander, and remove the stalks. To cook, simmer in a little water for 5-10 minutes until tender and then sieve or strain if desired.

Recipe: Strawberry Mousse (see p. 130).

Tangerines

Tangerines are another loose-skinned variety of citrus fruit, native to southern China and Laos. Similar in appearance to the satsuma, they have thinner skins and many pips. Prepare and use as for satsumas.

Recipe: Fresh Fruit Flan (see p. 125).

Ugli

The ugli fruit is a cross between the grapefruit and the tangerine, and is native to the East Indies. Uglis look like large, ugly grapefruit with thick, knobbly green and orange skins but the flesh is pink and sweet. They have very few pips. Prepare and use as for grapefruit.

Recipe: Use instead of grapefruit in Spinach Salad (see p. 94).

DRIED FRUIT

Apples	Currants	Mangoes	Prunes
Apricots	Dates	Peaches and nectarines	Raisins
Bananas	Figs	Pears	Sultanas

Drying is a useful way of storing perishable fruit and concentrating its nutritional value. The fruits are picked and either dried naturally in the sun or in dehydration units, which blast the fruit with hot air until all the moisture has evaporated.

Dried fruits are high in fibre, natural sugars, protein, vitamins A, B and C, iron, calcium and other minerals. They can be eaten raw as a snack or cooked in sweet and savoury dishes, desserts, cakes and biscuits. Dried fruits are an excellent source of natural sugar and sweeter than fresh fruit, so use them to help cut down on refined sugar.

Buying and storage

All dried fruit sold in retail shops should have a 'best before' stamp on the label. Although dried fruit can last for many months it is best to choose the freshest possible. Choose plump, unblemished fruit and check the labels for any additives (see below). Mixed dried fruit can be bought, but it is better to buy separate packets as these will usually be fresher.

All varieties of dried fruit should be stored in airtight containers, away from direct heat and sunlight. They will keep for up to a year, but are best eaten within 6 months.

Additives

There are two main additives used in the production of dried fruit; sulphur dioxide (E220) and a mineral spray.

To preserve some dried fruits and to prevent them from losing their bright colours, some manufacturers fumigate the fruit with sulphur dioxide (E220). This gas is poisonous and in excess can cause severe alimentary problems and possibly genetic mutations. It also destroys vitamin B in the fruit. Since the whole fruit is thoroughly fumigated it is impossible to remove all of the additive by washing, so buy unsulphured fruits whenever possible, especially if you are giving them regularly to children. Figs and dates are not usually sulphured.

Mineral oils are sometimes sprayed on to the fruits after they have been dried, to give them a glossy appearance and to prevent them from sticking together. However, these oils can prevent the body's absorption of vitamins A, D, E and K, and also calcium and phosphorus. Some manufacturers are now using vegetable oils instead, but buy untreated fruit whenever possible. If mineral oils have been used, remove by careful washing in warm water.

Drying fruit

Fruit can be dried at home in a low oven. Apples, apricots, peaches and pears are some of the most successful to do. Either leave whole or peel, core and slice as required. Apples are usually peeled and cut into rings; peaches, nectarines and apricots are either left whole (with their stones removed) or halved; pears can be left whole (cored or uncored) or sliced.

Heat the oven to a low temperature, about 60°C (150°F/Gas 2). Leave the oven door open if you have a gas or electric oven, as there should be plenty of air. If you have a solid fuel cooker this is unnecessary. Spread the fruit on to racks or thread on to cotton (this is particularly suitable for apple rings). Leave for several hours until well dried.

Soaking and cooking

Currants, raisins and sultanas are usually sold ready-washed and need no soaking, although they can be plumped up before use by soaking for a few minutes in hot water. Other dried fruit should usually be washed before use.

If you wish to reconstitute dried fruit by soaking, simply cover with water in a bowl and leave for about 6 hours or until puffed up. Boiling gently will speed up this process.

To cook dried fruit, boil in the soaking liquid for about 30 minutes until soft. They can then be puréed in a liquidizer if required.

DRIED FRUIT Per 100 g (4 oz)	Water	Protein	Fat	Carbohydrate	Fibre	Vitamin A	Vitamin B₁	Vitamin B₂	Vitamin B₃	Vitamin B₆	Vitamin B₁₂	Vitamin C	Vitamin D	Vitamin E	Folic acid	Iron	Calcium	Magnesium	Sodium	Potassium	Phosphorus	Zinc
	g	g	g	g	g	µg	mg	mg	mg	mg	µg	mg	µg	mg	µg	mg	mg	mg	mg	mg	mg	mg
Recommended daily allowance	N	80M 60W	N	N	25-30	750	1.5	1.5	18	1.5	3	30	2.5	8	200	12	500	250	2500	1500	500	15
Apples	N	0	**1.4**	61	3.2	N	0.05	0.1	0.4	0.11	0	**9**	0	N	N	1.4	26	N	4	480	44	N
Apricots	15	**4.8**	Tr	43.4	**24**	**3600**	Tr	0.2	3	0.17	0	Tr	0	N	14	4.1	92	65	56	**1880**	120	0.2
Currants	22	1.7	Tr	63.1	6.5	220	**0.1**	0.03	0.5	**0.3**	0	0	0	N	11	1.8	95	36	20	70	40	0.1
Dates	15	2	Tr	63.9	8.7	50	0.07	0.04	2	0.15	0	0	0	N	**21**	1.6	68	59	5	750	65	0.3
Figs	17	3.6	Tr	52.9	18.5	50	**0.1**	0.08	1.7	0.18	0	0	0	N	9	4.2	**280**	**92**	**87**	1010	92	**0.9**
Peaches	16	0.6	Tr	53	14.3	2000	Tr	0.19	**5.3**	0.1	0	Tr	0	N	14	**6.8**	36	54	6	1100	**120**	N
Prunes	**23**	2.4	Tr	40.3	16.1	1000	**0.1**	**0.2**	1.5	0.24	0	Tr	0	N	4	2.9	38	27	12	860	83	N
Raisins	22	1.1	Tr	64.4	6.8	30	**0.1**	0.08	0.5	**0.3**	0	0	0	N	4	1.6	61	42	52	860	33	0.1
Sultanas	18	1.8	Tr	**64.7**	7	30	**0.1**	0.08	0.5	**0.3**	0	0	0	**0.7**	4	1.8	52	35	53	860	95	0.1

KEY
All wholefoods are uncooked unless stated otherwise. Some wholefoods may not be included in the chart, as there is currently no nutritional data available.
g: grams **mg**: milligrams **µg**: micrograms **N**: no available data **Tr**: trace **M**: adult men **W**: adult women. The recommended daily allowances are averages and vary depending on age, occupation and metabolism. Figures in bold type indicate the wholefood with the highest level of nutrient.

Apples

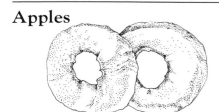

Available as rings and segments.

Dried apples are a good source of vitamin C, usually lost from other fruit in the drying process. They are often sold lightly sulphured.

To dry apple rings at home, peel, core and cut into rings. Then, heat in a 60°C (150°F/Gas 2) oven for several hours until well dried.

Dried apples can be eaten as a snack or used soaked and cooked in soups, sauces, cakes, desserts and puddings.

Recipe: Couscous Cake (see p. 141).

Apricots

Available whole, halved, in pieces, sulphured and unsulphured. Hunza apricots can also be bought.

Apricots have the highest protein content of all dried fruit, and are also high in vitamins A and B_2. Both sulphured and unsulphured apricots can be bought. Hunza or wild apricots have been cultivated for centuries by the Hunza tribe in the Himalayas, and are thought to be the best variety. Hunza apricots are small, pale brown in colour with an edible kernel. They are sold unsulphured.

Whole dried apricots can be eaten as they are, or soaked for a few hours until they expand. Halved apricots tend to be rather dirty and so wash well before eating or cooking. Apricot pieces cook quite quickly and are good for making jams and purées.

Use dried apricots as snacks or in soups, salads, curries, sweet and savoury dishes, puddings, cakes, jams and chutneys.

Recipe: Apricot & Orange Sago Cream (see p. 121).

Bananas

Available whole, sliced lengthwise and as banana chips.

Dried whole or sliced bananas have a high sugar content and are deliciously sweet and chewy. They are nutritionally superior to banana chips, which are small pieces of unripe banana which have been deep-fried in an oily sugar mix.

Use dried bananas as snacks or in curries, savoury dishes, puddings, cakes, jams, chutneys and pickles.

Recipe: Use 15 ml (1 tbsp) finely chopped banana instead of raisins in Fresh Vegetable Curry (see p. 106).

Currants

Available whole.

Currants are dried from a variety of black grape originating from Corinth. They are tiny, seedless, very sweet and are always sold unsulphured.

Currants can be eaten as a snack or used in salads, savoury dishes, puddings, cakes and mincemeat.

Recipe: Fruit & Malt Bread (see p. 153).

Dates

Available whole, unpitted and pressed into slabs.

Dried dates are extremely high in sugar and also contain vitamin A and some B vitamins. Plump, soft whole dates taste best but the pressed slabs or blocks are good for cooking and for making purées. If using these, make sure that no stones have been left inside.

Dates are unsulphured but are often treated with mineral oils to give them glossy skins, so buy untreated dates if possible or ones which have been treated with vegetable oils.

Use dried dates as snacks or chopped in salads, savoury dishes, puddings, cakes, jams, chutneys and pickles.

Recipe: Date & Oat Bars (see p. 141).

Figs

Available whole.

Figs have a high sugar content and are rich in protein, B vitamins and minerals, particularly calcium and magnesium. They are also a natural laxative. The best figs are dark brown with thin skins, often indicated by a sugary crusting on the surface.

Figs can be eaten as a snack or chopped in salads, savoury dishes, puddings, cakes, jams, chutneys and pickles.

Recipe: Brandy Fruit Cake (see p. 137).

Mangoes

Available sliced.

Dried mangoes are usually available in long slices and are very sweet. They have often been sulphured, so look for unsulphured mangoes if possible.

Use chopped in salads, sweet and sour dishes, curries, puddings, cakes, jams, chutneys and pickles.

Recipe: Use instead of apricots in Barley, Fruit & Vegetable Pollo (see p. 99).

Peaches and nectarines

Available whole and halved.

Dried peaches and nectarines have a similar appearance and use, although nectarines are rather smaller. Both perhaps lack the flavour and aroma of the fresh fruit, but they are an excellent source of iron and any unpleasant smell will disappear after soaking. They are often sulphured and some varieties (particularly from China) may be preserved in sugar.

Use dried peaches and nectarines as you would apricots; as snacks and in soups, salads, savoury dishes, puddings, cakes, jams, chutneys and pickles.

Recipe: Rich Muesli (see p. 70).

Pears

Available whole and halved.

Dried pear halves are tasty and retain much of the texture and flavour of the fresh fruit. If dried whole, the core, skin and pips can be removed after soaking if liked. Dried pears are often sulphured, and some varieties (particularly from China) may even have been preserved in sugar.

To dry pears at home, first halve and core (there is no need to peel). Then, heat in a 60°C (150°F/Gas 2) oven for several hours until well dried.

Dried pears can be eaten as a snack or used in compôtes, savoury dishes, puddings, cakes, jams and chutneys.

Recipe: Rich Muesli (see p. 70).

Prunes

Available whole, unpitted, pitted and tenderized.

Prunes are a dried variety of black-skinned plum, grown specifically for drying purposes. They are low in sugar and are also a natural laxative. Tenderized prunes have been partially cooked. Some prunes have been treated with mineral oils, so wash carefully or find untreated prunes if possible, or the cake may sink.

Prunes can be used whole or puréed, in compôtes, stuffings, puddings, cakes, jams and confectionery.

Recipe: Prune & Raspberry Whip (see p. 128).

Raisins

Available whole.

Raisins are dried grapes, and are available in a number of varieties. Lexia raisins are from Australia, and are juicy and sweet with their seeds removed. Muscatel raisins are also large, pale in colour and seedless. Small black seedless raisins are also available.

Raisins are usually unsulphured although some may have been treated with mineral rather than vegetable oils. Generally, raisins should be washed and sorted before using, but dry carefully if they are to be used in a cake mixture, or the cake may sink.

Eat raisins raw or use in salads, sweet and savoury dishes, curries, puddings, cakes, pickles and chutneys.

Recipe: Curried Coleslaw (see p. 90).

Sultanas
(Golden/White raisins)

Available whole.

Sultanas are dried, seedless white grapes. Large, pale and succulent, they are sweeter than raisins and currants. Sultanas have often been sulphured and treated with mineral oils to give them a shiny appearance, but some (for instance Australian sultanas) are unsulphured and have been treated with vegetable oils instead, which are much better.

Use sultanas as you would currants and raisins, especially when the dish requires a sweeter taste.

Recipe: Barley, Fruit & Vegetable Pollo (see p. 99).

NUTS

Almonds
Brazil nuts
Cashew nuts
Chestnuts

Coconuts
Hazelnuts
Macadamia nuts
Peanuts

Pecan nuts
Pine nuts
Pistachio nuts
Pumpkin seeds

Sesame seeds
Sunflower seeds
Tiger nuts
Walnuts

The term nut is used to describe any seed or fruit with an edible kernel in a hard, usually brittle, shell. All the more common varieties of nuts are included in this section, as well as those seeds which are generally used in the same way as nuts: pumpkin, sesame and sunflower seeds.

Nutritional value

Nuts are extremely nutritious, providing large amounts of protein and many essential vitamins and minerals. Nuts are also high in carbohydrate, fats, oils and fibre, so should not be eaten in excess. However, most nuts (except coconut and pine nuts) contain a certain amount of linoleic acid, which is thought to help counteract the possible build-up of cholesterol from any saturated fats and oils.

Fortunately, shelled nuts from reputable wholefood shops are not subjected to additives, although it is always best to check. Commercially packaged nuts are often treated with preservatives, inhibitors and dyes, however. You should also beware of snack-type nuts which are coated in saturated fats, roasted and often covered with large quantities of salt, thereby considerably reducing their nutritional value.

Storage

When buying nuts, you should check for freshness and only buy in small quantities. Because of their high fat and oil content they can turn rancid if left too long. Unshelled nuts will keep up to 6 months, but seeds and shelled nuts should be kept in an airtight container in a cool, dry and dark place. Chopped and ground nuts will go stale more quickly, and should ideally be eaten within 4-6 weeks.

Usage

Nuts can be eaten raw or added to all sorts of dishes, both savoury and sweet. They can be used whole or chopped in salads, purées, casseroles, roasts, stuffings, cereals, bakes and confectionery. They are generally available in a variety of forms: in their shells, or shelled and whole, slivered, chopped, flaked or ground. Most are interchangeable, but the whole nuts are usually fresher.

You may wish to blanch whole nuts to remove the skins more easily. To do this, immerse in boiling water for a few minutes and then pop the nuts out of their skins. For grinding whole shelled nuts, use a small grater or mill.

Roasting nuts

Many recipes call for roasted nuts. This accentuates the flavour of the nut although it somewhat reduces the nutritional value. Vegetable oil, spices, honey or tamari can also be added to the roasting nuts to alter the flavour.
1 Heat the oven to 190°C (375°F/Gas 5).
2 Spread the nuts evenly on a baking tray and bake for about 5 minutes, shaking occasionally until they are light golden-brown and crisp.
3 Remove from the oven and leave to cool.

NUTS Per 100 g (4 oz)	Water	Protein	Fat	Carbohydrate	Fibre	Vitamin A	Vitamin B₁	Vitamin B₂	Vitamin B₃	Vitamin B₆	Vitamin B₁₂	Vitamin C	Vitamin D	Vitamin E	Folic acid	Iron	Calcium	Magnesium	Sodium	Potassium	Phosphorus	Zinc
	g	g	g	g	g	µg	mg	mg	mg	mg	µg	mg	µg	mg	µg	mg	mg	mg	mg	mg	mg	mg
Recommended daily allowance	N	80M 60W	N	N	25-30	750	1.5	1.5	18	1.5	3	30	2.5	8	200	12	500	250	2500	2500	500	15
Almonds	5	16.9	53.5	4.3	14.3	0	0.24	**0.92**	2	0.1	0	Tr	0	20	96	4.2	**250**	260	6	860	440	3.1
Brazil nuts	9	12	61.5	4.1	9	0	1	0.1	1.6	0.17	0	Tr	0	6.5	N	2.8	180	**410**	2	760	590	4.2
Cashew nuts	5	17.2	45.7	27.9	1.5	60	0.43	0.25	1.8	N	0	Tr	0	N	N	3.8	38	267	15	464	390	N
Chestnuts	**52**	2	2.7	**36.6**	6.8	0	0.2	0.22	0.2	0.33	0	Tr	0	0.5	N	0.9	46	33	11	500	74	N
Coconuts – desiccated	2.3	5.6	62	6.4	**23.5**	0	0.06	0.04	0.6	N	0	0	0	N	N	3.6	22	90	28	750	160	N
– fresh	42	3.2	36	3.7	13.6	0	0.03	0.02	0.3	0.04	0	**2**	0	0.7	9	2.1	13	52	17	440	94	0.5
Hazelnuts	41	7.6	36	6.8	6.1	0	0.4	N	0.9	0.55	0	Tr	0	**21**	72	1.1	44	56	1	350	320	2.4
Macadamia nuts	N	7	55	8	2	0	0.15	0.1	1	N	0	0	N	N	N	1.5	40	N	N	200	180	N
Peanuts	5	24.3	49	8.6	8.1	0	0.9	0.1	16	0.5	0	Tr	0	8.1	**110**	2	61	180	6	680	370	3
Pecan nuts	3	9.2	**71.2**	14.6	2.3	**130**	0.86	0.13	0.9	0.2	0	**2**	0	N	N	2.4	73	N	Tr	603	289	N
Pine nuts	6	**31.1**	47.4	11.6	0.9	N	0.62	N	N	N	0	N	0	N	N	N	N	N	N	N	N	N
Pistachio nuts	6	19.3	54	15	2.4	60	0.7	0.2	1.5	N	0	0	0	N	N	**14**	140	N	N	750	525	N
Pumpkin seeds	4	29	46.7	15	1.9	70	0.24	0.19	2.4	N	N	N	N	N	N	11.2	51	N	N	N	**1144**	N
Sesame seeds	5	26.4	54.8	6.4	9.1	40	0.72	0.09	**12.6**	N	0	N	0	N	N	7.8	131	347	**40**	407	890	**10.3**
Sunflower seeds	5	24	47.3	19.9	3.8	50	**1.96**	0.23	5.4	**1.2**	0	N	0	N	N	7.1	120	N	30	**920**	837	N
Walnuts	24	10.6	51.5	5	5.2	0	0.3	0.13	1	0.73	0	Tr	0	0.8	66	2.4	61	130	3	690	510	3

KEY
All wholefoods are uncooked unless stated otherwise. Some wholefoods may not be included in the chart, as there is currently no nutritional data available.
g: grams **mg:** milligrams **µg:** micrograms **N:** no available data **Tr:** trace **M:** adult men **W:** adult women.   The recommended daily allowances are averages and vary depending on age, occupation and metabolism.   Figures in bold type indicate the wholefood with the highest level of nutrient.

Almonds

Available unshelled, shelled, blanched, slivered, flaked, roasted, chopped and ground.

Almond trees, with their beautiful pink and white blossom, are native to the Middle East. There are two types of almonds, bitter and sweet. Bitter almonds are broader and shorter than the sweet variety. Their bitter flavour is due to the presence of prussic acid, a highly volatile and poisonous substance which can only be removed by heating. You should therefore avoid eating raw bitter almonds. Their main use is in the production of almond oil (see p. 49) and almond essence (see p. 51).

Sweet almonds are extensively used in European and Eastern cookery. The nut has a thin, brown skin which can be eaten, but it is usually peeled away after roasting or blanching.

Almonds have the highest calcium content of all nuts, and are also high in protein and vitamin B_2. Use almonds whole and chopped in salads, dips, sweet and savoury dishes, cakes, puddings and biscuits. Flaked almonds can be tossed in butter and spices for a cocktail snack.

Recipe: Rhubarb & Almond Mousse (see p. 129).

Brazil nuts

Available unshelled, shelled, chopped and roasted.

Brazil nuts are native to the tropical regions of Bolivia, Brazil and Venezuela and grow along the banks of the Orinoko and Amazon rivers. The enormous wild brazil trees grow to heights of 45-60 metres (150-200 feet), producing large coconut-type shells inside which the seeds, or brazil nuts, are wedged like segments of a fruit. Brazil nuts are rich and nutritious, but because of their high fat and oil content they can easily go rancid, so you should buy in small quantities.

Eat as a snack or use in nut rissoles, stuffings, cakes, some savoury dishes and confectionery.

Cashew nuts

Available shelled, roasted, chopped and salted.

Cashew nuts originated in Brazil. A tree crop, the kidney-shaped nut grows underneath a false fruit or 'cashew apple', which is often eaten in preference to the cashew itself. The nut has two shells, in between which is a caustic oil which can cause blisters and skin irritation if it touches the body. To render this oil harmless, the nuts are shelled and roasted before being sold.

They are usually eaten as a snack but are delicious in stuffings, Chinese dishes, cakes and desserts. The nuts are also made into cashew nut butter (see p. 50).

Recipe: Cashew Cream (see p. 132).

Chestnuts
(Sweet chestnuts)

Available unshelled, shelled, peeled, dried, ground and puréed.

Edible chestnuts are sweet chestnuts, native to southern Europe. They should not be confused with the nuts of the horse chestnut, which are inedible. Both the outer and inner skins should be removed before eating by boiling or roasting. They are always cooked before eating.

Sweet chestnuts can be eaten boiled, steamed, roasted or stewed in a variety of sweet and savoury dishes, or they can be dried and ground to produce chestnut flour, which is delicious in bread, pancakes or porridge.

Recipe: Chestnut & Prune Roast (see p. 104).

Coconuts

Available unshelled, flaked, desiccated and as creamed coconut.

The coconut is the fruit of the coconut palm, native to the Tropics.

Coconut meat can be eaten fresh or dried, and the 'milk' inside the coconut makes a refreshing and nutritious drink. The dried flesh (often known as *copra*) may be flaked or compressed into hard cakes known as creamed coconut or coconut cream. Coconut can be used in curries, bakes and confectionery. It is extremely rich in oils and fats however, and should perhaps be eaten in moderation.

Recipe: Carrot & Coconut Cake (see p. 140).

Hazelnuts
(Cobnuts/Filberts)

Available unshelled, shelled, roasted, chopped and ground.

Hazelnuts, cobnuts and filberts all belong to the same family of plants. They originated in the Mediterranean and are now cultivated in most temperate areas of Europe, particularly Italy, France and Turkey.

The nuts grow in clusters, and are partially covered by a green helmet-shaped skin. They are particularly high in vitamins B_6 and E. Hazelnuts can be eaten on their own or used in bakes and confectionery. The nuts can also be made into hazelnut butter (see p. 50).

Recipe: Banana Nut Cake (see p. 136).

Macadamia nuts
(Queensland nuts)

Available whole: unshelled, shelled, roasted and salted.

Macadamia nuts are native to Australia and are now also widely cultivated in Hawaii. Outside the country of origin, they are usually only available shelled and roasted. They look like pale hazelnuts and have a very sweet, oily flavour. Like brazil nuts, they have a very high fat and oil content, so go rancid quickly. They are usually eaten as a snack but are delicious in salads or sweet dishes.

Recipe: Fennel & Tomato Salad (see p. 91).

Peanuts
(Groundnuts/Monkey nuts)

Available unshelled, shelled, peeled, roasted and salted.

The peanut is actually a legume, the seed of an annual pod-bearing plant originating in South America. The nuts are encased in a dry, fibrous shell. Peanuts are highly nutritious, and can be eaten raw or roasted. They are used in peanut butter (see p. 50) and groundnut oil (see p. 49).

Peanuts can be eaten as a snack or added to salads, sweet and savoury dishes, cakes, puddings and biscuits.

Recipe: Flapjacks (see p. 142).

Pecan nuts

Available unshelled, shelled, roasted, chopped and salted.

Pecan nuts are indigenous to North America and were a staple food for the American Indians. They have a smooth reddy-brown or golden shell, and the nut inside resembles a walnut in appearance, although the taste is rather milder.

Pecan nuts are widely used in sweet and savoury American cooking, and can be added to salads, stuffings, cakes, biscuits and confectionery.

Recipe: Stuffed Aubergines with Tomato Sauce (see p. 115).

Pine nuts
(Pine kernels/Indian nuts/Pignolas)

Available raw, roasted and salted.

Pine nuts are the edible seeds of a number of pine trees, mainly the stone pine. They are native to the Mediterranean.

Pine nuts grow unshelled and the tiny, creamy-yellow oblong-shaped seeds have a rich, slightly turpentine flavour. They are eaten raw, like peanuts, or can be used in soups, sauces, salads, rice dishes, stews and stuffings. In Italy they are used in the traditional pesto sauce for pasta, and they are used in many Middle Eastern rice dishes.

Recipe: Add to Fennel & Tomato Salad (see p. 91).

Pistachio nuts

Available unshelled and shelled.

These green nuts in their semi-split shells are native to the Middle East and Central Asia. The naturally golden shell is sometimes dyed red for decorative effect.

Pistachio nuts are often eaten as a salted snack, served with or without their shells. They are often added to confectionery and halva (see p. 51) or used as a garnish for desserts.

Recipe: Brown Rice Risotto (see p. 100).

Pumpkin seeds

Available unhusked and husked.

These small, flat green seeds are extremely nutritious, being high in protein, fats and minerals.

Pumpkin seeds can be eaten raw or cooked in both sweet and savoury dishes, and can also be sprouted (see p. 23).

Recipe: Granola 2 (see p. 69).

Sesame seeds
(Benne seeds)

Available unhusked.

The sesame plant is probably African in origin and is now grown commercially in the Middle East, the Far East and Mexico. The tiny beige seeds are eaten whole (they do not need to be husked), and are high in zinc, sodium and vitamin B_3.

Sesame seeds are most commonly processed into a fine, pale sesame oil (see p. 49). They are also often made into tahini, which is a thick cream-coloured sesame paste (see p. 50), gomashio or sesame salt (see p. 50) and halva, a sweet sesame cake made with either sugar or honey (see p. 51).

Use whole sesame seeds in bread and cakes or in savoury and sweet dishes. They have a delicious nutty flavour which blends well with most fruit, grains, vegetables and beans. Sesame seeds may also be sprouted successfully (see p. 23).

Recipe: Sesame Honey Bars (see p. 145).

Sunflower seeds

Available unhusked and husked.

Sunflowers belong to the daisy family and probably originated in or around Mexico. The tall, erect plants with their large sun-like flowers were cultivated and worshipped by the Incas. They are now mainly grown for sunflower oil (see p. 49).

Sunflower seeds are very nutritious, being rich in protein, the vitamin B group and minerals, particularly potassium. They may also be sprouted (see p. 23).

The seeds can be bought ready-husked in most wholefood shops, and have a sweet nutty flavour. They are delicious in savoury dishes, salads, breads, cakes and puddings or sprinkled over foods as a garnish.

Recipe: Sunflower Bars (see p. 145).

Tiger nuts
(Earth almonds)

Available whole or ground.

These are not in fact true nuts, but are rhizomes of a plant native to Africa. They are small, brown and knobbled in appearance, and have a flavour reminiscent of almonds. The chufa nut is similar to the tiger nut, and is more common in Europe. It is used in the Spanish drink *horchata de chufa*.

Eat tiger nuts raw as a snack or add to stuffings, cakes, sweet puddings, desserts and confectionery.

Walnuts

Available unshelled, shelled, chopped and ground.

Walnut trees are native to the Middle East and were taken to Europe by the Romans. There are many varieties but two main types of walnut, the European and the Black. European walnuts are sometimes called English or Persian walnuts. Black walnuts are native to America and are slightly larger, with a harder thicker shell and a stronger flavour.

Walnuts are used to make walnut oil (see p. 49), which has a pronounced flavour and is used for salad dressings. Immature green walnuts are available pickled in vinegar, and are used in the popular Mexican dish *chiles en nogada*. Walnuts contain some vitamin B_6 and folic acid, unusual in nuts.

Walnuts can be eaten as a snack or used in stuffings, salads, cakes, bakes, puddings and confectionery.

Recipe: Baked Avocado with Stilton & Walnuts (see p. 98).

SEAWEEDS

Agar-agar ☐   Dulse ☐   Laver   Nori ☐
Arame ☐   Hiziki ☐   Macrocystis porphyra   Wakame ☐
Carrageen ☐   Kombu ☐   Mekabu

☐ Pictured opposite page 48

Seaweeds grow abundantly in all the oceans and have been used as food, medicine and fertilizer for many thousands of years. They have a long tradition of use in Japan but have still to be fully appreciated in the West. If you are not familiar with their use, you can experiment with some of the recipes in this book and you should find the different varieties a valuable addition to your diet.

There are many varieties of seaweeds, with differing tastes and uses. Some have a strong sea flavour whereas others are mild and sweet. Some seaweeds, such as agar-agar or carrageen, produce a clear tasteless jelly which can be used in place of animal gelatine.

Nutritional value

Nutritionally seaweeds rate highly. They are high in protein, containing essential amino acids, and are rich in minerals and trace elements, particularly iodine, calcium, potassium and iron. They also contain sizeable amounts of vitamins A, B, C and D, including vitamin B$_{12}$, which is only found in three other plant foods (alfalfa, comfrey and fermented soya bean products such as miso and tamari).

Seaweeds are also high in sodium, however, especially when cooked with shoyu or tamari, and they should not be eaten too frequently by people with high blood pressure.

Storage

Seaweeds are best bought ready-cleaned and dried from wholefood shops. They will keep indefinitely unopened, but once open store in an airtight container and use within a few months.

Soaking

Most seaweeds need a preliminary soaking before use, unless they are going to be cooked in a stew or soup. In the preparation and cooking instructions which follow it is suggested that the water used for soaking is thrown away. This is to reduce the strong, salty sea flavour of some seaweeds. However, this water does contain many useful nutrients, so do make use of it if you wish, either for cooking the seaweeds or in soups and stocks.

SEAWEEDS Per 100 g (4 oz)	Water	Protein	Fat	Carbohydrate	Fibre	Vitamin A	Vitamin B$_1$	Vitamin B$_2$	Vitamin B$_3$	Vitamin B$_6$	Vitamin B$_{12}$	Vitamin C	Vitamin D	Vitamin E	Folic acid	Iron	Calcium	Magnesium	Sodium	Potassium	Phosphorus	Zinc
	g	g	g	g	g	µg	mg	mg	mg	mg	µg	mg	µg	mg	µg	mg	mg	mg	mg	mg	mg	mg
Recommended daily allowance	N	80M 60W	N	N	25-30	750	1.5	1.5	18	1.5	3	30	2.5	8	200	12	500	250	2500	2500	500	15
Agar-agar	**20**	2.3	0.1	**74.6**	0	0	0	0	0	N	✱	0	N	N	N	5	400	N	N	N	8	N
Arame	19	7.5	0.1	60.6	9.8	50	0.02	0.2	2.6	N	✱	0	N	N	N	12	1170	N	N	N	150	N
Dulse	17	N	3	N	0.7	N	N	N	N	N	✱	N	N	N	N	6.3	567	N	N	N	22	N
Hiziki	17	5.6	0.8	42.8	**13**	150	0.01	0.2	**4**	N	✱	0	N	N	N	**29**	**1400**	N	N	N	56	N
Kombu	15	7.3	1.1	54.9	3	430	0.08	0.32	1.8	N	✱	11	N	N	N	N	800	N	**2500**	N	150	N
Nori	11	**35.6**	0.7	44.3	4.7	**11000**	**0.25**	**1.24**	10	N	✱	**20**	N	N	N	12	260	N	600	N	**510**	N
Wakame	16	12.7	1.5	51.4	3.6	140	0.11	0.14	10	N	✱	15	N	N	N	13	1300	N	**2500**	N	260	N

KEY
All wholefoods are uncooked unless stated otherwise. Some wholefoods may not be included in the chart, as there is currently no nutritional data available. **g**: grams **mg**: milligrams **µg**: micrograms **N**: no available data **Tr**: trace **M**: adult men **W**: adult women. The recommended daily allowances are averages and vary depending on age, occupation and metabolism. Figures in bold type indicate the wholefood with the highest level of nutrient. ✱ Exact figure unknown but thought to be very high.

Agar-agar
(Kanten)

Agar-agar is the Malay word for jelly. It is obtained from a variety of seaweeds and is mainly manufactured in Japan. Agar-agar is a natural, unflavoured vegetable gelatine and is used as an alternative to animal gelatine. It is available in powder or flake form. The powdered varieties may be chemically processed, so the flakes are preferable.

Preparation and cooking

For a firm jelly, put 15 ml (1 tbsp) of agar-agar in a saucepan with 575 ml (1 pt) of cold water, fruit juice or stock. Gently bring to the boil and simmer for 5 minutes. Remove from the heat, pour into a serving bowl and refrigerate for 4 hours or until set. Use 10 ml (2 tsp) for a delicate jelly.
Recipe: Rhubarb & Almond Mousse (see p. 129).

Arame

This is a good seaweed to begin with if you are not familiar with the taste and texture of seaweed, and it is particularly rich in calcium. Arame has a mild, sweet flavour and is grown abundantly in the seas around Japan. It is harvested in early spring and is parboiled, sun-dried and then shredded into thin strands to make it easier to cook and use.

Preparation and cooking

Put a handful of arame in a bowl and cover with boiling water. Leave to stand for 5 minutes and then pour off the soaking liquid.

Add soaked arame to soups, stews or savoury dishes, and cook for a further 20-30 minutes. If you wish to cook it separately for salads or as a side vegetable, put it in a saucepan and cover with fresh cold water. Add 15 ml (1 tbsp) of shoyu or tamari for flavouring, bring to the boil and simmer gently for 20-30 minutes or until tender. A little garlic or grated root ginger can also be added during cooking, if liked. Eat hot or cold.
Recipe: Miso & Arame Soup (see p. 77).

Carrageen
(Irish moss)

Carrageen is grown in temperate North Atlantic coastal waters, in the seas around northern France, Ireland and New England. It is usually used for its gelling and setting properties, but the fan-like leaves can be cooked and eaten as a vegetable if desired.

The United States is the principal manufacturer of the by-product carrageenan, or E 407, which is an emulsifying, thickening and gelling additive used widely in commercial ice creams, jellies, biscuits, milk shakes, frozen desserts and some infant formulas. Although E 407 is from a natural substance it can cause intestinal problems if eaten in excess.

Preparation and cooking

For use as a vegetable, prepare and cook as for arame (see p. 43).

For use as a setting agent in moulds or blancmanges, first put 25 g (1 oz) of carrageen in a bowl. Pour over boiling water and leave to stand for 15 minutes. Pour off the soaking liquid and put the seaweed in a saucepan. Add 575 ml (1 pt) of fresh cold water, bring to the boil and simmer gently for 30 minutes.

Strain the cooking liquid off into a separate saucepan. Add your fruit, vegetables or flavouring as desired (depending on whether you require a sweet or savoury mould) and heat for a further 10 minutes. Pour into a serving bowl and refrigerate for 4 hours or until set.

Dulse

This is another North Atlantic seaweed, grown and eaten in the coastal areas of Canada and North America, Iceland and Ireland. It has large, dark red flat leaves and no matter how long it is cooked it still remains tough and chewy with a strong salty flavour. It is perhaps not a seaweed for beginners. It can be cooked as a vegetable or eaten raw.

Preparation and cooking

Put a handful of dulse in a bowl, cover with boiling water and leave to stand for 20 minutes. Pour off all the soaking liquid and put the seaweed in a saucepan. Cover again with cold fresh water and flavour with 15 ml (1 tbsp) shoyu or tamari if liked. Bring to the boil and simmer for 40-50 minutes.
Recipe: Dulse Soup (see p. 75).

Hiziki

This seaweed is from Japan, and has been used there for many hundreds of years. It is hand-picked and allowed to dry in the sun before being coarsely shredded. Hiziki is extremely high in iron and calcium and has a sweet delicate flavour. It can be cooked with vegetables or by itself.

Preparation and cooking

Put a handful of hiziki in a bowl, pour over boiling water and leave to stand for 20 minutes. Pour off the soaking liquid.

Add the seaweed to soups, stews or savoury dishes and cook for a further 30 minutes. If you wish to cook it separately as a side vegetable or for a salad, put in a saucepan and cover with fresh cold water. Add a little tamari, grated ginger or garlic for flavouring, bring to the boil and simmer for 30 minutes. Hiziki can be eaten hot or cold.
Recipe: Seitan with Hiziki (see p. 113).

Kombu

Kombu comes from Japan's northern seas, enjoying the cold Arctic currents. It has a strong sweet flavour and comes in thick black-green strips. Kombu is especially high in sodium but contains calcium and vitamins A and C, and makes a nutritious stock for soups and savoury dishes. It is also used as a tea-like infusion in Japan.

Preparation and cooking

For use as a vegetable or to eat in soups, salads or savoury dishes, first put 2 strips of kombu in a bowl. Pour over boiling water and leave to stand for 20 minutes. Pour off the soaking liquid and put the kombu in a saucepan. Cover with fresh cold water and add a little tamari and root ginger to flavour. Bring to the boil and simmer gently for 30 minutes.

For use as a stock, put 1 strip of kombu in a saucepan with about 450 ml (16 fl oz) of cold water. Bring to the boil and simmer gently for 30 minutes. Strain the liquid off and use it as a tasty, nourishing base for soups, stews and other savoury dishes.
Recipe: Kombu Surprise (see p. 84).

Laver

Laver is a red seaweed grown in the waters around South Wales and Ireland. It grows close to the shore and can be gathered at low tide.

Laver has the appearance of spinach, and is a traditional breakfast food in South Wales, where it is rolled in oatmeal, fried and served with bacon and eggs. It has a very strong seaweed flavour and is not recommended for those just beginning to experiment with seaweeds in their diet.

Prepare and use as for dulse.

Macrocystis porphyra

This is the variety of seaweed most often used in the preparation of kelp tablets and powders. Some people like to take these tablets as a daily nutritional supplement or to sprinkle a little of the powder on to savoury dishes.

Mekabu

A Japanese seaweed, mekabu is a black-green seaweed similar to kombu. It is available in curled, dried strips. It is used mainly in soups, salads and as a garnish.

Prepare and use as for kombu.

Nori

Nori is a close relative of laver and is used extensively in Japanese cuisine. It is cultivated on bamboo frames in shallow bays and inlets around the coast of Japan. After harvesting, the broad leaves are spread out on bamboo racks, sun-dried and then hand-pressed to form thin sheets.

Nori is extremely high in protein and minerals, and is usually crumbled over vegetables and savoury dishes as a garnish or wrapped in whole sheets around grains, vegetables and pickles. It can also be soaked and cooked.

Preparation and cooking

For use as a vegetable, cook as for arame.

For sprinkling purposes, take a sheet of nori between your fingers or with a pair of tongs and gently wave it over an open flame or electric ring. In a matter of seconds the nori will turn a dark green and take on a crisp texture. Remove from the heat, leave to cool and then crumble with your hands.

For wrapping purposes, lightly toast the sheets of nori as above and mould around rice or a stuffing of your choice.
Recipe: Nori & Spinach Rolls (see p. 85).

Wakame

Wakame is another Japanese seaweed with an appearance and flavour very similar to kombu, though rather softer. It is especially high in protein, iron and calcium. Wakame is a good seaweed for beginners, as it is close in taste to a green vegetable.

Preparation and cooking

Put 2 strips of wakame in a bowl, pour over boiling water and leave to stand for 20 minutes. Pour off the soaking liquid and cut out the central veins. Cut into small pieces as a salad, or cook as a vegetable. To cook, put in a saucepan, cover with fresh cold water, bring to the boil and simmer for 10-15 minutes.
Recipe: Wakame (see p. 119).

DAIRY PRODUCE

Butter   Eggs   Sour cream
Buttermilk   Ghee   Soya milk
Cheese   Margarine   Yogurt
Cow's milk   Smetana
Cream   Solid vegetable fat

Milk, cream, butter, cheese and eggs have been consumed since animals were first domesticated, and in the West they form about a third of our calorie intake. These animal products provide many nutrients, and are a highly concentrated form of energy. Milk, for instance, provides milk protein, calcium and vitamins; eggs supply complete protein, containing all the essential amino acids (see p. 8), and cheese is another good source of protein.

Dairy products can form a valuable part of a wholefood vegetarian diet, particularly because of the complete protein and vitamin B_{12} which they contain, rare in plant foods. However, in recent years there has been strong evidence that for health reasons our intake of fats should be reduced, and of animal fats in particular, which are contained not only in meat but in dairy products.

Animal fats and disease

Fats provide over twice as much energy, weight for weight, as carbohydrates and proteins. Comparatively little fat is needed, therefore, to provide the necessary energy. Any excess fat can lead to obesity, which increases the likelihood of diabetes, high blood pressure, arthritis and gall bladder disease.

Excessive consumption of fat has also been linked with degenerative disease and heart disease, such as atherosclerosis, a restriction in the flow of blood to the heart caused by narrowing, or thickening, of the heart arteries. This narrowing is caused by the build-up of cholesterol deposits. Other arteries can be blocked in the same way, and may lead to other circulatory problems.

Cholesterol is contained in saturated fatty acids (see below). Although some cholesterol is needed by the body for the formation of certain hormones, any excess may build up in the arteries. Medical evidence suggests that reduction of fat intake would significantly reduce heart disease and that fat should form only about 30 per cent of energy intake.

Dairy products have sometimes been found to have other adverse effects. Cheese and other dairy foods are mucus-forming in some people, leading to sinus problems and migraine. Other people are allergic to milk protein, resulting in breathing problems, catarrh or eczema. Some are allergic to milk sugar (lactose), resulting in cramps and diarrhoea.

Saturated and unsaturated fatty acids

Fats can be divided into three basic types: saturated, mono-unsaturated and polyunsaturated. Saturated fatty acids (or saturated fats) are mainly found in food from animal sources: full-fat milk, cheese, eggs, cream and butter. Cholesterol is contained in these saturated fatty acids.

Unsaturated fatty acids are of two types, mono-unsaturated and polyunsaturated. These are found mainly in liquid vegetable oils and soft margarines. Although they add to the daily fat intake, they contain no cholesterol.

Polyunsaturated fatty acids contain three essential acids: linoleic acid, oleic acid and arachidonic acid. Linoleic acid is of particular importance as it enables the body to synthesize other fatty acids from food. It is also thought actually to help lower the level of cholesterol in the blood. It is sometimes recommended therefore that saturated fat is eaten in conjunction with twice its amount of polyunsaturated fat.

Cutting down

There is no need to cut out dairy products altogether from your diet. If you are aware of the need to keep your intake down, and are aware of their presence in many processed foods (look at the labels), there are nutritional benefits to be gained from including some dairy products in your diet. However, because of all the medical information, many people are choosing to decrease their consumption of dairy products and/or look for substitutes.

Most dairy products have low-fat versions, such as skimmed milk, skimmed milk soft cheese and low-fat cheese. Yogurt and smetana (a low-fat version of soured cream) can be used instead of full-fat cream in cooking and desserts.

There are also dairy alternatives made from plant or vegetable sources, which contain less saturated fat. Mono-unsaturated or polyunsaturated fatty acids are found in many vegetable oils, also used in the manufacture of margarines. However, it should be remembered that the process of hydrogenation, which is used to solidify fats and oils to make hard margarine, actually converts unsaturated fats into saturated fats.

Alternatives

As well as the low-fat substitutes such as skimmed milk, yogurt and soft cheese mentioned above, there are a number of non-dairy products which can be used successfully as dairy substitutes. Soya milk, included in this section because of its usage, is a nutritious and tasty cholesterol-free substitute for cow's milk, although it has a distinctive flavour which may seem strong at first. Also a product of the soya bean, tofu (see p. 51) can be used in many dishes to replace both cheese and eggs. It comes in both a firm and soft form, the former being similar to cheese in consistency. Soft tofu can be beaten into ingredients as a binding agent instead of eggs, and it is often used in non-dairy cheese-cakes instead of cream cheese. Another non-dairy binding agent is tahini (see p. 50), which can be beaten into dishes mixed in a little water.

Smoked tofu and tempeh, another soya bean product (see p. 51) have a stronger flavour and can be used instead of strong cheese. Vegetable oils (see p. 49) can be used for cooking instead of butter or margarine.

Storage

Most dairy products and substitutes should be kept in the refrigerator. Pasteurized milk will keep for about 4-5 days; cream will keep for 2-3 days, but should be covered or it will harden. Margarines and butter keep well, and eggs will keep for 3-4 weeks in a cool place or the refrigerator. To store cheese, keep wrapped in foil or waxed paper in a cool place or in a temperate part of the refrigerator (the salad box is ideal). Take out the cheese and stand at room temperature for about 1 hour before serving.

DAIRY PRODUCE Per 100 g (4 oz)	Water	Protein	Fat	Carbohydrate	Fibre	Vitamin A	Vitamin B_1	Vitamin B_2	Vitamin B_3	Vitamin B_6	Vitamin B_{12}	Vitamin C	Vitamin D	Vitamin E	Folic acid	Iron	Calcium	Magnesium	Sodium	Potassium	Phosphorus	Zinc
	g	g	g	g	g	µg	mg	mg	mg	mg	µg	mg	µg	mg	µg	mg	mg	mg	mg	mg	mg	mg
Recommended daily allowance	N	80M 60W	N	N	25-30	750	1.5	1.5	18	1.5	3	30	2.5	8	200	12	500	250	2500	2500	500	15
Butter, salted	15	0.4	82	Tr	0	470	Tr	Tr	Tr	Tr	Tr	Tr	0.76	2	Tr	0.2	15	2	870	15	24	0.15
Buttermilk	N	3.5	0.08	4.8	0	4	0.04	0.18	0.08	0.4	0.22	0.2	N	N	N	0.04	120	N	128	136	92	N
Cheese – Cheddar	37	26	33.5	Tr	0	205	0.04	0.5	0.1	0.08	1.5	0	0.26	0.8	20	0.4	800	25	610	120	520	**4**
– cottage	79	13.6	4	1.4	0	18	0.02	0.19	0.08	0.01	0.5	0	0.02	N	9	0.1	60	6	450	54	140	0.47
– cream	46	3.1	47.4	Tr	0	220	0.02	0.14	0.08	0.01	0.3	0	0.03	1	5	0.1	98	10	300	160	100	0.5
– Edam	44	24.4	22.9	Tr	0	135	0.04	0.4	0.06	0.08	1.4	0	0.18	0.8	20	0.2	740	28	980	160	520	**4**
– Feta	56	16.8	19.9	Tr	0	20	0.03	0.11	0.2	N	1.4	0	Tr	N	15	0.2	384	20	**1260**	70	N	1.1
– Parmesan	28	**35.1**	29.7	Tr	0	195	0.02	0.5	0.3	0.1	1.5	0	0.27	0.9	20	0.4	**1220**	**50**	760	150	**770**	**4**
– Stilton	28	25.6	40	Tr	0	230	0.07	0.3	N	N	N	0	0.31	1	N	0.5	360.	27	1150	160	300	N
Cow's milk – skimmed	**91**	3.4	0.1	5	0	Tr	0.04	0.2	0.08	0.04	0.3	1.6	Tr	Tr	5	0.05	130	12	52	150	100	0.36
– whole	88	3.3	3.8	4.7	0	18	0.04	0.19	0.08	0.04	0.3	1.5	0.02	0.09	5	0.05	120	12	50	150	95	0.35
Cream – double	49	1.5	48.2	2	0	220	0.02	0.08	0.04	0.02	0.1	0.8	0.28	1	2	0.2	50	4	27	79	21	0.17
– single	72	2.4	21.2	3.2	0	98	0.03	0.12	0.07	0.03	0.2	1.2	0.12	0.4	4	0.3	79	6	42	120	44	0.26
Duck eggs	71	13.2	14.2	0.7	0	185	0.16	0.4	3.2	N	4.5	0	N	N	17	3.6	64	N	191	**258**	N	0.8
Goat's milk	87	3.3	4.5	4.6	0	0	0.04	0.15	0.19	0.04	Tr	1.5	0.06	N	1	0.04	130	20	40	180	110	0.3
Hen eggs – whites	88	9	Tr	Tr	0	0	0	0.43	2.7	Tr	0.1	0	0	0	1	0.1	5	11	190	150	33	0.03
– whole	75	12.3	10.9	Tr	0	Tr	0.09	0.47	3.7	**0.11**	1.7	0	1.75	1.6	2.5	2	52	12	140	140	220	1.5
– yolks	51	16.1	30.5	Tr	0	Tr	**0.3**	**0.54**	**4.8**	0.3	**4.9**	0	**5**	**4.6**	**52**	**6.1**	130	15	50	120	500	3.6
Margarine	16	0.7	92	1	0	**900**	0	0	0	Tr	Tr	0	7.94	8	Tr	0	23	N	1100	26	18	N
Sour cream	N	2.7	18	**32**	0	720	0.04	0.14	0.08	N	N	N	N	N	N	N	96	N	38	52	72	N
Soya milk	N	3.6	1.32	2	0	36	0.03	0.03	0.36	N	0	0	N	N	N	0.32	N	N	N	N	44	N
Yogurt	86	5	1	6.2	0	5	0.05	0.26	0.12	0.04	Tr	0.4	Tr	0.03	2	0.09	180	17	76	240	140	0.6

KEY

All wholefoods are uncooked unless stated otherwise. Some wholefoods may not be included in the chart, as there is currently no nutritional data available. **g:** grams **mg:** milligrams **µg:** micrograms **N:** no available data **Tr:** trace **M:** adult men **W:** adult women. The recommended daily allowances are averages and vary depending on age, occupation and metabolism. Figures in bold type indicate the wholefood with the highest level of nutrient.

Butter

Butter is made by separating the cream from whole milk and churning it until it coagulates. Like milk, it contains calcium, milk protein, milk sugar and minerals. Its fat content is usually 80 per cent, and it is twice as high in saturated fatty acids and cholesterol as milk. Most commercially produced butters have added salt and colouring; salt as a preservative to increase shelf life and colouring to make them more appealing to the eye. Buy unsalted and untreated butters whenever possible.

Butter is usually used as a spread, but it has a wide range of culinary uses. It is used for sautéeing, sauces, bakes, flavoured butters and many other dishes.
Recipe: Apple, Soya & Almond Pudding (see p. 120).

Buttermilk

Buttermilk was originally the sour residue left over from making butter, but most commercial buttermilk is now made from pasteurized skimmed milk with an added culture to sour and thicken it. Easily digestible, buttermilk contains the protein and minerals of whole milk but hardly any of the fat. However, it also has a lower vitamin A content than whole milk.

Use buttermilk as a drink on its own, in baking and confectionery.

Cheese

Cheese is extremely nutritious, being rich in protein, fats, vitamins A and B, iron, calcium, phosphorus, potassium and sodium. However, cheese made from whole milk can be mucus-forming and is high in cholesterol, and so should be eaten in moderation or substituted with low-fat cheese when possible.

There are many types of cheese: fresh, soft, semi-hard, hard, blue and smoked. Fresh cheeses are made by dripping soured milk through cheesecloth until only the curd remains. The unripened curd is eaten shortly after it is made. These cheeses include ricotta, cottage cheese, Mozzarella, cream cheese, quark, fromage blanc and curd cheese. They have a high moisture content and are comparatively low in fat. Soft cheeses have been briefly ripened, and so are slightly firmer but still spreadable. They have a high moisture and fat content, though lower than hard cheese, and include such cheeses as Brie, Camembert and Feta.

Semi-hard and hard cheeses have been matured for a long time, often for many months, for their flavours to develop. These cheeses have a low moisture content and may contain up to 50 per cent fat. They include such cheeses as Cheddar and Parmesan.

Some cheeses contain an added substance called rennet, which is an enzyme found in calves' stomachs used to curdle and set the milk. Obviously, these cheeses are not acceptable to some vegetarians, but in recent years non-animal rennet has appeared and a wide range of vegetarian cheese is now available in most wholefood shops.

Cheese can be used in soups, soufflés, sandwiches, salads, savoury bakes and sweet dishes. Use according to type and requirement. Hard cheeses such as Cheddar are good for sauces or melting on toast; soft cheeses such as Mozzarella and Gruyère are good for fondues; fresh cheeses such as curd or quark are good in cheesecakes. Feta, Roquefort and other crumbly cheeses can be used in salads.
Recipe: Stuffed Baked Mushrooms (see p. 86).

Cow's milk

Milk is an extremely nutritious food, full of easily assimilated animal protein, calcium, iron and some B vitamins. For those wishing to pursue a meatless diet, milk is particularly useful because it contains vitamin B_{12}.

However, full-fat milk can be mucus-forming and is high in saturated fatty acids (and therefore cholesterol), which can lead to thickening of the arteries and heart disease. It may also contain hormones and traces of spray chemicals and pesticides which have been ingested by the cows.

A variety of skimmed and semi-skimmed milks are now available where all or most of the fat and cream have been removed. Whereas whole full-fat milk contains about 3-8 per cent fat, semi-skimmed milk contains half that amount and skimmed milk only 0·1 per cent. However, it should be remembered that skimmed milk loses its fat-soluble vitamins, namely A, D and E. Fortified skimmed milk is available which has these vitamins added. Milk can also be bought in powdered form, both whole and skimmed.

Goat's milk is sometimes used by people allergic to cow's milk. It does contain more phosphorus, calcium and magnesium than cow's milk, but it is just as high in fats.
Recipe: Apricot & Orange Sago Cream (see p. 121).

Cream

As milk cools after milking, the fat rises to the surface. This is creamed off and either used as cream or churned to make butter.

Cream is extremely high in saturated fatty acids, although the fat content will vary depending on the type of cream. Single cream contains a minimum of 18 per cent fat; sterilized (tinned) milk contains a minimum of 23 per cent fat. Whipping cream contains 35-42 per cent fat and double and extra thick cream contain a minimum of 48 per cent fat.

Cream is usually used in sauces, soups, desserts and puddings. It can be substituted with smetana or Greek-style yogurt.
Recipe: Baked Bananas with Yogurt Sauce (see p. 121).

Eggs

Eggs are extremely nutritious, containing all the essential amino acids needed to form a complete protein (see p. 8), as well as iron, calcium, phosphorus, potassium and some B, E and K vitamins. However, eggs do have a very high cholesterol content, which in excess can lead to thickening of the arteries and heart disease. As a rough guide, 4 eggs per week is probably enough for the body to handle, although small children, invalids and older people may eat a few more.

Many vegetarians will only eat free-range eggs because of the cruelty of battery farming. Although nutritionally they are the same, the taste of free-range eggs is generally thought to be better. There is no difference between white and brown eggs, since the shell colour relates only to the breed of hen. Duck eggs are slightly larger and richer than hen's eggs, and should be eaten very fresh if used.

Eggs are an extremely versatile food. They can be boiled, scrambled, poached, coddled, fried or made into omelettes. Added to other ingredients, they act as a raising or setting agent for cakes, sauces, custards, soufflés, mousses or pastries. They can bind croquettes and burgers and can be used as a glaze for breads and pastries. Yolks on their own add a rich creamy flavour to certain dishes and egg whites whipped separately add a delicious lightness to desserts.
Recipe: Baked Eggs with Coriander (see p. 81).

Ghee

There are two types of ghee, real ghee made from clarified butter and vegetable ghee made from hydrogenated vegetable oils.

To make your own real ghee, simply melt butter and filter through muslin. Vegetable ghee is made from coconut, sesame, groundnut or mustard oils. Because vegetable ghee is hydrogenated it is not much lower in cholesterol than ghee made from clarified butter. Both, however, are free from additives.

Unlike butter, ghee can be heated to a high temperature without burning, making it suitable for frying and cooking. It will leave food crisp, dry and light.
Recipe: Fresh Coriander Dhal (see p. 105).

Margarine

The commercial production of margarine as a cheap alternative to butter began in the 1870s. It was invented by a French chemist, Monsieur Mega-Mouries, and its popularity soon spread throughout Europe and America.

Margarines range from those containing significant amounts of animal fats, whey and other dairy products to pure varieties using only vegetable fats and oils. The former, like butter and lard, contain saturated fats and therefore cholesterol. The latter are high in polyunsaturated fatty acids and low in cholesterol. They contain linoleic acid, essential for the synthesis of fats from other fat-containing food in the body.

When buying margarine, look for the words 'vegetable oils and fats' (not just 'oils and fats'), and buy unhydrogenated brands. Hydrogenation turns polyunsaturated fatty acids into saturated fatty acids in order to harden the product, so you may as well eat butter as far as cholesterol is concerned. Usually, the softer the margarine, the higher the polyunsaturated fat content.

Watch out also for additives in margarine, such as flavouring agents, yellow food pigments, emulsifiers, preservatives and salt. In Britain, since 1940, all margarines must be fortified with vitamins A and D.

Use margarine as you would use butter: for sauces, savouries, puddings, cakes, adding to cooked vegetables and for spreading on bread and toast.

Smetana

Smetana is made from a mixture of skimmed milk and single cream, and can be used as a low-fat substitute for cream or sour cream. Two types of smetana are available, smetana and creamed smetana.

Solid vegetable fat

This is the vegetarian alternative to lard or suet. It is made from hydrogenated vegetable oils, which does mean that it contains saturated fatty acids and therefore cholesterol.

Sour cream

Sour cream is cream which has been inoculated with a lactic acid culture. It is used in desserts, sauces, dressings and some savoury dishes. For a low-fat alternative, use smetana or a mixture of cream and natural yogurt.

Soya milk

Soya milk looks very similar to cow's milk and has a slightly sweet, nutty flavour and creamy texture. Soya milk is made by soaking soya beans until they are thoroughly saturated and then grinding them up with boiling water. The liquid is strained off and heated before refrigeration.

Compared with cow's milk, soya milk has more protein, much more lecithin, less fats, no carbohydrates, no vitamin B_{12} and less calcium. It is easily digested and is useful for those allergic to cow's milk.

Some commercial soya milks taste rather bitter, but if you do not like the taste of one brand, try another as they all differ slightly. Some brands may contain added sugar, so check first.

Soya milk can be drunk on its own or used in soups, sauces, savouries, milk shakes, puddings and cakes.
Recipe: Strawberry Mousse (see p. 130).

Yogurt

Yogurt, a fermented milk product, has grown in popularity in the West over the past few years. In the Middle East, Far East and eastern Europe, the nutritional and medicinal properties of yogurt have been known for hundreds of years.

Nutritionally, yogurt is similar to milk, containing protein, calcium, iron and some A and B vitamins, including a little vitamin B_{12}. Yogurt bacteria breaks down the milk sugar to produce a lactic acid, which means that it is easier to digest than cow's milk and has a beneficial effect on the digestive system.

Commercial yogurts often contain additives, preservatives and colouring agents, so check first. Greek-style yogurt is strained through muslin or cheesecloth, and has a creamy, sweet taste. It is an excellent substitute for cream.

Yogurt can be made from any milk, but goat's milk yogurt is even more digestible than cow's milk yogurt as it more closely resembles human milk. Eat yogurt on its own, plain or flavoured, or use in dressings, soups, savoury dishes and desserts.
Recipe: Cheesecake (see p. 122).
Home-made yogurt
Yogurt is simple, delicious and economical to make at home. There are many commercial yogurt-makers on the market but a wide-necked thermos flask will give as good a result. Fresh cow's or goat's milk can be used.

First, take 575 ml (1 pt) fresh milk and heat in a saucepan until just below boiling point. This is necessary because dairy herds are often given antibiotics, which then appear in the milk. These antibiotics can fight the yogurt bacteria and need to be killed by heating. (UHT milk has, however, been heat-treated.)

Let the milk cool until it is just above body temperature (it should feel just warm to the fingers). Mix in a large tablespoon of natural live yogurt and pour into a wide-necked thermos. Secure the lid and leave for 12 hours. Then, refrigerate for a few hours and use as desired. Reserve a large spoonful of yogurt for the next batch.

Herbs (See p. 53)

Bay leaves (see p. 53) are usually available whole, and are popular in stocks.

Mint (see p. 54) has a distinctive, fresh taste and pleasant aroma.

Marjoram (see p. 54) is often used in stuffings.

Oregano (see p. 55) is very aromatic and is popular in Italian and tomato dishes.

Dill weed (see p. 54) is commonly used as a garnish and in Scandinavian dishes.

Parsley (see p. 55) is high in vitamins and minerals.

Coriander leaves (see p. 54) are used in many Eastern savoury dishes.

Rosemary (see p. 55) is a very aromatic herb with a strong flavour.

Basil (see p. 53) is often used in tomato-based dishes.

Chervil (see p. 53) has a delicate, spicy taste popular in France.

Thyme (see p. 55) has a subtle, sweet flavour and is good with vegetables.

Chives (see p. 54) are best eaten raw and fresh, and have a mild onion flavour.

Sage (see p. 55) is quite strong in flavour and so should be used sparingly.

Tarragon (see p. 55) is delicious chopped and added to salads and soups.

diet. Salt is also included, but substitutes and alternatives are given if you wish to reduce your sodium intake.

Other savoury products described in this section include kuzu, a natural thickener, nut butters, seitan, a highly nutritious form of wheat protein, and pickled plums from Japan.

Sweet products

Sweeteners add to the taste and appeal of many dishes, and are used in baking, sweet dishes, desserts, confectionery and drinks. The most commonly used sweetener is now sugar, but there are many alternative sweeteners available.

VEGETABLE OILS	SATURATED FATTY ACIDS	MONO-UNSATURATED FATTY ACIDS	POLYUNSATURATED FATTY ACIDS
Corn oil	Low	Medium	High
Groundnut oil	Low	High	Medium
Olive oil	Low	High	Low
Safflower oil	Low	Low	High
Sesame oil	Low	Medium	Medium
Soya oil	Low	Low	High
Sunflower oil	Low	Medium	High
Walnut and almond oils	Low	Medium	High

OILS

Oils are liquid fats extracted from plant or animal substances. There are many types of oil, with differing flavours, colours and uses. A large range of vegetable oils extracted from nuts, seeds and beans are described below.

Methods of oil extraction
The purest, finest oil is obtained by cold pressing. There may be three cold presses, the first being the superior. The first press of olive oil is often called 'virgin oil'. Cold pressed oils are unrefined and have the best taste and highest nutritional value.

Semi-refined oils are usually oils made from secondary pressings under heat, to obtain larger quantities of oil. Nutritionally they are inferior to cold pressed oils.

Refined or 'pure' oils have usually been highly processed. Some oil extraction methods may use chemical solvents such as hexane to break down the outer husk of the seed and thus obtain a higher extraction rate. These solvents also deodorize and bleach the oil. Some oils are also heated and treated with anti-oxidants, which help prevent the oil from becoming rancid. However, this process also converts any polyunsaturated fats into saturated fats. These extraction techniques decrease the nutritional value of the oils.

Storage
Cold pressed oils should be stored in cool, dark places and not bought in huge quantities unless you use them very fast. Once opened, oils may become rancid after a month, except for sesame oil (see below). Oils may go opaque and solidify in the refrigerator, but will quickly liquify if stood at room temperature. Refined oils will keep for longer, about 3 months.

Corn oil

Extracted from sweetcorn, this is a good all-round oil with a mild flavour, suitable for all types of cooking and baking. It is a common ingredient in margarine. Cold pressed corn oil is high in polyunsaturated fatty acids.
Recipe: Mung Bean Casserole (see p. 109).

Groundnut oil

Groundnut oil or peanut oil is a good all-round oil. It has a mild flavour and is excellent for deep-frying as it can be heated to a high temperature without burning. It can be used in all sweet and savoury dishes. Groundnut oil is fairly low in polyunsaturates, however. It is frequently used in margarine manufacture and for canning purposes.
Recipe: Black Bean Chilli (see p. 100).

Olive oil

Olive oil is usually fairly thick with a golden or greenish-brown colour and a very distinctive flavour, varying with the country of origin. Virgin olive oil is the best, and usually a golden colour. Pure olive oil is from the second pressing and is usually a darker green colour.

Olive oil is most often used for salad dressings although it can be used for general savoury cooking. It is not suitable for deep-frying or for use in cakes and pastries. For optimum nutritional value, combine cold pressed olive oil with cold pressed safflower oil, because olive oil is relatively low in polyunsaturated fatty acids and safflower oil is high.
Recipe: Gazpacho (see p. 76).

Safflower oil

Safflower oil is often confused with sunflower oil, but they actually come from different plants belonging to the same botanical family. Cold pressed safflower oil is pale in colour with a delicate, but distinctive flavour. It is extremely nutritious, being high in polyunsaturates and containing more linoleic acid than any other oil listed.

Safflower oil is particularly nutritious when combined with olive oil for salad dressings. It can be heated to a high temperature without burning, which makes it suitable for deep-frying and use in other savoury dishes, although cold pressed safflower oil is not recommended for puddings, cakes and pastries because of its strong flavour.
Recipe: Brown Rice Salad (see p. 89).

Sesame oil

Sesame oil has a slightly nutty flavour and is made from toasted sesame seeds. There are two types, one rather dark, used in Chinese cooking, and a paler variety which is used in Indian cooking.

Sesame oil contains a substance called sesamol which prevents it from becoming rancid. It is also fairly high in polyunsaturates.

This is a good all-round oil which can be heated to a high temperature without burning, making it suitable for deep-frying. It can be used successfully in cooking most sweet and savoury dishes.
Recipe: Smoked Tofu Appetizer (see p. 86).

Soya oil

Soya oil is pale with a very mild flavour and it is recommended for salads and all types of cooking. It keeps well if kept in a cool place, and is high in polyunsaturates. Soya oil is used for the majority of the cooking at the Neal's Yard Bakery.
Recipe: Basic Wholewheat Sponge Cake (see p. 136).

Sunflower oil

Cold pressed sunflower oil has a pale yellow colour and a delicate flavour. It is a good substitute for safflower oil, being high in linoleic acid and mono-unsaturates. It is an all-round oil which can be used for salad dressings, frying and other savoury uses, puddings and baking. Sunflower oil is often used in the manufacture of margarine.
Recipe: Mayonnaise (see p. 96).

Walnut and almond oils

These can occasionally be found in wholefood shops. They each have a very distinctive, nutty flavour and are best used only in uncooked dressings. Both are high in polyunsaturates, walnut oil being the higher. Walnut oil is also rich in iodine.
Recipe: Sweetcorn & Mushroom Salad (see p. 95).

SAVOURY PRODUCTS

Brewer's yeast

Brewer's yeast is a by-product in the production of beers and spirits. It is extremely nutritious, being high in protein and minerals, especially iron, potassium and phosphorus. It is also extremely rich in B vitamins, which is important as most foods are only high in one particular B vitamin. (B vitamins are synergetic, and are most effective when eaten together.)

Brewer's yeast may be sprinkled over soups and savoury dishes, enjoyed on its own or used in drinks. Start using brewer's yeast in moderation, for example about 2·5 ml ($\frac{1}{2}$ tsp) per day, and gradually build up to 10-15 ml ($\frac{1}{2}$-1 tbsp) per day as you get used to it.
Recipe: Pep-up Drink (see p. 61).

Gomashio
(Sesame salt)

Gomashio is made by grinding roasted sesame seeds very finely and adding sea salt, usually in a ratio of 10 parts sesame seeds to 1 part salt. It is widely used in Japan for sprinkling on top of food in preference to salt, and is useful for those wishing to reduce their salt intake. Gomashio has a light, nutty flavour and is a delicious addition to any savoury dish.
Recipe: Seitan with Hiziki (see p. 113).

Kuzu

Kuzu comes from the roots of a plant which grows in the mountains of Japan. The deep roots are soaked in cold running water until only the starchy white 'kuzu' remains. This is ground into a powder. In Japan, kuzu is used for preventing colds, strengthening weak constitutions, relaxing muscles and toning up the digestive system.

Kuzu can be used just as one would use cornflour or arrowroot: for thickening soups, sauces and gravies, or as a glaze for desserts and puddings.
Recipe: Cherry Pie (see p. 123).

Miso

Miso is made by fermenting soya beans, rice, barley or wheat under pressure for 1-2 years, gradually adding sea salt until a thick paste has formed. It is extremely nutritious, being rich in complete protein (see p. 8), minerals and some B vitamins.

Hacho miso is made from soya beans, **genmai miso** from soya beans and brown rice, **mugi miso** from soya beans and barley, and **natto miso** from soya beans, barley, ginger and seaweed. Hacho and natto miso contain the most protein, although hacho is extremely high in sodium. All contain a fair amount of calcium. Genmai miso is lightest in colour and contains slightly less salt than the others.

Use miso as a stock for soups and sauces, as a savoury spread or in stews and casseroles as a flavouring. Because it contains living bacteria and enzymes from the fermentation, which are easily destroyed by boiling, miso is generally added at the end of cooking.
Recipe: Lettuce, Cucumber & Miso Soup (see p. 76).

Nut butters

Nut butters are blended mixtures of whole shelled nuts and oil, and have both savoury and sweet uses. Peanut butter is probably the most well known, but hazelnut and cashew nut butters (sometimes called creams) are also available. Nutritious and tasty, nut butters can easily be made at home.

Put about 225 g (8 oz) shelled peanuts, hazelnuts or cashew nuts in a blender, add 15 ml (1 tbsp) of vegetable, groundnut or sesame oil and blend to a paste. The mixture can be blended until chunky or smooth, depending on your preference.

If buying nut butters or creams, check that they are not hydrogenated. This process prevents rancidity but also turns mono-unsaturated and polyunsaturated fatty acids into saturated fatty acids (see p. 45). Commercial nut butters also often contain added sugar, salt, and preservatives.

Use nut butters on toast and in sandwiches, or add to sweet and savoury dishes, breads, sauces, cakes and biscuits.
Recipe: Gado-gado (see p. 106).

Salt
(Sodium chloride)

Salt is the mineral sodium chloride, either evaporated from the sea or mined from primeval sea deposits in the land. The three basic types of salt are described below.

Sodium, together with potassium, is essential for the healthy functioning of the human body. The kidneys monitor the amount of sodium in the blood and excrete or retain liquid as necessary to maintain the correct amount. However, we only need about 4 grams of salt a day and too much salt can be damaging. Excess salt will increase the volume of blood in the vessels and this overloading of the circulatory system causes the tiny arteries to constrict, in order to prevent themselves from being damaged. This leads to increased pressure in the larger vessels and hypertension or high blood pressure can occur, sometimes resulting in strokes and heart disease.

Many ethnic groups with a low sodium intake have no incidence of hypertension, whereas those with a high sodium intake, such as Japan, have a high incidence of hypertension. There are certain situations when additional salt in the diet is appropriate. Excessive sweating, through physical exertion or ill health, causes sodium to be lost through the urine and skin and pregnant women should also take rather more salt than usually necessary. However, as a general rule it is clear that our sodium intake is too high and should be reduced where possible.

All the salt we need can be obtained from fresh foods, but salt and other sodium-based additives are frequently added to a huge range of convenience foods, from salted snacks to sweet jams and marmalades. The habit of heavily salting food at the table is also unnecessary, but our taste buds have become so accustomed to salt in food that we often find it difficult to appreciate flavours without it.

Reducing salt intake is only a matter of practice, however, and there are a number of low-salt flavourings which can be used instead. Gomashio, miso, tamari and shoyu are nutritious and although they contain salt, less is used. Salt substitutes, often consisting of potassium salt or a mixture of sodium and potassium salt, are also available for those wishing to cut down on sodium.

Table salt

Commercial table salt is made by pumping water into underground mines and vacuum-drying it to evaporate the water and thus obtain salt. This salt is then very finely ground and additives such as starch or phosphate of lime to prevent caking may be added. This processing removes all the trace elements.

Rock salt

Veins of salt from prehistoric seas are found deep in the ground, sandwiched between layers of ancient rock. This is rock salt, sold in varying degrees of coarseness. Refined rock salt is often called kitchen, lump or block salt, and contains no additives.

Sea salt

Sea or bay salt is formed by the evaporation of water from salt pans. Because it is from sea water it contains iodine, not found in land-mined salts. Usually sold in crystals, sea salt is thought by many to have the best flavour. Atlantic sun-dried sea salt is also considered superior to Mediterranean sea salt.

Iodized salt

Iodized salt is land-mined salt to which iodine has been added. Some leading food experts believe this is preferable to sea salt because of the increasing pollution of the seas.

Seitan

Seitan is wheat gluten, the sticky strands of protein contained in the starchy part of the grain. It is obtained by first mixing wheat flour (any type) with water until a soft dough is formed. This is then kneaded to allow the strands of gluten to form. The dough is then washed under running water until only the shiny white gluten remains.

Seitan is very high in protein. It can be bought at most wholefood shops and is generally a brown or beige colour. This is because it is marinated with tamari, seaweed and ginger before packaging to make it more appetizing.

Use seitan in soups, pâtés or stews. It is especially good with grain and bean dishes. Chop into bite-sized pieces, or slice finely as required.
Recipe: Seitan with Hiziki (see p. 113).

Tahini

Tahini is a thick creamy paste made from finely ground sesame seeds and sesame oil. It has been popular in the Middle East for many hundreds of years and both dark and light tahinis are available. The dark variety is made from unhusked sesame seeds and has a slightly bitter flavour, but it is more nutritious than the light variety which is made from husked sesame seeds.

Tahini can be used in sauces, pâtés or puddings; eaten with vegetables, beans or grains; or simply spread on bread for a delicious and nutritious snack. It can also be used as a

substitute for eggs if a binding agent is required. Use 10 ml (2 tsp) tahini in a little water for each egg used.
Recipe: Apple & Butter Bean Pâté (see p. 80).

Tamari and shoyu

These liquids are naturally fermented soya sauces, produced in the manufacture of miso. Japanese in origin, they are rich in protein, minerals, especially sodium, and some vitamins. They also improve circulation, aid digestion and promote the growth of healthy bacteria in the intestines.

Tamari has a stronger flavour than shoyu, and because it is only made from soya beans, salt and water, it is gluten-free. Shoyu is made from soya beans, wheat, salt and water and is less concentrated than tamari. Neither should contain any artificial additives. Beware, however, of some brands of manufactured soya sauce which contain caramel, artificial flavouring and refined salt.

Tamari and shoyu are delicious sprinkled over steamed vegetables, grains or beans. They can also be used in cooked savoury dishes, as bases for marinades, or added to sauces and salad dressings.
Recipe: Carrot & Orange Soup (see p. 73).

Tempeh

Tempeh is another fermented soya bean product. Soaked and boiled soya beans are treated with a fungus, wrapped in banana leaves and then left to ferment. It sounds unsavoury but tempeh has a rich, cheese-like flavour and is a strong natural antibiotic.

Tempeh is usually cut into thin slices or cubes, shallow-fried in oil and eaten dipped in tamari flavoured with grated root ginger and chopped garlic.
Recipe: Fried Tempeh with Orange Sesame Sauce (see p. 106).

Tofu
(Bean curd)

Tofu is soya bean curd. It is made by crushing soaked and cooked soya beans into a smooth paste and adding a curdling or setting agent, usually nigari (which mainly consists of calcium sulphate). It is made in wooden presses and once set must be kept in clean water, (changed daily), and eaten within a week.

Tofu, like soya milk, is extremely nutritious, containing protein, iron, calcium and B vitamins. It also contains unsaturated fatty acids and is free from cholesterol. It is usually available in three forms, silken, soft and firm. Silken tofu has been lightly pressed, and is used for blending into other ingredients. Soft tofu is slightly firmer and firm tofu has been heavily pressed. Firm tofu has a consistency similar to cheese. Smoked tofu is also available and has a strong smoky flavour.

Tofu has a bland, subtle flavour and is extremely versatile. It can be used in sweet and savoury dishes, dips and spreads, or can be eaten on its own with a sauce or marinade. It retains its setting property when cooked, so makes a perfect substitute for eggs when making flans or cheesecakes.
Recipe: Marinated Tofu (see p. 84).

Umeboshi plums

These are salty pickled plums from Japan. They are usually pickled for at least two years before eating. Their sharp pungent flavour is due to the presence of lactic acid, produced by the micro-organisms. This acid will help remove unwanted bacteria from the alimentary canal in the body and aids digestion.

Umeboshi plums can be cooked with grains, added to savoury dishes or simply eaten on their own after a meal to help digestion.
Recipe: Seaweed Rolls (see p. 113).

Vegetable stock cubes

These are the vegetarian answer to meat stock cubes. They contain vegetable oils or fats, yeast extract, vegetable protein, starch, dehydrated vegetables, lactose, spices and salt. Vegetable concentrates are similar, but are sold in soft paste form.

Some brands can be extremely salty, although salt-free cubes are available in some shops. If you follow a vegan diet, check for the addition of lactose or milk sugar, which you may not want to include in your diet.

Vegetable cubes can be added to soups and savoury dishes in place of water or stock to give extra flavour. Vegetable concentrates can be used in stocks, hot drinks or for spreading on toast.
Recipe: Carrot & Rice Soup (see p. 73).

Vinegars

Vinegars are a neat solution of acetic acid produced by the fermentation and oxidation of natural carbohydrates. They are usually obtained from the fermentation of cider, wine and malt alcohols, hence the different cider, wine and malt vinegars. Wine vinegar is rather stronger than the other vinegars, and can be red or white depending on the colour of the grape used in fermentation. A popular grain vinegar is brown rice vinegar, used widely in the Far East.

The vinegars often reflect the major raw product in each country of origin. If you wish, use rice vinegar in Oriental recipes, malt vinegar in traditional English recipes, wine vinegar in Mediterranean recipes and cider vinegar in American recipes.

Flavoured vinegars are also available, with added herbs or spices such as tarragon, dill, rosemary, chilli or peppercorns.

Use vinegars in salad dressings, sauces, sweet and sour dishes and dips. They are an essential ingredient in chutneys and pickles because of their preservative properties.
Recipe: Leeks Vinaigrette (see p. 84).

Yeast extracts

Yeast extracts are dark brown and are a mixture of brewer's yeast and salt. They have the same protein, minerals and vitamins as brewer's yeast with the addition of trace elements from the salt. They are therefore very nutritious but high in sodium, so should be used in moderation.

Yeast extracts are delicious spread on bread and toast, or they can be added to soups, stocks and savoury dishes as a flavouring.
Recipe: Millet Casserole (see p. 108).

SWEET PRODUCTS
Carob powder

Carob powder or flour is ground from carob beans, which are contained in the large pods of the Mediterranean carob tree.

The taste of carob is fairly similar to that of cocoa powder, and it can be used instead of cocoa or chocolate in recipes. Unlike cocoa and chocolate, carob has no caffeine, has a lower fat content and provides some calcium and phosphorus.

Carob can be used to flavour cakes, sweets, puddings and sweets. Use sparingly as it is much sweeter than cocoa powder.
Recipe: Carob & Sunflower Mousse (see p. 122).

Essences

Essences are highly concentrated extracts, usually of fruit, nuts and plants. They are extracted by steam distillation or by maceration in water and alcohol. Essences commonly used for flavouring are vanilla, almond, orange blossom, rose, pear, peppermint and coffee.

Pure essences are available at most wholefood shops. Take care to buy a pure essence and not one containing preservatives, artificial colours or flavourings.

Essence is very concentrated so only use 1 or 2 drops as needed to flavour cakes, pastries, biscuits, custards and drinks.
Recipe: Macaroon Cake (see p. 143).

Fruit concentrates

To make fruit concentrate, fresh fruit is first crushed to make fruit juice, which is concentrated at a low temperature to retain its flavour and nutritional value. A centrifugal process is then used to separate the juice from the flesh.

More and more natural fruit concentrates are now appearing on the market, the most common being apple concentrate. Other fruit concentrates available are cherry, blackcurrant, pear and raspberry. All these are in fact mixed with some apple concentrate, but it does not interfere with their flavours. They are available in liquid form or in a highly concentrated spread, the most common being pear and apple spread.

Fruit concentrates are free from preservatives, colouring and artificial flavourings and will keep in a cool dark place or refrigerator.

Use as a sweetening agent in cakes, puddings, bread, biscuits, savouries, salad dressings and ice lollies or use simply as a refreshing drink diluted with filtered water. Fruit concentrates are very strong, so use in small amounts.
Recipe: Apple & Butter Bean Pâté (see p. 80).

Halva

Halva is a sweetmeat made from crushed sesame seeds flavoured with honey. It is popular in the Middle East and Mediterranean countries. Some halvas have pistachio nuts or chopped fruit added. Make sure that you do not buy halva sweetened with refined sugar.

Eat halva as a snack on its own (it is very sweet so eat in moderation), or sprinkle over desserts and puddings or add to ice cream.

Honey

Honey is made from the nectar of various flowers and plants taken into the bee's stomach where enzymic action converts the complex sugar molecules of the nectar into simple sugars. Once back in the hive this sugar solution is deposited in the honeycombs. Honey is extracted from the honeycombs by centrifugal force, and is then usually filtered before being packed.

Honey contains some protein, vitamins and most minerals, and is particularly good for invalids, athletes and children because the sugar can enter straight into the bloodstream, providing instant energy. Honey is sweet, nourishing and easy to digest, and has natural antiseptic, antibiotic and laxative properties.

There are many types of honey, each with a slightly different colour and flavour depending on the flower or plant visited by the bee. Honeys are often available in both honeycomb and liquid form. The choice is a matter of personal preference, but choose pure un-filtered honeys rather than blended honeys where possible. Make sure of the quality of the honey. In an attempt to produce cheap honey some manufacturers place white sugar solutions close to the hives, so the bees no longer fly any distance in search of plant nectars. The essential enzymic reactions do not take place and the honey is nutritionally inferior. Some manufacturers also heat the combs to obtain the maximum amount of honey, which decreases the nutritional value.

Honey may deepen in colour and crystallize due to age or lowering of temperature. To make it runny again, put the jar in a bowl of warm water and store in a warmish place.

Use honey instead of sugar in cakes, breads, puddings, pastries, scones, drinks and glazes. Remember that honey is sweeter than sugar, so use less if substituting in a recipe.
Recipe: Granola 2 (see p. 69).

Malt extract
(Barley syrup)

Malt extract is a natural sugar obtained from malted cereal grains, usually barley. The malted grains (see p. 11) are ground and soak-ed in water, which is then heated and reduced to a syrup. Malt extract is not as sweet as sugar, but does contain B vitamins and iron.

Malt extract can be used instead of sugar and honey in cakes, puddings and drinks and it is often given to children as a nutritional supplement.
Recipe: Date & Oat Bars (see p. 141).

Maple syrup

This delicious syrup is obtained from certain North American maple trees, chiefly the sugar maple and the black maple. The clear sap is extracted through small tapholes in the bark by vacuum pumping. It is then boiled in an open pan until only a thick dark syrup remains. Between 150 and 190 litres (30-50 gallons) of maple sap is needed to make 5 litres (1 gallon) of maple syrup.

Maple syrup is mainly sucrose but it does contain some potassium and calcium. Beware of products calling themselves maple syrup which are actually white sugar-based syrups with maple syrup flavouring added.

Apart from pouring over pancakes, waffles and ice cream, maple syrup can be used to sweeten cakes, puddings and pastries. It can even be used in savoury sauces and vinai-grette dressings.
Recipe: Banana Frozen Yogurt (see p. 122).

Mirin

Mirin is a sweet brown liquid, a natural sweetener which has been used in Japan for centuries. To make it, a rice mould is added to *koji* (sweet brown rice). This mould breaks down the sugar in the grains over a period of 6 months or more. This resulting sweet liquid is then diluted with pure spring water to produce mirin.

Always boil mirin for 1 minute before use. Use it to sweeten vegetable dishes and sauces or as a marinade or glaze. A traditional Japanese marinade is made by boiling a little mirin for 1 minute and then adding shoyu, grated root ginger and brown rice vinegar or lemon juice.

Molasses

Molasses is a by-product of refined sugar and is sometimes known as black treacle, although this is usually a blend of molasses and golden syrup. Molasses is a thick black syrup and is rich in minerals, particularly iron, calcium, phosphorus and potassium.

Blackstrap, or dark, molasses is thicker, richer and more nutritious than plain molasses, as it is less refined. It is usually used in cooking. Light molasses has a milder flavour and is usually used as a table syrup.

Molasses can be used in place of sugar or honey to sweeten cakes, pastries, puddings or savoury dishes and it is often an ingredient in nourishing pick-me-up drinks. It is not as sweet as refined sugar.
Recipe: Bran Muffins (see p. 137).

Sugar
(Sucrose)

Sugar or sucrose is extracted from two main sources; sugar cane and sugar beet, and three minor sources; maple trees, date palms and sorghum cane.

Separating the sucrose from the stems of the sugar cane is a complex process, involving crushing and grinding to release the sweet juice and treatment with chemicals or lime to clarify the liquid. This liquid is reduced by evaporating through boiling and then centri-fugal force is used to separate out the crystal-lized raw brown sugar. The residue is molasses. The brown raw sugar is treated further with lime, carbon dioxide and sulphur dioxide to produce refined white sugar. Sugar from sugar beet is obtained in a similar way, al-though brown sugar cannot be produced from sugar beet.

Refined white sugar contains no nutrients, only calories. Consumption of refined sugar has rocketed in the last hundred years, to the detriment of our health. It is not only con-sumed in drinks, on cereals and in baking but is a hidden additive in many processed foods. Apart from the better-known physical effects of obesity, tooth decay and diabetes, too much refined sugar can actually reduce the level of nutrients in our body, in particular calcium and vitamin B. Hyperactivity in children and some kinds of metal depression in adults are also being linked with excessive sugar intake.

If you must use sugar, raw, unrefined sugars are better than white as they contain a little fibre. Demerara is light brown in colour and contains approximately 2 per cent molasses. Beware of some brands which are white sugar dyed with caramel. Muscovado is much darker in colour, being only partly refined, and is nutritionally superior as it contains approxi-mately 13 per cent molasses.

Sugar-free jams

Over the past few years various sugar-free jams and marmalades have become available. By sugar-free, the manufacturers mean that there is no refined sugar in the product. They are usually made from fruit concentrates, which are high in natural fruit sugars.

Sugar-free jams tend not to be as sweet as traditional sugar jams and it may take a little while to get used to this. Once opened, they should be refrigerated and consumed within 10 days. Use them on bread, toast and scones or in puddings, cakes and custards.
Recipe: Bakewell Tart (see p. 134).

HERBS

Basil ☐
Bay leaves ☐
Bergamot
Borage
Bouquet garni
Burnet
Chervil ☐
Chives ☐

Comfrey
Coriander leaves ☐
Dill weed ☐
Fennel leaves
Fenugreek leaves
Fines herbes
Garlic
Lemon balm

Lemon verbena
Lovage
Marjoram ☐
Mint ☐
Mixed herbs
Nasturtiums
Oregano ☐
Parsley ☐

Rosemary ☐
Sage ☐
Tansy
Tarragon ☐
Thyme ☐
Winter savory

☐ Pictured opposite page 49

Herbs are the edible leaves, flowers, seeds, stems and roots of non-woody plants which are used for flavouring and garnishing food. Garlic is included in this section because of its similar usage to many herbs, although it is strictly a bulb vegetable.

Each herb has a distinctive taste and aroma. It takes a little time (and possibly a few disasters) to learn the strengths and flavours of the different herbs, but it is well worth the effort. An understanding of herbs can greatly enhance your cooking and open up limitless creative possibilities in the kitchen.

There is little doubt that fresh herbs are far superior to dried. However, unless you have your own herb garden many herbs are often unavailable and in this case the dried versions are perfectly palatable if used correctly. If a recipe calls for 5 ml (1 tsp) of a fresh herb, use 2·5 ml ($\frac{1}{2}$ tsp) of the dried herb instead.

Drying herbs

Foliage herbs should be harvested just before flowering, when the leaves are most numerous and flavourful and before the spores have formed. Pick the stems early in the morning, after the dew has dried and before the hot summer sun evaporates the essential oils.

Either lay the herbs on wire screens or tie in loose bundles and place in large brown paper bags, fastening the mouth of the bag around the stems. Leave until the herbs are quite dry and will fall easily from their stems.

Crumble the herbs into small pieces by hand or through a coarse sieve. The herbs can then be finely ground with a pestle and mortar if desired. Most fresh herbs will dry well except for parsley, chervil and chives, but these can be frozen (see p. 65).

Storage

Freshly cut herbs keep best if their stems are put in a glass of water. They can also be frozen if desired (see p. 65). Dried herbs should be kept in opaque, airtight jars away from direct sunlight and heat. If purchasing, buy a little at a time to ensure maximum freshness and flavour.

Basil

Basil originated in India and has large, rounded, bright green leaves. The herb has a sweet delicate flavour and aroma. It is especially popular in Italy where it is used in the traditional pesto sauce. It is best eaten fresh but retains its strength and flavour when dried.

Culinary uses

Basil is delicious in curries and spicy dishes as well as in soups, salads, casseroles and bakes. It combines particularly well with tomatoes, artichokes, peas, eggs and cheese.

Recipe: Minestrone (see p. 77).

Bay leaves

Bay leaves come from the sweet bay tree, a variety of laurel native to the Mediterranean.

Bay leaves are tough and leathery and can be used fresh or dried. They have a strong flavour which needs long cooking before it is released. Ground bay leaves are available but the whole leaves, fresh or dried, are preferable.

Culinary uses

Bay leaves can be used to flavour curries and spicy dishes, soups, casseroles, sauces and stocks. Remove the leaves before serving, and be careful not to use too many. Bay leaves also make good garnishes for pâtés and bakes.

Recipe: Aduki Bean Soup (see p. 72).

Bergamot
(Bee balm/Oswego)

Bergamot is a member of the mint family, and is native to America. It is now also widely grown in Europe. There are many varieties of bergamot, and both the flowers and the leaves can be used. It has a distinctive, strong flavour and can be used fresh or dried.

Culinary uses

Use chopped bergamot leaves in salads, soups, sauces and dressings. Fresh bergamot flowers, when in season, make a beautiful garnish. The leaves can also be used to make tea (see p. 59 for the method).

Borage

Borage is native to the Middle East and is now grown all over Europe. When in season, borage has bright blue flowers. Both the leaves and the flowers are used in cooking.

Culinary uses

Borage has a slightly cucumber-like taste. Chop finely and add to soups, dips, dressings, sauces, salads and drinks.

Bouquet garni

This is a ready-prepared mixture of herbs, either tied together in a bundle or chopped and tied into small muslin or cheesecloth bags. Packets of the loose mixed herbs are also sometimes available. The herbs used in a bouquet garni are traditionally bay leaves, parsley and thyme, but other herbs may also be added.

Culinary uses

Bouquet garni is used widely in French cooking in many soups, casseroles and bakes. The herbs combine well with peppers, courgettes, aubergines, potatoes, leeks, onions and many other vegetables as well as most grains and beans. Remove the bunch or bag before serving the dish.

Recipe: Use instead of mixed herbs in Mung Bean Casserole (see p. 109).

Burnet
(Salad burnet)

Burnet is a small herb with tiny, scalloped leaves. Native to Europe, it is popular in French and Italian cooking. The leaves can be used fresh or dried, but the flavour is best when fresh and young.

Culinary uses

Burnet has a flavour similar to borage, and is also used in soups, dips, dressings, sauces, salads and drinks.

Chervil

Chervil originates from southern Russia and the Middle East. It is a very popular herb in Europe, particularly France, and grows well in temperate climates. It is similar in appearance to parsley and has a slightly spicy taste, rather like tarragon. It can be eaten fresh or dried but dried chervil does not retain its flavour as well as the fresh.

Culinary uses

Chervil can be used in soups, salads, stuffings, casseroles and other savoury dishes. It is particularly delicious in milk-based sauces and with eggs, cheese, salad vegetables, spinach, greens, potatoes, grains and beans.

Chives

Chives are native to Europe, and are a member of the onion, leek and garlic family. Their long, bright green, grass-like leaves have a mild oniony or garlicy flavour. Chinese chives have larger leaves and a slightly stronger flavour.

Chives are best eaten fresh, and ideally home-grown. They can be dried or frozen, the latter being preferable.

Culinary uses

Chopped chives are delicious in clear soups, salads and many savoury dishes, and they can also be used as a garnish. They can be mixed with butter for spreading on potatoes or hot bread, and are often used in soups and egg and cheese dishes.

Recipe: Melon & Tomato Salad (see p. 91).

Comfrey

Native to Europe and Asia, comfrey is related to the borage plant. It has large, wide green leaves. Both the leaves and the roots can be used, fresh or dried.

Comfrey is extremely nutritious, due to the great length of its roots, which can grow as long as 3 metres (10 feet). This enables the plant to draw up many minerals and nutrients usually only available to trees. Comfrey is high in the B vitamin group, including B_{12}, which is rare in plant foods.

Culinary uses

Use comfrey chopped fresh or dried in salads, soups, dips and savoury dishes. It has a flavour rather like borage. The leaves can also be used to make tea (see p. 59).

Coriander leaves
(Chinese parsley)

A member of the carrot family, the coriander plant is Middle Eastern in origin and now grows in Europe, the Mediterranean and America. The soft, feathery leaves are sometimes known as Greek or Chinese parsley. They have a distinctive aroma and a fresh, strong taste. (For coriander seeds, see p. 57.)

Culinary uses

Fresh coriander leaves may be chopped and used in salads and savoury dishes, or sprinkled as a garnish over soups and starters. Use in dishes with an Oriental flavour.

Recipe: Baked Eggs with Coriander (see p. 81).

Dill weed

Dill is native to Europe and western Asia, and is now grown all over the world. It is very popular in Scandinavia. Dill has green, feathery leaves, which are often used as a garnish in the same way as parsley. Dill leaves or dill tops are best eaten fresh although dried dill still retains a little of its distinctive flavour. Dill seeds are also available.

Culinary uses

Dill leaves are wonderful in salads or sprinkled over soups and other savoury dishes. The flavour goes particularly well with mushrooms, leeks, cauliflower, tomatoes, courgettes and most grains and beans. Try adding fresh dill to cream sauces and mayonnaise.

Recipe: Stuffed Baked Mushrooms (see p. 86).

Fennel leaves

Fennel is native to Europe and is a tall, feathery herb with small dark green leaves. The large fennel root is eaten as vegetable (see p. 28). Fennel leaves have a slightly aniseed aroma and flavour.

Culinary uses

Use fennel leaves in soups, salads and stuffings, or as a garnish.

Fenugreek leaves
(Methi)

The leaves of the fenugreek plant, or methi, are often eaten as a vegetable in parts of the Far East and North Africa, although the fresh leaves are seldom found in Western countries. However, they are available in dried form. They have a milder flavour than the fenugreek seeds (see p. 57).

Culinary uses

Use fenugreek leaves in soups and savoury dishes, particularly curries. They have a slightly bitter flavour.

Recipe: Use instead of cumin in Onion Bhajis with Yogurt Sauce (see p. 86).

Fines herbes

This is a ready-prepared mixture of chopped dried herbs, usually chervil, parsley, tarragon and chives.

Culinary uses

Fines herbes can be used in many savoury dishes such as soups, sauces and casseroles.

Garlic

Garlic is one of the oldest cultivated plants in the world, probably originating in Central Asia. It is an important ingredient in many great cuisines of the world. Choose firm, tightly packed 'heads' of garlic, preferably with large cloves.

Garlic has a strong pungent flavour and can sometimes smell on the breath. Used in moderation, garlic can enhance many savoury dishes and is extremely versatile. Fresh garlic is best, but dried flakes and powder are available.

Culinary uses

Garlic can be eaten raw or cooked. Peel and then crush or finely chop the raw cloves for use in salads, salad dressings, soups and sauces. When cooking garlic, add towards the end of cooking for the best results. Boiled garlic will have a milder flavour, but if fried in oil the flavour will become very pungent.

Garlic can be used in a number of Asian, Oriental and Mediterranean dishes, and it will blend well with most vegetables and grains.

Recipe: Garlic & Onion Soup (see p. 76).

Lemon balm
(Balm)

Lemon balm is native to the Mediterranean, and has oval-shaped, textured leaves. Available fresh or dried, it has a distinctive lemony aroma and flavour.

Culinary uses

Use lemon balm generously in soups, savoury salads, sauces, drinks and fruit salads. The leaves can be used to make tea in the same way as lemon verbena (see p. 60).

Lemon verbena

This herb is native to South America, and is now also grown in parts of Europe. It is sometimes confused with lemon balm, but has longer, smoother leaves of a darker green. It is available fresh or dried.

Culinary uses

Lemon verbena has a fresh, lemony flavour and can be added to many light sauces, dressings, salads, soups, drinks and fruit dishes. It is also used to make tea (see p. 60).

Lovage
(Love parsley)

Lovage is a large, celery-like plant native to southern Europe. The whole plant is used, leaf, seed and root. It has a strong, aromatic flavour and is available as fresh leaves and root or as dried root.

Culinary uses

Lovage can be cooked whole, in the same way as celery (see p. 28). It can also be chopped and added to soups, sauces and salads.

Marjoram
(Sweet/Knotted marjoram)

Marjoram is native to the Mediterranean and has a sweet, delicate flavour when used in moderation. It has a high tannin content, so can taste slightly bitter if overused.

Marjoram is available fresh or dried. If using fresh marjoram, be sure to wash well because it grows very close to the ground and the downy leaves can easily pick up dust.

Culinary uses

The fresh herb is delicious chopped and sprinkled over salads or cooked vegetable dishes, and the dried herb can be added to any combination of vegetables, grains and beans. Marjoram combines particularly well with nut, egg and tomato dishes. A pinch of marjoram can also be added to salad dressings, sauces and mayonnaise.

Recipe: Cream Cheese Dip (see p. 82).

Mint

There are many varieties of mint, the most common being spearmint, applemint, peppermint and horsemint. They are native to the Mediterranean and western Asia, but are now grown worldwide. The dried herb can be used if no fresh is available.

Spearmint is common garden mint, and is used for culinary purposes. Applemint is a downy leaved variety with a fine flavour, also used in cooking. The peppermint is usually used for the strong pungent oil which is extracted from the herb, but dried leaves are available.

Culinary uses

Common garden mint (spearmint) is used in sauces and drinks, and with potatoes, peas and other grains and vegetables. It is often used as a garnish and is extensively used in Middle Eastern dishes such as Tabouleh. Applemint can be used in a similar way.

Peppermint oil can be used in drinks and sweets. The dried peppermint leaves can be used to make mint tea (see page 60). Horsemint is usually used in curries and chutneys.

Recipe: Citrus Cocktail (see p. 81).

Mixed herbs

This is a ready-prepared mixture of dried herbs, usually marjoram, thyme, parsley, basil and rosemary.

Culinary uses

Mixed herbs can be used in many savoury soups, stocks and casseroles, and most vegetable, grain and bean dishes.

Recipe: Mung Bean Casserole (see p. 109).

Nasturtiums

Native to Peru, nasturtiums are usually grown as a garden flower. Both the brilliant orange-red flowers and the large bright green leaves can be eaten, and have a peppery, cress-like taste. Nasturtiums are usually eaten fresh.

Culinary uses

Leave the flowers and leaves whole or chop if desired and add to salads and sandwiches.

Oregano
(Wild marjoram)

Oregano is rather larger than marjoram, and has an aromatic flavour. Native to Asia, Europe and North Africa, it is used extensively in Italian and Greek cooking, and is usually the predominant herb in pizzas.

Culinary uses

Like marjoram, oregano can be used for almost any savoury dish. It blends perfectly with tomatoes, raw or cooked, and is delicious with cheese dishes, pasta, grains, beans and most vegetables. Be careful not to use too much as it is quite strong.

Dried oregano has a stronger flavour than fresh and it can be used at any point during cooking, although a pinch added just before serving brings out the best flavour.

Recipe: Red Bean Salad (see p. 93).

Parsley

Parsley is Mediterranean in origin. There are several varieties, including broad leaved parsley, curly leaved parsley and Neopolitan parsley with thick stems. Best eaten fresh, parsley is extremely nutritious, being high in vitamins A, B, C and E as well as some minerals (see the nutritional chart on p. 26).

Culinary uses

Most of the nutrients are stored in the stems, so be sure not to discard all of these. Parsley can be chopped and sprinkled over salads or hot vegetable dishes, and its bright green colour is very decorative.

Parsley can also be used in sauces, soups, stuffings and savoury dishes. It combines very well with other herbs. If using in a hot dish, add towards the end of cooking.

Recipe: Creamed Cauliflower Soup (see p. 73).

Rosemary

Rosemary is native to the Mediterranean, and grows wild on many cliffs and shorelines there. The hard, spiky leaves contain oil of camphor, and fresh rosemary can have an intoxicating aroma and flavour.

Rosemary has a strong, pungent flavour and is best eaten fresh, although dried is still quite tasty. Dried is available as leaves and powder.

Culinary uses

Rosemary needs a while to cook for its flavour to come through, so add it at the beginning of cooking. It is particularly good with root vegetables and grains, and can also be used to help counteract the oiliness of a dish. Use sparingly, however, as it can overpower the flavour of the other ingredients.

Recipe: Rye Grain & Vegetable Broth (see p. 78).

Sage

Sage originated in the northern Mediterranean but now grows extensively in most temperate regions. There are several varieties. Sage is a welcome addition to a garden because it attracts honey bees, therefore helping pollination of the other plants. The soft greeny-grey leaves can be used fresh or dried, but use cautiously because they have a very strong flavour and a high tannin content, which, when used in excess, causes a bitter taste.

Culinary uses

Sage is commonly used in stuffings, but it can also be used sparingly in spicy dishes and sauces. A few fresh leaves in a summer punch can be very refreshing.

Recipe: Chestnut & Prune Roast (see p. 104).

Tansy

Tansy is native to Europe, but is now also common in America. It has narrow, feathery leaves and a very distinctive flavour. Tansy is usually eaten fresh.

Culinary uses

Add chopped fresh tansy to dips, cottage or cream cheese, dressings, salads and fruit salads. It combines particularly well with eggs.

Tarragon

The tarragon plant is native to southern Europe. There are two main culinary varieties, the French and the Russian. French tarragon is superior and its pungent aniseed-like flavour is used extensively in French cooking.

French tarragon has to be grown from cuttings, since the plant itself produces no seed. It is not easy to grow and needs careful attention to begin with, but once established it will thrive. It can be used fresh or dried, the fresh being preferable. The dried herb is available as whole leaves and ground.

Culinary uses

Fresh tarragon is delicious chopped and sprinkled over salads and mild-flavoured vegetables, and is particularly good with tomatoes, eggs, asparagus or cream cheese. It can be added at any stage of cooking, as the longer it cooks the more flavourful it becomes. Tarragon is also a lovely addition to salad dressings, mayonnaise, and white and tomato-based sauces.

Recipe: Tiny Stuffed Tomatoes (see p. 87).

Thyme

This is another herb with Mediterranean origins which now grows successfully in all temperate areas. There are over 50 varieties, the main culinary herbs being garden thyme, wild thyme and lemon thyme. Lemon thyme is often preferred as its flavour is less strong.

Thyme has a high tannin content, so should be used sparingly to avoid a bitter taste.

Culinary uses

The subtle, sweet flavour of thyme blends well with most vegetables, grains and beans. It is particularly good with courgettes, aubergines and peppers. If using the dried herb, add at the beginning of cooking. Fresh thyme should be added towards the end of cooking, or sprinkled on top of the dish before serving.

Winter savory

Winter savory is native to the Mediterranean, and has thin, small leaves and an aromatic, peppery flavour. Summer savory is similar and is thought by some to have an even better flavour. Savory is available fresh or dried.

Culinary uses

Use chopped winter savory as a seasoning or in vegetable, bean and grain dishes. It is a rather strong herb so should perhaps be used in moderation.

SPICES & SEEDS

Alfalfa seeds ☐
Allspice ☐
Anise-peppers
Anise seeds
Asafoetida ☐
Caraway seeds
Cardamom ☐
Cayenne pepper ☐

Celery seeds ☐
Chilli ☐
Chinese five-spice ☐
Cinnamon ☐
Cloves ☐
Coriander seeds ☐
Cumin seeds ☐
Curry powders ☐

Fenugreek seeds ☐
Garam masala ☐
Ginger ☐
Juniper berries ☐
Linseeds ☐
Mixed spice
Mustard seeds ☐
Nutmeg and mace ☐

Paprika ☐
Peppercorns ☐
Poppy seeds ☐
Saffron ☐
Star anise ☐
Turmeric ☐
Vanilla pods

☐ Pictured opposite page 64

Spices are basically the dried seeds, leaves, flowers, roots and barks of edible aromatic plants. Described in this section are many of the spices and seeds commonly used in cooking. As mentioned in the herb section, it may take you a little time to familiarize yourself with all the different flavours and usages, but once you master the art of spicing, a mere touch can transform a dish.

Grinding spices
Many spices and seeds can be bought ready-ground. This can be useful for the very hard spices but in general it is better to

buy the whole spices or seeds and grind them yourself. A pestle and mortar is a good investment for this purpose. If you wish, the whole spices or seeds can be roasted or dry-fried before grinding, to release their aromatic oils and improve their flavour. Heat gently so as not to burn the delicate spice.

Storage
All whole or ground spices and seeds should be kept in opaque, airtight jars, away from direct sunlight or heat. Ready-ground spices do deteriorate and lose their flavours more quickly, so only buy in small quantities and use within 6 months.

Alfalfa seeds
(Lucerne)
Alfalfa is an extremely important food supplement, being highly nutritious. It contains a high proportion of protein, vitamins and minerals, including vitamin B_{12}, which is essential to a healthy diet and usually only available in meat, fish and dairy products. Alfalfa seeds can also be sprouted (see p. 23).
Culinary uses
The tiny light brown seeds can be sprinkled over savoury dishes, breads and pastries, or added to cakes and desserts.

Allspice
(Jamaica pepper/Pimento berries)
Allspice is the brown sun-dried berry from the pimento tree, indigenous to Central America and the West Indies. It is not a mixture of several spices, as is often thought, but is similar in flavour to cinnamon, cloves and nutmeg and is an ingredient in mixed spice. Allspice is available as whole berries or ground.
Culinary uses
Allspice is widely used in Central and South American cooking and can also be used in soups, savoury dishes, pickles, cakes, puddings and pastries.
Recipe: Evelyn's German Potato Soup (see p. 75).

Anise-peppers
(Szechwan peppers)
Anise-peppers are the dried red berries of a tree native to China, and should not be confused with anise seeds. They are hot and aromatic, popular in Chinese cooking, and are an ingredient in Chinese five-spice powder.
Culinary uses
Use in savoury Chinese and Oriental dishes, and in spicy soups, sauces and casseroles.

Anise seeds
(Aniseed/Sweet cumin)

The anise plant belongs to the carrot family, and originates from Greece and Egypt. Both the fresh leaves and the seeds are used as a spice, and they have a distinctive liquorice flavour. The seeds are used whole or ground.

The oil extracted from anise seeds is used to make alcohol: *pastis* in France, *ouzo* in Greece and *raki* in Turkey. The oil is also used as a substitute for liquorice extract in sweets.
Culinary uses
Anise seeds can be used in curries, spicy dishes, puddings, cakes and pastries, confectionery and drinks. Use sparingly and add at the beginning of cooking.
Recipe: Black Bean Chilli (see p. 100).

Asafoetida
Asafoetida is a sticky resin extracted from the stems of a plant native to Asia. It is used widely in Oriental and Eastern cookery, but is still quite hard to find in Western countries.

The resin is pale brown or yellow in colour and extremely hard. You need a hammer or a very hard object to break off tiny chips, which should then be ground. It is easier to buy resin ready-ground, although some brands often contain artificial colouring.
Culinary uses
Use asafoetida sparingly in savoury dishes. It is a very smelly spice, somewhat similar to strong garlic, and should be kept in an airtight container away from other spices. Asafoetida can also be used as a salt substitute.
Recipe: Fresh Coriander Dhal (see p. 105).

Caraway seeds
Caraway is a member of the carrot family and is native to Europe and Asia. The thin crescent-shaped seeds have a strong characteristic flavour which people tend to either love or hate. They are used whole.
Culinary uses
You can use caraway seeds in bread, curries, pastries and cakes. Use sparingly and add at the beginning of cooking.
Recipe: Unroasted Buckwheat Casserole (see p. 117).

Cardamom
Cardamom is a member of the ginger family, native to India and grown in most tropical countries. It is usually quite expensive because harvesting occurs sporadically, as the pods ripen at different times. The large green, black or white pods contain black seeds, and you can buy as whole pods, whole seeds or ground. Ground cardamom is one of the ingredients in garam masala.
Culinary uses
Cardamom has a very strong, aromatic flavour. It can be used whole or ground in curries, savoury dishes, rice, puddings and cakes.
Recipe: Aubergine & Potato Curry (see p. 98).

Cayenne pepper
Cayenne pepper is a variety of chilli powder ground from certain hot red chilli peppers native to Central America. Some commercial brands also contain added salt and spices.
Culinary uses
Cayenne pepper can be used in the same way as chilli powder, although it is rather hotter. Add sparingly to soups, white sauces, curries and spicy dishes.
Recipe: Fresh Vegetable Curry (see p. 106).

Celery seeds

These are the dried seeds of the celery plant, native to Italy. Celery seeds have a slightly sharp, bitter flavour, reminiscent of the vegetable. Celery salt is made by combining crushed celery seeds with refined salt, and is used as a seasoning.

Culinary uses
Use sparingly in savoury soups, stocks, casseroles and vegetable stews.

Chilli

Chillies are an extremely pungent, fiery hot variety of pepper native to South America. They are grown widely in all tropical regions of the world and can be eaten fresh or dried and used whole or ground. Dried flaked chillies are also available. Commercial chilli powder is usually a blend of ground chilli and other spices.

Culinary uses
Chilli is used in Indian, Chinese, Mexican and West Indian dishes. Whole chillies can be minced finely (remove the seeds first) or used whole. Take great care to wash your hands well after preparation because they have a stinging action on the skin. If using whole chillies in cooking, remove them before serving. Chilli powder should be added at the beginning of cooking and used sparingly.
Recipe: Black Bean Chilli (see p. 100).

Chinese five-spice

This is a mixture of ground anise-peppers, star anise, cassia (a type of cinnamon), cloves and fennel seeds. It has a faint liquorice flavour and is commonly used in Chinese cookery.

Culinary uses
Add a little Chinese five-spice to noodles or brown rice, or use in curries and Chinese-style cooked vegetables.

Cinnamon

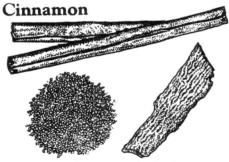

Cinnamon is the aromatic bark of a variety of laurel tree native to Sri Lanka and southern India. Available as sticks, quills and ground.

Culinary uses
Cinnamon can be used in Oriental, African and Indian savoury dishes. Ground cinnamon is commonly used in the West for flavouring sweet dishes, desserts and cakes. The sticks can be used to flavour drinks and syrups, and are removed before use.
Recipe: Christmas Puddings (see p. 124).

Cloves

Cloves are the hard, dried flower buds of an evergreen tree of the myrtle family, native to Southeast Asia. Pink when they are picked, the buds turn reddy-brown after sun-drying. They are very aromatic and can be used whole or ground. Ground cloves are the powdered 'heads' of the whole cloves.

Culinary uses
Cloves have a strong pungent flavour, so use sparingly. They can be used in spicy, sweet or savoury dishes, mulled wines and punches, sauces, cakes, mincemeat, puddings, biscuits and pastries.
Recipe: Baked Apples (see p. 121).

Coriander seeds

Coriander seeds are the dried, roasted fruit of a small annual plant originating from southern Europe and the Middle East. The mild, aromatic seeds can be bought whole or ground. Coriander leaves (see p. 54) have a quite different flavour.

Culinary uses
Coriander seeds are used in many Arabian and Eastern dishes, and can be added to a number of savoury dishes, curries, desserts, puddings and pickles.
Recipe: Aubergine & Potato Curry (see p. 98).

Cumin seeds

Cumin is a member of the carrot family, originating from North Africa. The seeds resemble caraway seeds in appearance, but have a quite different flavour, being hot and pungent. They are widely used in Central American, North African and Asian cooking. Ground cumin is also available, and is a main ingredient in curry powder.

Culinary uses
Cumin has a strong, spicy flavour and is best added at the beginning of cooking. It is a common ingredient in curries and is also delicious in dips, yogurt relishes, soups, salads, savoury and sweet dishes. Cumin is also used as a pickling spice.
Recipe: Potato & Beetroot Soup (see p. 78).

Curry powders

Curry powders are ready-prepared mixtures of ground coriander, turmeric, cumin, chilli and other aromatic spices. Each manufacturer has an individual recipe. Curry powders can be mild, medium or hot, depending on how much chilli is used. Curry pastes are also available, which usually contain fresh chillies, onion and ginger as well as dry spices.

Culinary uses
Curry powder or paste can be added to soups, savoury rice and bean dishes, curries, sauces and mayonnaise.
Recipe: Butter Bean Salad (see p. 90).

Fenugreek seeds

The fenugreek plant is native to the Middle East and western Asia and produces bitter-sweet, yellow rectangular seeds. Fenugreek seeds are available whole or ground and may also be sprouted (see p. 23). Fenugreek leaves are used as a herb (see p. 54).

Culinary uses
Many Indian dishes call for fenugreek seeds and they can be used in chutneys and pickles. They should be added at the beginning of cooking and used in moderation.
Recipe: Add ground to Joey's Egg Curry (see p. 108).

Garam masala

Garam masala is a mixture of several spices ground together. Like curry powder, there is no standard recipe. Garam masala can be bought, but it is even better to make your own as described below:

15 ml (1 tbsp) cardamom seeds
5 ml (1 tsp) whole cloves
5 cm (2 in) stick, or 10 ml (2 tsp) ground, cinnamon
10 ml (2 tsp) cumin seeds
2·5 ml ($\frac{1}{2}$ tsp) black peppercorns
$\frac{1}{4}$ whole nutmeg

If liked, first roast or dry the spices together in a dry frying pan. Put all the ingredients through a fine mill or coffee grinder and store away from direct sunlight in an airtight jar. This mixture will keep for a couple of months.

Culinary uses
Add to curries, spicy Indian dishes, vegetable, grain or bean dishes towards the end of cooking. Garam masala can also be added to sauces or mayonnaise.
Recipe: Onion Bhajis with Yogurt Sauce. (see p. 86).

Ginger

Fresh ginger is the knobbly, cream-coloured root of a sturdy herbaceous plant, native to Southeast Asia and now common in most tropical areas. It is used extensively in Indian, Asian, Japanese, Caribbean, African and West Indian cookery.

The fresh ginger root should be scraped gently to help preserve the essential oils close to the surface and then cut into small pieces, sliced thinly or grated. The root is also available dried, whole or sliced, and needs to be soaked before using.

The dried root is also available ground, but only buy a little at a time as the strong pungent 'gingery' flavour does not keep well. Stem ginger can also be found in crystallized form or preserved in syrup.

Culinary uses
Fresh or dried ginger can be added to soups, salad dressings, Chinese stir-fries, savoury dishes, puddings, cakes, jams, chutneys and pickles. Stem ginger is often used in puddings and confectionery.
Recipe: Peach & Pear Crumble (see p. 127).

Juniper berries

Juniper is an evergreen shrub native to the northern hemisphere and found in many parts of America, Europe and Asia. The dried bluish-black fruits or berries of the shrub are available whole.

Culinary uses
Juniper berries have a sharp, pungent flavour and can be used in pickles and chutneys. They are good for counteracting oily dishes.

Linseeds

Linseeds are the tiny, shiny brown oval-shaped seeds of the flax plant, itself grown for fibre in the production of linen.

Linseeds are mainly used in the production of oil, for industrial purposes as well as consumption. The whole seeds are also available however, and are nutritionally valuable as they are rich in three essential fatty acids. They have a distinctive smooth, nutty flavour.

Culinary uses
Linseeds may be added to bread dough, or sprinkled over the top of loaves before baking.
Recipe: Three-seed Bread (see p. 156).

Mixed spice

This spice is a ready-prepared mixture of nutmeg, cinnamon, ginger and allspice.

Culinary uses
Mixed spice is commonly used in cakes, scones, puddings and pastries but can also be added to savoury dishes, especially curries.
Recipe: Baked Bananas with Yogurt Sauce (see p. 121).

Mustard seeds

The mustard plant grows, both wild and cultivated, in the Mediterranean region. There are two types of mustard seeds generally available, black (brown) and white (yellow). Both have a characteristic hot, pungent flavour although the white seeds are milder than the black. They are both available whole. Ground mustard (dry mustard powder) is usually from a mixture of black and white seeds.

The commercial mustards bought as a relish are made from mustard seeds. Wholegrain mustard contains the whole seeds and is often flavoured with herbs, spices, wines and sweeteners, such as tarragon, green peppercorns, allspice, white wine and honey.

Culinary uses
Mustard seeds are frequently added to Indian, African and Asian dishes, either whole or crushed. Fry them at the beginning of cooking in hot oil, to release their essential oil which carries the flavour. Ground mustard can be used for sauces, dressings and chutneys.
Recipe: Leeks Vinaigrette (see p. 84).

Nutmeg and mace

The evergreen nutmeg tree originated in Indonesia and is grown in most tropical areas.

Nutmeg is the dried kernel or seed of the plant and mace is its dried outer covering. Always buy whole nutmegs if you can and grate them yourself with a cheese grater, although ready-ground nutmeg is available.

Mace is available in pressed, flat 'blade' form and ground. Mace has a brighter, more orange colour than nutmeg.

Culinary uses
Nutmeg and mace make delicious and aromatic additions to soups, curries, sauces or pickles. They can also be used in puddings, cakes and pastries. Although similar in aroma and flavour, mace is slightly stronger.
Recipe: Cream of Mushroom Soup (see p. 74).

Paprika

Paprika is ground from a variety of peppers native to South America. Paprika can vary in taste from mild to hot, and in colour from reddy-brown to bright red. It is a popular spice in Hungarian cookery. Buy ready-ground, but in small quantities so that it is as fresh as possible.

Culinary uses
Use paprika generously in dips, soups, savoury dishes and white sauces. It should be added at the beginning of cooking to bring out its full flavour. Paprika can also be used uncooked, sprinkled over dishes as a garnish.
Recipe: Egg & Avocado Mayonnaise Dip (see p. 82).

Peppercorns

Peppercorns come from the pepper vine, native to Asia. They are available green, black and white. Green peppercorns are the unripe berries of the plant, usually sold in brine. Black peppercorns are sun-dried green peppercorns and have a strong, pungent flavour. White peppercorns are the fully ripened berries of the plant, sun-dried and with the red outer skin removed. They have a milder, more aromatic flavour. White pepper is relatively recent, only becoming fashionable when some great French chefs decided that tiny specks of black pepper ruined the aesthetic beauty of their creamy white sauces.

Both black and white peppercorns are available whole or ground. Freshly ground pepper will have the best flavour.

Culinary uses
Add whole or ground peppercorns to savoury dishes, sauces, dressings, marinades and pickles. Ground pepper is used as a seasoning for most savoury dishes.
Recipe: Hummus (see p. 83).

Poppy seeds

These tiny blue-black or white seeds come from the opium poppy flower, but have no hallucinogenic properties. Native to the Middle East, the seeds are very popular in Russian, Jewish and Eastern cookery. They have a sweet, mild flavour and aroma.

Culinary uses
Poppy seeds are delicious added to sweet and savoury dishes, either sprinkled on top or added at the beginning of cooking. They can also be used in baking to decorate bread and confectionery.
Recipe: Joey's Egg Curry (see p. 108).

Saffron

Saffron is one of the most expensive spices available. The yellow-red strands are the dried stamens of an Asian crocus, and it can take 75,000 hand-harvested stamens to make just 450 g (1 lb) of saffron. It is available in strands or as powder, but the latter is sometimes adulterated.

Culinary uses
Saffron has a delicate, aromatic flavour, and is used in soups, rice dishes, cakes, biscuits and breads. A pinch of saffron added to a pan of cooking rice will turn it a vibrant yellow-orange. If using saffron for flavouring, add at the end of cooking, dissolved in a little water.
Recipe: Add to Brown Rice Risotto (see p. 100).

Star anise

This small, dried star-shaped pod is from an evergreen tree of the magnolia family, originating from China. The small oval seeds are contained in the pod, in the points of the star. Both the pods, whole or cracked, and the whole or ground seeds are available.

The flavour of star anise is reminiscent of liquorice, and is similar to that of anise seeds. It is now used for the extraction of anise oil.

Culinary uses
Ground star anise is an ingredient of Chinese five-spice powder. It can be used in spicy dishes, curries, puddings, cakes and biscuits or in recipes requiring anise seeds.
Recipe: Use in Black Bean Chilli (see p. 100).

Turmeric

Turmeric is the ground root from a plant of the lily family, native to Southeast Asia, usually only found ground in a bright yellow powder. It has a mild aromatic flavour and will colour food a bright yellow (it is sometimes known as 'poor man's saffron'). Be careful not to use too much or the food may taste bitter.

Culinary uses
Turmeric is a basic ingredient in most curry powders. It can be cooked in many grain, bean or vegetable dishes and can be used in chutneys and pickles. Turmeric can also be used sparingly to add colour to cakes and rice. Add at the beginning of cooking in small amounts.
Recipe: Onion Bhajis with Yogurt Sauce (see p. 86).

Vanilla pods

Vanilla pods come from a type of climbing orchid native to Central America. The pod is picked before the seeds inside mature, and then cured. It is used whole. To obtain the vanilla flavour from the pod, immerse it in the liquid to be used in the recipe. The longer the infusion, the stronger the flavour. Pods are reusable, so remove, rinse and pat dry, and store in an airtight jar.

Culinary uses
Vanilla pods can be used to flavour drinks, sweet sauces, puddings, cakes, custards, ice creams and confectionery.
Recipe: Add to Rice Pudding (see p. 130).

HERB TEAS

Bancha tea
Camomile tea ☐
Coltsfoot tea
Comfrey tea ☐

Fennel tea ☐
Lemon verbena tea
Linden tea ☐
Luaka tea

Mint tea
Mu tea ☐
Nettle tea ☐
Raspberry leaf tea ☐

Rosehip tea ☐
Twig tea ☐
Vervain tea ☐

☐ Pictured opposite page 65

Drink is an important part of the wholefood diet and should not be overlooked. Many commercial drinks such as fruit squashes or fizzy drinks contain high amounts of sugar as well as colourants, flavourings, preservatives and other additives. Alcohol is not only high in sugar but dehydrates the body, depleting it of B vitamins and, in excess, damaging the liver. Coffee and tea both contain caffeine, which can be damaging in large doses. Caffeine acts as an immediate stimulant, making the heart beat faster and more irregularly. It raises the blood pressure and insulin level, and is also thought to prevent the body's absorption of some vitamins and minerals, particularly B vitamins and iron. Tea also contains tannin, which can cause constipation in excess.

For all these reasons, it is recommended that you cut down your intake of sugared drinks, alcohol, coffee and tea. Herbal teas offer a wholesome alternative to the more commonly used tea and coffee, and have been drunk for their pleasant flavours and therapeutic effects for thousands of years. They can form a beneficial part of the daily diet, helping to calm, stimulate or cleanse the body in a gentle and natural way.

Listed here are a few of the most common herbal teas. Their therapeutic values are briefly mentioned. Some teas are taken only for their medicinal effects but most can be enjoyed purely for their pleasant and delicate flavours. Their therapeutic effects are not, of course, guaranteed, and should not be considered as a substitute for your doctor's advice. Other health drinks, including fruit and vegetable juices and caffeine-free coffees, are described in the next chapter (see p. 61).

Herbal teas can be made from dried or fresh herbs. Many are now marketed in handy sachets, which can be very convenient but also quite expensive. All herbal teas should be stored in opaque airtight containers.

Making herbal teas

As a general rule for an average strength of tea, use 5 ml (1 tsp) of dried herbs or 15 ml (1 tbsp) of crushed fresh herbs to each cup of boiling water (preferably filtered). Pour over the boiling water and leave the tea to steep for 3-5 minutes before straining and drinking. If a stronger tea is desired, add more herbs to the pot or cup rather than increasing the steeping time. Over-steeping can ruin the delicate flavour and alter the beneficial effect of the tea.

For herbal teas made from seeds rather than leaves, the proportions are 5 ml (1 tsp) of crushed seeds to each cup of water. Put the seeds and water in a saucepan and boil together for 5 minutes before straining and drinking.

If you are making herb tea in a teapot, use a china pot rather than a metal one as the latter can affect the flavour of delicate teas. Do not leave for too long or the herb tea may stew.

All herbal teas can be drunk hot or cold. If drinking cold, be sure to strain before cooling. A little honey may be added as a sweetener if desired.

Bancha tea

Bancha tea is a macrobiotic green tea from Japan. It is prepared from the leaves of the tea bush, picked after 3 years of growth.

Bancha tea has a slightly smoky flavour and is a soothing, relaxing tea. It is low in caffeine and tannin and high in calcium. Leftover bancha tea can be reheated and drunk later.

To prepare bancha tea, use 5-10 ml (1-2 tsp) of tea to 1 cup water. Put the tea and water in a saucepan, bring to the boil and simmer for 20 minutes. Strain and drink.

Camomile tea

Camomile is a daisy-like plant native to Europe, which can be found growing wild all over Europe and America. Only the flower-heads, either dried or fresh, are used.

Camomile tea is very good for soothing upset stomachs and relieving flatulence and indigestion. It is said to help regulate monthly periods for women and is good for fever and restlessness in children.

Externally, camomile tea is beneficial as a facewash to keep skin soft and supple, as a mouthwash to soothe inflamed gums or mouth ulcers, and as a hair rinse for fair hair.

Coltsfoot tea

The roots, leaves and flowers of coltsfoot may be used in the preparation of tea. It is sometimes known as 'British tobacco', since the dried and crushed leaves are sometimes smoked or taken as snuff to relieve cold symptoms.

Coltsfoot is an excellent remedy for coughs, colds, phlegm, catarrh and associated bronchial diseases.

Externally, coltsfoot tea can be used for insect bites, leg ulcers, burns and swellings.

Comfrey tea

Comfrey tea is made from the dried, crushed leaves of the comfrey plant. It is a mild tea and is nutritionally valuable, being high in the B vitamin group, including the rare vitamin B_{12}, and many minerals.

Comfrey tea is a powerful remedy for coughs, colds, catarrh, inflammation of the lungs and other associated bronchial diseases. It is also helpful for digestive and intestinal problems such as dysentery and diarrhoea.

Externally, comfrey tea can be used for bruises, cuts and insect bites.

Fennel tea

The fennel plant is tall and feathery, with yellow seeds and a bulbous root eaten as a vegetable (see p. 28). Generally the fennel seeds are used to make fennel tea, although the leaves, roots and flowers may also be used.

Fennel tea is good for soothing upset stomachs, especially after food poisoning. It relieves abdominal cramps and flatulence, and is particularly good for children. It can also help expel mucus from the sinuses or lungs and is an effective soothing tea for those suffering from bronchitis or asthma. Fennel tea may also be taken for menstrual problems and is said to help stimulate the flow of milk in breast-feeding mothers.

Externally, warm fennel tea makes an excellent gargle for hoarseness, coughs or for sore throats.

Lemon verbena tea

Similar in flavour to vervain, lemon verbena is a larger plant with thick, bushy leaves and branches. It is indigenous to South America.

Lemon verbena tea has a powerful, stimulating effect and is useful in cases of depression, lethargy and mental exhaustion. It will help to sooth fevers, neuralgia and migraines and is also useful in reducing acid or wind in the stomach causing cramps or indigestion.

Linden tea
(Lime flower tea)

There are two varieties of linden plant, the American and the European. Infusions can be made from both the flowers and the leaves.

Linden tea is excellent for relaxing and encouraging sleep, especially for those suffering from chronic insomnia, anxiety attacks, nervous tension and irritability. It may also be taken for coughs, colds, sore throats and influenzas. Its diuretic properties make it useful for mild kidney and bladder problems, gout and rheumatism.

Externally, preparations made from the linden bark are soothing for skin irritations and burns.

Luaka tea

This tea comes from the high mountainous parts of Sri Lanka. It is not strictly a herbal tea, but contains significantly less caffeine and tannin than other 'black' teas.

Mint tea

There are many varieties of mint (peppermint, spearmint, applemint, horsemint, etc.), native to the Mediterranean and western Asia and now growing prolifically in most parts of the world. It is commonly used as a herb (see mint, p. 54).

Mint tea is a tonic. It is often recommended as a substitute for 'black' tea and coffee and it has a general stimulating and soothing effect on the nervous system. For these reasons it is particularly useful for children, old people and those recovering from illness or disease. It is also used to help heartburn, irritability, migraine, headaches, stomach cramps, nausea and vomiting.

Externally, an infusion of mint may be added to the bath to relieve itchy or irritating skin conditions. Gargling with mint tea can relieve toothache and helps freshen the breath.

Mu tea

Mu tea is a macrobiotic tea formulated in 1963 by George Ohsawa, a practitioner of oriental medicine and philosophy who founded the macrobiotic movement.

There are two types of mu tea, one made from a combination of 9 natural herbs and the other from 16 natural herbs. It has a strong, aromatic flavour.

Mu tea is a natural tonic increasing vitality and strength. It is specifically good for wheezing coughs and other respiratory problems where there is difficulty in breathing.

To prepare mu tea, use 5-10 ml (1-2 tsp) of tea to 1 cup water. Put the tea and water in a saucepan, bring to the boil and simmer for 20 minutes. Strain and drink.

Nettle tea

Many people think of nettles as annoying weeds and do not realise their numerous culinary and medicinal uses. All parts of the plant may be used to prepare the tea.

Nettle tea can act as a gentle blood purifier and may be taken for rheumatism, gout, kidney and urinary problems. It is also helpful in stopping excessive bleeding or haemorrhaging. It can increase milk flow in nursing mothers and can help regulate monthly periods or bring them on when overdue.

Used externally, nettle is an ingredient in many beauty products helping to cleanse the skin and reduce acne and eczema. Nettle tea is also an excellent hair tonic.

Raspberry leaf tea

This tea is made from the leaves of a variety of mild raspberry.

The tea has a mild purgative effect and is useful for cases of dysentery and diarrhoea, especially in children (although many children do not take readily to the taste and prefer fennel tea). Raspberry leaf tea can be taken by women to help regulate or decrease menstrual flow, or during pregnancy to help tone the uterus and prevent miscarriage. This tea has been taken by pregnant women in China for thousands of years.

Rosehip tea

Rosehips are the fruit of wild roses and are exceptionally high in vitamin C.

Rosehip tea is an excellent remedy for coughs, colds, sore throats, runny noses, influenzas and other bronchial infections. It may also be taken for chronic inflammation of the digestive tract, dysentery and diarrhoea.

Twig tea
(Kukicha tea)

Twig tea is made from the same plant as bancha tea, but is prepared from the twigs rather than the leaves. The twigs are picked from the bottom of the tea bush after just 3 years of growth.

Prepare and use as for bancha tea.

Vervain tea

Although similar to lemon verbena, vervain is a different plant with tinner leaves and branches and smaller flowers. It is indigenous to Europe.

Vervain tea acts as a general tonic, helping to cleanse the system.

Externally, vervain tea may be used as a gargle for sore throats and tonsillitis. It is used in some medicinal concoctions for ulcers, burns, cuts and bruises.

HEALTH DRINKS

CAFFEINE-FREE COFFEES
Dandelion coffee ☐
Decaffeinated coffee
Grain coffee ☐

FRESH FRUIT AND VEGETABLE JUICES
Apple juice ☐
Beetroot juice ☐
Carrot juice ☐
Celery juice ☐

Cucumber juice ☐
Lettuce juice ☐
Orange juice ☐
Parsley juice ☐
Spinach juice ☐
Watercress juice ☐

MILK AND YOGURT DRINKS
Lassis ☐
Milk shakes ☐
Pep-up drink ☐

☐ Pictured opposite page 65 or 80

Described in this section are some of the caffeine-free coffees available, as well as a selection of nutritious fresh fruit and vegetable juices and delicious health drinks made from milk, yogurt and fruit.

CAFFEINE-FREE COFFEES

Dandelion coffee

Dandelion coffee is made from the ground, roasted roots of the dandelion plant. It can be bought ready-ground.

Preparation
Use 5 ml (1 tsp) of dandelion coffee for each cup needed. Put the coffee in a saucepan and dry roast for 2-3 minutes. Add the water and simmer for 10 minutes. Strain and drink with or without milk.

Decaffeinated coffee

In recent years techniques have been developed which remove the caffeine from coffee with chemical solvents. Unfortunately, these chemicals are not totally removed from the coffee, and it is possible that they are harmful.

Grain coffees and coffee substitutes

There are many grain coffees on the market. They are mixtures of ground and toasted whole grains, grain products, fruit, roots and natural sweeteners. Some common ingredients are barley, oats, millet, wheat, rye, bran, chicory, figs, malt and molasses.

Preparation
Put 5 ml (1 tsp) coffee into a cup, pour over boiling water and add milk if desired.

FRESH FRUIT AND VEGETABLE JUICES

As well as being delicious, fresh juices are extremely beneficial to the body, being highly concentrated in nutrients. Any fruit or vegetable can be juiced, and all have diuretic and laxative properties. Juices of particular value are described below. Of course, their therapeutic effects are not instantaneous or guaranteed, and should not be considered as a substitute for your doctor's advice.

Juices should not be drunk in huge quantities as they are so concentrated. About 275 ml (½ pt) or less a day will be plenty, particularly with some of the more acid fruit.

Citrus fruit can be squeezed by hand but you will need a special juicing machine (see p. 62)

for most of the other fruit and vegetables. To use, wash the fruit or vegetables, top and tail, core and chop as necessary (there is no need to peel) and feed into the juicer.

Apple juice

Apple juice, like most fruit and vegetable juices, has diuretic and laxative properties. It is good for general cleansing of the system.

Beetroot juice

This is thought to build up red blood cells in the body, useful in cases of anaemia. It also cleanses the liver, kidneys and gall bladder and may be helpful for women with menstrual problems or infertility.

Carrot juice

Carrot juice cleanses the digestive system, promoting vitality and a feeling of well being. It is a good skin cleanser and digestive aid, and is also believed by some to help break down ulcerous or cancerous growths. Carrot juice should not be taken in excess as it can be poisonous in large quantities.

Celery juice

This cleans away waste in the intestinal tract and is thought to be helpful in cases of arthritis, varicose veins and heart disease.

Cucumber juice

Cucumber juice has natural cleansing and diuretic properties. It is thought to promote hair growth, to regulate blood pressure and to alleviate arthritis and rheumatism.

Lettuce juice

Lettuce juice is high in iron, and is therefore helpful for women with heavy menstruation. It is also a natural relaxant and mild diuretic.

Orange juice

This juice is high in vitamin C, which is thought to help prevent coughs and colds. Orange juice can be fairly acid and should not be drunk in large quantities.

Parsley juice

Parsley juice is thought to stimulate the thyroid and adrenal glands and is helpful in urinogenital and kidney disorders.

Spinach juice

Spinach juice is a wonderful remedy for constipation. It is high in oxalic acid, which increases peristalsis.

Watercress juice

Watercress juice is a good general cleanser and purifier of the body.

MILK AND YOGURT DRINKS

Milk shakes

Commercial milk shakes are often filled with sugar, synthetic colouring and even synthetic flavouring. However, milk shakes can be just as enticing and also nutritious if you make them yourself from natural ingredients.

275 ml (½ pt) whole milk, skimmed milk or soya milk
50-100 g (2-4 oz) fresh fruit, stoned and chopped roughly if necessary
a little sweetener if liked

Blend all the ingredients until smooth.

Lassis

Lassis are similar to milk shakes but are made from yogurt instead of milk. They are a delightful alternative to milk shakes and are very quick and simple to make.

Plain lassis are usually made with an equal mixture of natural yogurt and water, whisked together with a hand whisk or fork, and sweetened or salted as desired.

275 ml (½ pt) natural yogurt
50-100 g (2-4 oz) fresh fruit, stoned and chopped roughly if necessary
a little sweetener
a little grated citrus rind or grated nuts

Blend all the ingredients until smooth.

Pep-up drink

This is a wonderful way to start the day, giving you a good balance of protein, vitamins and minerals.

275 ml (½ pt) milk, whole, skimmed or soya
275 ml (½ pt) fruit or vegetable juice
15 ml (1 tbsp) brewer's yeast

Mix all the ingredients together in a glass.

KITCHEN EQUIPMENT

Although you do not need a wide range of kitchen equipment in wholefood cookery, the following may be useful.

Blender

An electric blender can be used to blend pâtés, purées, soups, sauces and drinks and also to grate nuts and breadcrumbs. Vegetable purées are particularly beneficial because the vegetables only need to be be lightly cooked before blending, thus retaining most of their nutritional value. Only fill to about two-thirds from the top, as the contents will rise up.

Chopping boards

Wooden chopping boards are preferable as knives do not blunt so quickly. After use, a wooden board should be lightly washed and left to dry in a warm, dry place.

Food processor/mixer

A food processor or mixer is not really essential unless you are cooking with large quantities of food. However, it will enable you to mix cakes, bread and many other sweet and savoury dishes in a very short time, leaving you free for other things. A good food processor should be able to chop, grind, shred and slice. Useful attachments for a food mixer are a shredder for vegetables and cheese, and a dough hook for breads and pastry.

Garlic press

For some recipes sliced or chopped garlic is required, and a knife should be used, but for crushed garlic a press is a great help.

Grater

A small hand grater is invaluable for grating vegetables (especially the root varieties), cheese, hard fruit, nutmeg, root ginger and citrus rind. The upright box type is best.

Juicer

A juicer is essential if you want to make your own fresh fruit and vegetable juices. It liquidizes the produce, separating the fresh juice from the pulp. It can be used for most fruit and vegetables, although citrus fruit can also be squeezed by hand or with a citrus juicer.

Knives

Good, sharp, well-weighted knives are a joy to work with. Sharpen them regularly with a knife sharpener for the best results. Stainless steel knives usually last longer than those made from carbon steel.

Longer knives are best for chopping and slicing; shorter knives for peeling. Serrated knives are useful for slicing soft produce.

Pans

Pans should be made of stainless steel, stainless steel with copper bottoms, enamel, iron, or enamelled iron. Glass or ceramic pans can cook rather unevenly. Avoid aluminium pans which leave a poisonous deposit on food. At the Neal's Yard Bakery stainless steel pans are preferred, but if using these, be careful not to scratch them as small amounts of metal can escape into the food.

The best pans are fairly heavy with tightly fitting lids and secure handles, preferably of a different, heat-resistant material.

Potato masher

This can be used for roughly puréeing any vegetable or soft fruit and for mixing up dips and sauces.

Pressure cooker

A pressure cooker is a good investment for wholefood cooking, as it will cook dried beans, grains and root vegetables in a fraction of the time normally taken. It is particularly good for dried beans as it makes the initial fast boiling for some beans unnecessary. It can also be used for soups, stocks, stews and rice puddings. Pressure-cooking is not recommended for soft vegetables as they overcook.

Choose one made from stainless steel rather than aluminium if possible, as aluminium oxides can dissolve into the food.

Salad sprouter

Although it is very simple to sprout beans, grains and seeds in a jam jar (see p. 23), a salad sprouter is well worth having if you are planning to sprout beans regularly. Because it has 3 layers it is possible to sprout 3 varieties of beans simultaneously.

Steamer

A steamer is important. Most vegetables retain more of their shape, flavour and nutritional value when steamed. There are quite a few good steamers on the market; the best are usually metal and 'petal-shaped', expanding to fit the size of the saucepan. If you don't have a steamer, you can use a metal colander inside a saucepan with a tightly fitting lid.

Tins

Baking tins are available in many shapes and sizes, and it is useful to have a selection. Cake tins can be round or square with varying depths and widths. The most commonly used size is 20 cm (8 in) wide. Loose-bottomed or spring-release cake tins are particularly useful. Flan tins (for tarts, flans and quiches) are shallow, round tins with removable bases.

A loaf tin can be used for both bread and cakes. The most commonly used sizes are for a 400 g (14 oz) loaf: 15 cm × 9 cm × 7.5 cm (6 in × 3½ in × 3 in) and for a larger 800 g (1 lb 12 oz) loaf: 18 cm × 11.5 cm × 8.5 cm (7¼ in × 4½ in × 3½ in).

A Swiss roll tin, patty tins and a baking tray are useful for biscuits, small cakes and tarts.

Vegetable mill

This is used for puréeing vegetables. It is adjustable so that varying degrees of coarseness can be achieved.

Water filters

There are two basic types of water filter generally available. One can be attached to your tap, so that all the water is filtered. The other is a jug through which you pour the water you wish to be filtered.

Filters will remove most of the chlorine (added intentionally) and most of the lead, mercury and cadmium (added unintentionally by water passing through old metal pipes). Use water filters for drinking water, making tea and for all water used in cooking.

Whisks

Hand whisks are basic kitchen utensils, used for stirring, mixing and beating. Use a wire balloon whisk for whisking egg whites, stirring sauces and whipping cream, and a rotary whisk for whipping cream, beating eggs and other light mixtures. A flat whisk is best for mixing together dry ingredients. For large quantities, such as cake mixtures, you may prefer to use a food processor or mixer.

Wok

These are Chinese pans designed for quick stir-frying. Made of thin metal and rounded, the heat reaches all parts of the pan, cooking food quickly and evenly. They are usually made from carbon iron, and can have wooden or iron handles.

Woks are usually balanced on a stand over the heat. Some varieties are flat-bottomed and do not need a stand. These are particularly suitable if you are using an electric ring.

Miscellaneous

Other useful kitchen utensils are wooden spoons, a rolling pin, a vegetable brush, spatulas, scales, a wire rack (for cooling bakes), a mortar and pestle (for grinding seeds), a rotary grater (for grinding nuts), a measuring jug, a colander, a sieve, a salad spinner, a zester (for citrus rind), an ice cream scoop, small brushes (for egg or oil glazes), oven gloves and a clock.

FREEZING

Home freezing is a good way of storing surplus produce and ready-prepared dishes, and is particularly useful if you cook for a large family, lead a busy life or grow your own produce. Most fresh vegetables, fruit, raw foods and cooked dishes can be frozen successfully if you follow the guidelines given here.

The best freezer wrappings are heavy-duty or double-thickness polythene bags, cling film or foil. If the wrappings are too thin, the food will deteriorate more quickly. Containers should be rigid, preferably plastic, and well-sealed. Label bags and containers before freezing for easy identification.

Fresh vegetables

All vegetables for freezing should be as young and tender as possible. If they are from your own garden or allotment, pick them first thing in the morning and blanch and freeze them immediately to preserve as much of their nutritional value as possible. If you are buying vegetables, choose the freshest available. Always prepare and blanch vegetables before freezing to preserve the colour, flavour and texture.

Most fresh vegetables freeze well, but there are some exceptions. Salad vegetables such as lettuce, cucumber, tomatoes, endive, chicory, avocados, watercress, radishes, peppers and celery do not freeze well, and also 'wet' vegetables such as swedes and boiled potatoes. Too much water is lost during thawing and they will become limp and soft.

Preparation and blanching

Clean the vegetables well. Top and tail, break into florets, cut into small pieces or leave whole, as appropriate.

Blanching destroys the enzyme which would otherwise spoil the colour and flavour of the vegetable. There are two methods, water blanching and steam blanching.

Water blanching is the immersion of raw vegetables in fast boiling water for a given time (see the chart below). For blanching 450 g (1 lb) of vegetables you will need about 4.4 l (8 pts) of fast boiling water. Put the prepared vegetables in a wire basket or sieve and lower into the water. The water should be brought back to the boil within 1 minute. Start timing when it begins to boil vigorously.

For steam blanching, put the prepared vegetables in a steamer with a tightly fitting lid and steam vigorously over boiling water for the given time (see the chart below).

When blanching is complete, remove the vegetables from the water and cool thoroughly in cold water. Drain well.

Freezing

Having prepared, blanched, cooled and drained your vegetables, pack in plastic bags or containers, in small or large quantities according to use. Take care to eliminate all the air.

Thawing and cooking

Most frozen vegetables can be cooked straight

Continued on page 65

VEGETABLE	WATER BLANCHING	STEAM BLANCHING	STORAGE TIME
Artichokes, globe	8 minutes Add 15 ml (1 tbsp) lemon juice.	12 minutes	12 months
Asparagus	2-4 minutes, depending on size.	3-6 minutes	10 months
Aubergines	6 minutes Cut in 2 cm (1 in) cubes.	9 minutes	10 months
Beetroots: small **large**	5-10 minutes, until completely cooked.	5-10 minutes, until completely cooked.	6 months 6 months
Broad beans	3 minutes	4½ minutes	12 months
Broccoli	3-5 minutes, depending on size.	4½ minutes, depending on size.	12 months
Brussels sprouts	4 minutes	6 minutes	12 months
Cabbages	1 minute Shred finely.	1½ minutes Shred finely.	6 months
Calabrese	As for broccoli.		
Carrots	3 minutes Leave whole if small or cut into 2 cm (1 in) slices.	4½ minutes Leave whole if small or cut into 2 cm (1 in) slices.	12 months
Cauliflowers	4 minutes Break into florets. Add 15 ml (1 tbsp) lemon juice.	6 minutes Break into florets.	6 months
Celeriac	3 minutes Cut in 2 cm (1 in) pieces.	4½ minutes Cut in 2 cm (1 in) pieces.	6 months
Celery	3 minutes Cut in 2 cm (1 in) pieces.	4½ minutes Cut in 2 cm (1 in) pieces.	6 months
Chard	2 minutes	3 minutes	12 months

VEGETABLE	WATER BLANCHING	STEAM BLANCHING	STORAGE TIME
Courgettes	1 minute Cut in 1 cm (½ in) slices.	1½ minutes Cut in 1 cm (½ in) slices.	6 months
Fennel	3 minutes Cut in 2 cm (1 in) pieces.	4½ minutes Cut in 2 cm (1 in) pieces.	6 months
French beans	2-3 minutes	4-5 minutes	12 months
Jerusalem artichokes	4 minutes Leave whole or cut in 2 cm (1 in) pieces.	6 minutes Leave whole or cut in 2 cm (1 in) pieces.	8 months
Kohlrabi	3 minutes Cut in 2 cm (1 in) pieces.	4½ minutes Cut in 2 cm (1 in) pieces.	12 months
Leeks	1 minute Cut in 2 cm (1 in) slices.	1½ minutes Cut in 2 cm (1 in) slices.	3 months
Marrows, pumpkins and squashes	3 minutes Cut in 1 cm (½ in) slices.	4½ minutes Cut in 1 cm (½ in) slices.	6 months
Mushrooms	These are best sautéed for 1 minute in a little butter or oil, whole if button mushrooms or in 1 cm (½ in) slices if large. Cool and freeze.		3 months
Okra	2 minutes	3 minutes	6 months
Onions	2 minutes Chop, slice or leave whole as appropriate.	3 minutes Chop, slice or leave whole as appropriate.	2 months
Parsnips	2 minutes Cut in 1 cm (½ in) slices.	3 minutes Cut in 1 cm (½ in) slices.	12 months
Peas and mange tout	1 minute	1½ minutes	12 months
Peppers	2 minutes Cut in 1 cm (½ in) slices.	3 minutes Cut in 1 cm (½ in) slices.	12 months
Potatoes: new mashed	4 minutes —	6 minutes —	12 months 3 months
Runner beans	2 minutes Cut in 2 cm (1 in) lengths	3 minutes Cut in 2 cm (1 in) lengths.	12 months
Salsify	2 minutes Cut in 1 cm (½ in) pieces.	3 minutes Cut in 1 cm (½ in) pieces.	12 months
Seakale	1 minute	1½ minutes	6 months
Spinach	2 minutes	3 minutes	6 months
Sweetcorn: small cobs large cobs	4 minutes 6 minutes	6 minutes 9 minutes	12 months 12 months
Sweet potatoes	3 minutes Cut in 2 cm (1 in) pieces.	4½ minutes Cut in 2 cm (1 in) pieces.	12 months
Tomatoes	These are best frozen as tomato pulp. Skin and core the tomatoes and simmer in their own juice for 5 minutes. Cool and freeze.		12 months
Turnips	2 minutes Cut in 1 cm (½ in) pieces.	3 minutes Cut in 1 cm (½ in) pieces.	12 months
Yams	2 minutes Cut in 2 cm (1 in) pieces.	3 minutes Cut in 2 cm (1 in) pieces.	12 months

CONVERSIONS

The recipes which follow conform to the conversion tables given here. Recipes have been tested for accuracy, both for metric and imperial weights. All imperial measurements have been rounded up or down to within the nearest 5 grams. In the case of cakes and breadmaking, however, it is essential to use the exact measurement given, even though these may differ from conversions in other sections of the book.

Whichever type of measurement is chosen (i.e. metric or imperial), it is essential to keep to that measurement throughout the recipe.

Please note also that one teaspoon measures 5 millilitres. Some modern teaspoons hold rather less. Accurate measurements are particularly important in bread- and cakemaking.

WEIGHTS

IMPERIAL Ounces		METRIC Grams to nearest 25 g
$\frac{1}{4}$		8
$\frac{1}{2}$		15
$\frac{3}{4}$		20
1		25
2		50
3		75
4	$\frac{1}{4}$ lb	100
5		150
6		175
7		200
8	$\frac{1}{2}$ lb	225
9		250
10		275
11		300
12	$\frac{3}{4}$ lb	350
13		375
14		400
15		425
16	1 lb	450
32	2 lb	900
35	2 lb 3 oz	1,000/1 kilo

Note: All dishes cooked in the oven are placed on the middle shelf unless otherwise specified.

In cases where greasing a container is mentioned, butter, margarine or oil may be used.

LIQUID MEASUREMENTS

IMPERIAL Fluid ounces/pints		METRIC Millilitres
1		25
2		50
3		75
4		100
5	$\frac{1}{4}$ pt	150
6		175
7		200
8	$\frac{1}{2}$ pt	225
9		250
10		275
15	$\frac{3}{4}$ pt	425
20	1 pt	570
25	$1\frac{1}{4}$ pt	700
30	$1\frac{1}{2}$ pt	825
35	$1\frac{3}{4}$ pt	1,000/1 litre

1 tablespoon	15 ml
1 teaspoon	5 ml
1 cup	8 fl oz

OVEN TEMPERATURES

CENTIGRADE	FAHRENHEIT	GAS MARK
240	475	9
230	450	8
220	425	7
200	400	6
190	375	5
180	350	4
170 (160)	325	3
150	300	2
140	275	1
130 (120)	250	$\frac{1}{2}$
110	225	$\frac{1}{4}$
100	200	Low
80	175	Very low
70	150	Extra low

BREAKFASTS

For additional breakfast ideas, see Bran Muffins (p. 137),
Cheese Scones (p. 140) and the Bread Section (p. 147).
For breakfast drinks, see Herb Teas (p. 59)
and Health Drinks (p. 61).

◆

Granola 1

100 ml (4 fl oz) soya oil
100 ml (4 fl oz) malt extract
225 g (8 oz) regular oats
100 g (4 oz) jumbo oats
100 g (4 oz) wheat flakes
100 g (4 oz) rye flakes
50 g (2 oz) sunflower seeds
50 g (2 oz) chopped hazelnuts
25 g (1 oz) desiccated coconut (optional)
100 g (4 oz) raisins

Preparation 10 minutes
Cooking 1 hour
Makes about 1 kg (2 lb 3 oz)
Ⓥ

1 Heat the oven to 140°C (275°F/Gas 1).

2 Melt the oil and malt in a large saucepan.

3 Add all the rest of the ingredients except for the raisins. Mix well.

4 Spread the mixture on to 2 large trays and bake in the oven for 1 hour until the flakes are brown and crispy. Stir frequently to prevent sticking.

5 Remove from the oven and leave to cool. Stir a couple of times while cooling to stop the flakes from sticking together. Add the raisins and store in an airtight container in a cool place.

Serve with milk, yogurt, soya milk or fruit juice. Add a little fresh fruit, if wished.

Granola 2

100 ml (4 fl oz) soya oil
100 ml (4 fl oz) honey
200 g (7 oz) jumbo oats
250 g (9 oz) regular oats
75 g (3 oz) sunflower seeds
50 g (2 oz) sesame seeds
25 g (1 oz) pumpkin seeds
150 g (5 oz) chopped mixed nuts
30 ml (2 tbsp) wheat germ
100 g (4 oz) sultanas

Preparation 10 minutes
Cooking 1 hour
Makes about 1 kg (2 lb 3 oz)

1 Heat the oven to 140°C (275°F/Gas 1).

2 Melt the oil and honey in a large saucepan.

3 Add all the ingredients except for the wheatgerm and sultanas. Mix together well.

4 Spread the mixture on to 2 large trays and bake in the oven for 1 hour until the flakes are brown and crispy, stirring frequently to prevent sticking.

5 Remove from the oven and leave to cool. Stir a couple of times while cooling to stop the flakes from sticking together. Add the wheatgerm and sultanas and store in an airtight container in a cool place.

Serve with milk, yogurt, soya milk or fruit juice. Add a little fresh fruit, if wished.

Muesli Base

500 g (1 lb 2 oz) regular and/or
  jumbo oats
250 g (9 oz) barley flakes
250 g (9 oz) wheat flakes

Preparation 5 minutes
Makes about 1 kg (2 lb 3 oz)
Ⓥ

You can make this as rich or plain a muesli as you like, depending on the extra ingredients.

Combine the ingredients and store in an airtight jar in a cool place.

Add your own selection of dried or fresh fruit, nuts or seeds and serve with milk, yogurt, soya milk or fruit juice. Eat immediately or leave to soak overnight. Alternatively, cover with your choice of liquid, simmer gently for 5 minutes and eat warm.

Basic Muesli

250 g (9 oz) regular and/or
  jumbo oats
250 g (9 oz) rye flakes
250 g (9 oz) wheat flakes
250 g (9 oz) barley flakes
250 g (9 oz) raisins
250 g (9 oz) sultanas
250 g (9 oz) hazelnuts
250 g (9 oz) sunflower seeds
250 g (9 oz) dried apricots
150 g (5 oz) bran (optional)

Preparation 10 minutes
Makes 2.5 kg (4 lb 6 oz)
Ⓥ

Combine the ingredients and store in an airtight jar in a cool place.

Serve with milk, yogurt, soya milk or fruit juice and add a little fresh fruit, if wished. Eat immediately or leave to soak overnight. Alternatively, cover with your choice of liquid, simmer gently for 5 minutes and eat warm.

Gluten-free Muesli

500 g (1 lb 2 oz) rice flakes
500 g (1 lb 2 oz) millet flakes
250 g (9 oz) sunflower seeds
250 g (9 oz) raisins
250 g (9 oz) sultanas
250 g (9 oz) hazelnuts
250 g (9 oz) dried apricots
90 ml (6 tbsp) desiccated coconut
250 g (9 oz) soya bran (optional, for added fibre, see p. 14)

Preparation 10 minutes
Makes 2.5 kg (4 lb 6 oz)
(GF) (V)

Combine the ingredients and store in an airtight jar in a cool place.

Serve with milk, yogurt, soya milk or fruit juice and add a little fresh fruit if wished. Eat immediately or leave to soak overnight. Alternatively, cover with your choice of liquid, simmer gently for 5 minutes and eat warm.

Rich Muesli

250 g (9 oz) regular and/or
    jumbo oats
250 g (9 oz) rye flakes
250 g (9 oz) wheat flakes
250 g (9 oz) barley flakes
250 g (9 oz) raisins
250 g (9 oz) sultanas
250 g (9 oz) hazelnuts
250 g (9 oz) sunflower seeds
250 g (9 oz) chopped almonds
250 g (9 oz) cashew nuts
250 g (9 oz) dried apricots
250 g (9 oz) dried pears
250 g (9 oz) dried peaches

Preparation 10 minutes
Makes about 3 kg (6 lb 9 oz)
(V)

Combine the ingredients and store in an airtight jar in a cool place.

Serve with milk, yogurt, soya milk or fruit juice and add a little fresh fruit if wished. Eat immediately or leave to soak overnight. Alternatively, cover with your choice of liquid, simmer gently for 5 minutes and eat warm.

Basic Porridge

225 g (8 oz) jumbo oats
570 ml (1 pt) milk or water
a little salt (optional)

Preparation and Cooking 15-20 minutes
Serves 2

Porridge need not simply be made of oats: any flaked grain, meal or flour may be used.
    To prevent sticking, soak the oats for an hour or overnight in the liquid in which they are to be cooked. This will also reduce the actual cooking time.

1 Put the oats, milk and salt, if using, into a saucepan.

2 Bring to the boil, then lower the heat and simmer gently for 10-15 minutes until cooked, stirring frequently to prevent sticking.

Serve with a little milk or sweetener, if wished.

Pinhead Porridge

225 g (8 oz) pinhead oatmeal
900 ml (32 fl oz) milk or water or a
  mixture of both
a little salt (optional)

**Preparation and Cooking 45 minutes
(allow 12 hours for soaking)
Serves 2**

1 Put the pinhead oatmeal and milk in a saucepan. Leave to stand for 12 hours or overnight.

2 In the morning, bring to the boil, add the salt, if using, cover the pan and simmer over a low heat until the oats are tender and the liquid is absorbed. This will take about 45 minutes.

Serve immediately with a little milk or sweetener, if wished.

Soya & Oat Porridge

100 g (4 oz) jumbo oats
25 g (1 oz) soya grits
pinch of salt
200 ml (7 fl oz) soya milk
200 ml (7 fl oz) water

**Preparation and Cooking 15 minutes
(allow 12 hours for soaking)
Serves 2**

1 Put the oats, soya grits and salt in a saucepan. Pour over the soya milk and water. Set aside for 12 hours or overnight.

2 Bring the porridge mixture to the boil and simmer gently for 8-10 minutes until cooked, stirring frequently to prevent sticking.

Serve immediately with a little milk or sweetener, if wished.

Toasted Porridge

50 ml (2 fl oz) soya oil
100 g (4 oz) regular oats
50 g (2 oz) jumbo oats
50 g (2 oz) barley flakes
pinch of salt (optional)
500 ml (18 fl oz) water
200 ml (7 fl oz) milk

**Preparation and Cooking 20 minutes
Serves 2**

1 Heat the oil in a saucepan. Add the oats and barley flakes. Toast gently, stirring frequently for 2-3 minutes.

2 Add the salt, water and milk and bring to the boil. Turn the heat down and simmer gently for 15 minutes until cooked, stirring frequently to prevent sticking.

Serve immediately with a little milk or sweetener, if wished.

SOUPS

Note: Many of these soup recipes require a blender. Alternatively, unless the recipe specifies otherwise, you can use a potato masher. This will produce a coarser-textured soup.

◆

Aduki Bean Soup

450 g (1 lb) tomatoes
50 ml (2 fl oz) soya oil
2 onions, chopped
2 celery sticks, chopped
2 carrots, chopped
2 garlic cloves, crushed
15 ml (1 tbsp) tomato purée
1 bay leaf
10 ml (2 tsp) finely chopped fresh thyme
  or 5 ml (1 tsp) dried
1.4 l (2½ pt) vegetable stock or water
200 g (7 oz) aduki beans, soaked for
  4 hours
salt and black pepper
finely chopped fresh parsley, to garnish

**Preparation 20-25 minutes
(allow 4 hours for soaking the beans)
Cooking 1 hour
Serves 6**
ⓖⒻ Ⓥ

This hearty soup is equally delicious with mung beans or split peas. Serve with a sprinkling of grated cheese for extra nutrition.

1 Put the tomatoes in a bowl and pour over boiling water. Set aside for 10-15 minutes to allow the skins to soften.

2 Heat the oil in a large heavy-bottomed saucepan and add the onion, celery, carrot and garlic.

3 Pour the water off the tomatoes. Drain, peel and coarsely chop.

4 Add the tomatoes, tomato purée, bay leaf and thyme to the celery and carrot mixture.

5 Add the stock and the presoaked aduki beans and simmer for about 1 hour or until the beans are tender.

6 Adjust the seasoning and garnish with a sprinkling of fresh parsley.

Serve piping hot with wholewheat rolls.

Carrot & Orange Soup

45 ml (3 tbsp) soya oil
45 ml (3 tbsp) tamari
1 large onion, coarsely chopped
400 g (14 oz) carrots, coarsely chopped
juice and grated rind of 2 oranges
75 ml (3 fl oz) finely chopped
    fresh parsley
2 l (3½ pt) water
salt and black pepper

Preparation 10 minutes
Cooking 20 minutes
Serves 6-8
GF V

1 Heat the oil and tamari in a saucepan, add the onion and carrot and fry for 5 minutes until the onion is soft.

2 Add the orange juice and rind.

3 Reserve a little of the parsley for the garnish, and add the rest to the pan.

4 Pour over the water and simmer for 15 minutes. Put into a blender. Liquidize to a purée, then reheat.

5 Season to taste and garnish with the reserved fresh parsley sprinkled on top.

Carrot & Rice Soup

25 g (1 oz) butter or 30 ml (2 tbsp)
    soya oil
1 large onion, finely chopped
450 g (1 lb) carrots, finely chopped
1 l (1¾ pt) vegetable stock
5 ml (1 tsp) finely chopped fresh
    marjoram or 2·5 ml (½ tsp) dried
50 g (2 oz) cooked brown rice
salt and black pepper

Preparation 15 minutes
Cooking 30 minutes
Serves 4
GF

This soup is ideal for using up leftover brown rice.

1 Melt the butter in a medium-sized saucepan and add the onion and carrot.

2 Add the stock, marjoram and cooked rice and simmer gently for 30 minutes, stirring occasionally to prevent sticking.

3 Transfer the soup to a blender. Liquidize till smooth and season to taste.

Creamed Cauliflower Soup

1 small cauliflower
275 ml (½ pt) water
25 g (1 oz) butter
1 large onion, chopped
30 ml (2 tbsp) medium oatmeal
salt and black pepper
570 ml (1 pt) milk
15 ml (1 tbsp) finely chopped
    fresh parsley

Preparation and Cooking 25 minutes
Serves 4

1 Cut the cauliflower into small pieces, using as much of the stalk and leaves as possible.

2 Put the water in a medium-sized saucepan with a tightly fitting lid. Add the cauliflower and bring to the boil. Lower the heat a little and simmer for 5 minutes.

3 Melt the butter in a saucepan. Add the onion and cook for 3-5 minutes until soft.

4 Stir in the oatmeal and seasoning. Add the milk a little at a time taking care not to make any lumps.

5 Add the cauliflower and the water in which it was cooking and bring to the boil, stirring occasionally to prevent sticking. Cook for a further 5 minutes until tender.

6 Pour the mixture into a blender and liquidize till smooth. Return to the saucepan, add the parsley and warm through.

Cream of Mushroom Soup

1 large onion, finely chopped
50 g (2 oz) butter
450 g (1 lb) mushrooms, finely chopped
$\frac{1}{4}$ tsp grated nutmeg
2 garlic cloves, crushed
1 l (1$\frac{3}{4}$ pt) milk
salt and black pepper
finely chopped fresh parsley or
    mushroom slices, to garnish

Preparation 10 minutes
Cooking 20 minutes
Serves 4
(GF)

1 In a medium-sized saucepan, gently fry the onion in the butter till soft.

2 Add the mushrooms to the pan with the nutmeg and garlic.

3 Pour over the milk. Bring to the boil, then lower the heat and simmer gently for 20 minutes.

4 Transfer the soup to a blender and liquidize till smooth. Season to taste.

5 Garnish with a sprinkling of fresh parsley or finely chopped mushroom slices.

Serve immediately with fingers of cheese on toast and a fresh salad for a satisfying lunch.

Cream of Watercress Soup

25 g (1 oz) butter
1 large onion, finely chopped
450 g (1 lb) potatoes, peeled and
    finely chopped
2 bunches watercress
570 ml (1 pt) vegetable stock
570 ml (1 pt) milk
salt and black pepper
100 ml (4 fl oz) sour/fresh cream,
    to serve
watercress sprig, to garnish

Preparation 15 minutes
Cooking 45 minutes
Serves 4
(GF)

This recipe uses potatoes to thicken the soup.

1 Melt the butter in a large heavy-based saucepan.

2 Add the onion and cook for 3-5 minutes till soft.

3 Add the potatoes, watercress, stock and milk.

4 Bring to the boil. Lower the heat and simmer for 45 minutes.

5 Transfer the soup to a blender and liquidize till smooth.

6 Season to taste. Pour into individual bowls and serve with a swirl of sour or fresh cream and a sprig of fresh watercress on top.

Serve with wholewheat rolls or slices of Three-seed Bread (see p. 156).

Creamy Broad Bean Soup

225 g (8 oz) young broad beans, podded
25 g (1 oz) butter
1 onion, finely chopped
2 garlic cloves, crushed
30 ml (2 tbsp) fine wholewheat flour
1 l (1¾ pt) milk or a mixture of equal
    parts of milk and stock
salt and black pepper
100 ml (4 fl oz) sour cream, to serve

Preparation 5 minutes
Cooking 20 minutes
Serves 4

Choose small, tender broad beans for this recipe as the larger ones can be tough and floury.

1 Boil the broad beans for 6-8 minutes or steam for 8 minutes until cooked and tender.

2 In a medium-sized saucepan, melt the butter and sauté the onion and garlic for 5 minutes until the onion is soft.

3 Remove from the heat and mix in the flour. Gradually add the milk or milk and stock.

4 Pour this mixture into a blender with the cooked broad beans and liquidize till smooth.

5 Return to the saucepan and heat gently, stirring constantly until the soup begins to thicken. Cook for a further 2-3 minutes. Adjust seasoning, pour into individual bowls and add a swirl of sour cream.

Serve piping hot with warm wholewheat or rye rolls.

Dulse Soup

25 g (1 oz) dulse (see p. 44)
1 l (1¾ pt) boiling water
15 ml (1 tbsp) soya oil
1 onion, thinly sliced
50 g (2 oz) regular oats
salt and black pepper
30 ml (2 tbsp) shoyu (see p. 51)

Preparation 10 minutes
Cooking 30 minutes
Serves 6
(V)

1 Rinse the dulse in cold water and put in a bowl. Pour over the boiling water.

2 Heat the oil in a medium-sized saucepan and add the onion. Cook for 5 minutes until soft.

3 Add the oats and cook for 1 minute. Add the dulse with its water and seasoning. Bring to the boil, lower the heat and simmer for 30 minutes until the soup thickens.

4 Add the shoyu and serve immediately.

Serve with wholewheat rolls.

Evelyn's German Potato Soup

1 kg (2 lb 3 oz) potatoes, peeled and
    finely chopped
2 large onions, sliced into rings
12 allspice berries
1 l (1¾ pt) water
570 ml (1 pt) Greek-style yogurt
salt and black pepper

Preparation 15 minutes
Cooking 20 minutes
Serves 6
(GF)

1 Put the potatoes, onions and allspice berries in a large saucepan and cover with the water. Boil for 20 minutes or until the potatoes are tender.

2 Remove from heat, mash the potato mixture with a fork or potato masher or liquidize in a blender till smooth.

3 Stir in the yogurt and season to taste.

Garlic & Onion Soup

25 g (1 oz) butter
1 large onion, sliced into rings
225 g (8 oz) white cabbage, shredded
3 garlic cloves, crushed
30 ml (2 tbsp) tamari
1 l (1¾ pt) water
100 g (4 oz) grated cheese and a little
   finely chopped fresh parsley,
   to garnish

Preparation 10 minutes
Cooking 20 minutes
Serves 4
(GF)

This quick and easy soup can also be served with croûtons fried in herb butter.

1 Melt the butter in a medium-sized saucepan.

2 Add the onion rings.

3 Add the shredded cabbage.

4 Add the garlic, tamari and water and simmer gently for 20 minutes or until the vegetables are cooked.

5 Pour into individual bowls and serve piping hot with a little grated cheese and chopped parsley sprinkled on top.

Gazpacho

700 ml (25 fl oz) tomato juice
50 ml (2 fl oz) olive oil
50 ml (2 fl oz) wine vinegar
3 garlic cloves
1 small cucumber, finely chopped
1 small red pepper, finely chopped
1 small fennel, finely chopped
1 onion, finely chopped
4 sprigs fresh parsley
2 slices wholewheat bread
salt and black pepper

Preparation 10 minutes
Chilling 20 minutes
Serves 4-6
(V)

A blender is essential for this quick and easy soup. Be sure to chill thoroughly before serving.

1 Put half the tomato juice, with the olive oil, vinegar and garlic, into a blender and liquidize till smooth.

2 Add half the vegetables and parsley to the blender and liquidize till smooth. Transfer to a serving bowl.

3 Put the other half of the tomato juice and the remaining vegetables and parsley into the blender with the wholewheat bread. Liquidize till smooth. Transfer to a serving bowl.

4 Mix well and season to taste. Chill in the refrigerator for at least 20 minutes before serving.

Serve with crisp cheese croûtons.

Lettuce, Cucumber & Miso Soup

15 ml (1 tbsp) soya oil
15 ml (1 tbsp) finely chopped
   spring onions
225 g (8 oz) lettuce, shredded
225 g (8 oz) cucumber, finely chopped
1 garlic clove
10 ml (2 tsp) miso (see p. 50)
275 ml (½ pt) water
salt and black pepper
sour cream or Greek-style yogurt, to
   serve (optional)

Preparation 10 minutes
Chilling 2 hours
Serves 4
(GF) (V)

You will need a blender for best results.

1 Heat the oil in a medium-sized saucepan and add the spring onions.

2 Add the lettuce and cucumber to the saucepan and heat gently for 3-4 minutes until cooked.

3 Put the lettuce and cucumber into a blender with the garlic, miso and water. Liquidize till thoroughly mixed. Season to taste.

4 Pour into a bowl and chill in the refrigerator for about 2 hours or until quite cold. Top with a swirl of sour cream or Greek-style yogurt, if liked.

Serve with warm wholewheat bread.

Minestrone

50 ml (2 fl oz) olive oil
2 onions, finely chopped
2 carrots, finely chopped
2 celery sticks, finely chopped
225 g (8 oz) tomatoes, finely chopped
30 ml (2 tbsp) tomato purée
10 ml (2 tsp) finely chopped oregano or
    5 ml (1 tsp) dried
5 ml (1 tsp) finely chopped fresh basil or
    2.5 ml (½ tsp) dried
2 garlic cloves, crushed
1 l (1¾ pt) water
150 g (5 oz) cooked cannellini beans
50 g (2 oz) peas
50 g (2 oz) mushrooms
salt and black pepper
grated cheese, to garnish (optional)

**Preparation 15 minutes (allow extra
time for cooking the beans)
Cooking 25 minutes
Serves 4-6**
(GF) (V)

**Cannellini beans are traditionally added to this soup, but leftover
black-eyed, haricot or pinto beans taste just as good.**

1 Heat the oil in a heavy-based saucepan and add the onions,
carrots, celery and tomatoes.

2 Add the tomato purée, pregano, basil and garlic. Cook gently for
a few minutes.

3 Add the water and cannellini beans, and simmer for 20 minutes.

4 Add the peas and mushrooms. Simmer a further 5 minutes,
season to taste and garnish with grated cheese, if liked.

Miso & Arame Soup

25 g (1 oz) arame (see p. 43)
15 ml (1 tbsp) soya oil
1 onion, finely chopped
1 large carrot, finely chopped
1 celery stick, finely chopped
5 ml (1 tsp) grated root ginger
75 ml (3 fl oz) tamari
1 l (1¾ pt) water
30 ml (2 tbsp) finely chopped fresh
    coriander leaves
15 ml (1 tbsp) miso (see p. 50)

**Preparation 10 minutes
Cooking 30 minutes
Serves 4-6**
(GF) (V)

1 Put the arame in a bowl. Cover with boiling water and leave to
stand for 5 minutes.

2 Meanwhile, heat the oil and onion in a medium-sized saucepan.

3 Add the carrot and celery.

4 Add the drained arame, root ginger and tamari and simmer gently
for 5 minutes.

5 Add the water and simmer gently for 15 minutes.

6 Add the chopped coriander leaves and cook for a further
5 minutes. Do not overcook.

7 Remove from the heat and stir in the miso. Return to the stove
and heat to just below boiling.

Serve immediately with slices of Sunflower Seed Bread (see p. 155).

Parsnip Soup

25 g (1 oz) butter
450 g (1 lb) parsnips, finely chopped
1 large onion, finely chopped
570 ml (1 pt) milk
275 ml (½ pt) water
2.5 ml (½ tsp) grated nutmeg
salt and black pepper

Preparation 10 minutes
Cooking 30 minutes
Serves 4
(GF)

Carrots, broccoli, cauliflower or leeks can be substituted for parsnips in this rich and healthy soup.

1 Melt the butter and gently sauté the parsnip and onion for 5 minutes until tender.

2 Add the milk, water, grated nutmeg and seasoning and simmer for 25 minutes.

3 Transfer the soup to a blender and liquidize until smooth.

Serve piping hot with warm crusty rolls.

Potato & Beetroot Soup

50 g (2 oz) butter
1 large onion, finely chopped
450 g (1 lb) potatoes, chopped
2.5 ml (½ tsp) ground cumin (optional)
225 g (8 oz) cooked beetroot, peeled and chopped
825 ml (1½ pt) milk
salt and black pepper
finely chopped fresh parsley or coriander leaves, to garnish

Preparation 15 minutes
Cooking 20 minutes
Serves 4
(GF)

The bright pink colour of this soup makes it especially popular with children.

1 Melt the butter in a large saucepan.

2 Add the onion and fry for 5 minutes till soft.

3 Add the potatoes to the pan, together with the cumin, if using.

4 Add the beetroot.

5 Pour over the milk and simmer for 20 minutes or until the potatoes are tender.

6 Transfer to a blender and liquidize till smooth. Season to taste.

7 Garnish with a sprinkling of parsley or fresh coriander leaves.

Rye Grain & Vegetable Broth

30 ml (2 tbsp) soya oil
1 large onion, coarsely chopped
3 carrots, coarsely chopped
1 small cauliflower, coarsely chopped
10 ml (2 tsp) coarsely chopped fresh sage or 5 ml (1 tsp) dried
3 bay leaves
10 ml (2 tsp) coarsely chopped fresh rosemary or 5 ml (1 tsp) dried
salt and black pepper
225 g (8 oz) rye grains
1.1 l (2 pt) vegetable stock or water

Preparation 10 minutes
Cooking 2 hours
Serves 6
(V)

This hearty soup makes an excellent lunch or supper meal if served with creamy mashed potatoes or swedes. For extra nutrition, stir in a tablespoon of miso (see p. 50) before serving.

1 Heat the oil in a large heavy-based saucepan. Add the chopped vegetables, sage, bay leaves, rosemary and seasoning. Fry gently for 2-3 minutes.

2 Add the rye grain and water. Mix together well. Bring to the boil, then lower the heat and simmer for 2 hours.

Serve with wholewheat rolls.

Aubergine Pâté

1 large aubergine
30 ml (2 tbsp) yogurt
30 ml (2 tbsp) olive oil
2 garlic cloves, crushed
juice of 1 lemon
2.5 ml ($\frac{1}{2}$ tsp) finely chopped fresh basil
   or $\frac{1}{4}$ tsp dried
salt and black pepper

Preparation 10 minutes
Cooking 40 minutes
Serves 4
(GF)

1 Heat the oven to 200°C (400°F/Gas 6).

2 Cut the aubergine in half lengthwise and remove the fibrous stalk. Prepare as necessary (see p. 27).

3 Brush the aubergine halves all over with olive oil and bake in a greased baking tray for 40-45 minutes or until cooked.

4 Peel off the skin and mash the flesh or liquidize in a blender.

5 Add the yogurt, olive oil and garlic and mix well.

6 Add the lemon juice and basil to the aubergine mixture, season to taste, then serve in individual ramekins.

Serve hot or cold with wholewheat rolls or bread.

Baked Eggs with Coriander

a little butter or oil, for greasing
175 ml (6 fl oz) single cream
175 g (6 oz) soft cream cheese
30 ml (2 tbsp) finely chopped fresh
   coriander leaves
salt and black pepper
8 eggs
finely chopped fresh parsley, to garnish

Preparation 5 minutes
Cooking 7-10 minutes
Serves 8
(GF)

1 Heat the oven to 220°C (425°F/Gas 7).

2 Grease 8 ramekin dishes.

3 Mix together the single cream, cream cheese, coriander and seasoning.

4 Carefully break 1 egg into each ramekin dish.

5 Put 30 ml (2 tbsp) of the cream mixture on top of each egg.

6 Bake for 7-10 minutes or until the whites of the eggs are just set.

7 Sprinkle with a little chopped parsley and serve immediately.

Serve with hot crusty wholewheat rolls.

Citrus Cocktail

2 pink grapefruit
2 oranges
2 celery sticks, thinly sliced
2.5 ml ($\frac{1}{2}$ tsp) finely chopped fresh mint
   or $\frac{1}{4}$ tsp dried

Preparation 10 minutes
Standing 20 minutes
Serves 6
(GF) (V)

A light and refreshing start to a meal. Substitute other citrus fruit when in season.

1 Divide the grapefruit and oranges into separate segments over a bowl so as to catch any juice that might run out.

2 Cut the segments into bite-sized pieces and remove any pips.

3 Add the celery to the citrus fruits.

4 Add the mint and stir thoroughly. Allow to stand for at least 20 minutes before serving.

Cottage Cheese Cooler

450 g (1 lb) cottage cheese
1 celery stick, finely chopped
½ cucumber, finely chopped
1 small red pepper, finely chopped
1 carrot, grated
15 ml (1 tbsp) finely chopped fresh
   parsley
juice and grated rind of 1 lemon
5 ml (1 tsp) sesame seeds, to garnish

Preparation 10 minutes
Serves 4
(GF)

For this quick and simple recipe, you can use fresh lime juice instead of lemon and substitute sunflower for the sesame seeds.

1 Put the cottage cheese into a mixing bowl.

2 Add the celery, cucumber and red pepper.

3 Add the carrot and parsley.

4 Pour the lemon juice and rind over the cottage cheese mixture.

5 Mix everything together gently and turn into individual dishes. Sprinkle with sesame seeds.

Serve with hot Bran Muffins (see p. 137).

Cream Cheese Dip

450 g (1 lb) soft cream cheese
1 small red pepper, finely chopped
¼ cucumber, finely chopped
15 ml (1 tbsp) finely chopped
   fresh parsley
5 ml (1 tsp) mixture of finely chopped
   fresh thyme, basil and marjoram or
   2.5 ml (½ tsp) dried
2 garlic cloves, crushed
salt and black pepper

Preparation 10 minutes
Serves 6-8
(GF)

This rich starter also makes a good dip for buffets and parties.

1 Put the cream cheese into a mixing bowl.

2 Add the red pepper, cucumber and parsley.

3 Sprinkle over the herbs and garlic, mix well and season to taste.

Serve with hot wholewheat rolls or buttered fingers of toast and, if liked, a selection of cut, raw vegetables such as carrots, celery, cauliflower or cucumber.

Egg & Avocado Mayonnaise Dip

15 ml (1 tbsp) vinegar
juice of 1 lemon
2 eggs (or just the yolks for a thicker
   mixture)
5 ml (1 tsp) honey
15 ml (1 tbsp) finely chopped
   fresh parsley
90 ml (6 tbsp) olive oil
6 hard-boiled eggs, shelled
2 ripe avocados
salt and black pepper
pinch of paprika, to garnish

Preparation 10 minutes
Serves 6-8
(GF)

A useful dip for buffets or parties, this recipe also makes a good sandwich filling. If you do not have a blender, a wire balloon whisk can be used.

1 Put the vinegar, lemon, eggs, honey and parsley into a blender and liquidize till smooth.

2 With the blender still running, slowly pour in the olive oil till a smooth mayonnaise is formed.

3 Add the eggs and avocados and liquidize till all the ingredients are well mixed.

4 Adjust seasoning and serve garnished with paprika.

Serve with wedges of toast or bread.

Guacamole

3 avocados
1 large tomato, finely chopped
juice and grated rind of 1 lemon
pinch of chilli powder or cayenne
15 ml (1 tbsp) olive oil (optional)
salt and black pepper
black olives, to garnish

Preparation 10 minutes
Serves 6

This traditional Mexican dish needs really well-ripened avocados.

1 Put the avocado flesh into a mixing bowl and mash with a fork or a potato masher.

2 Add the tomato, lemon juice and rind.

3 Sprinkle over the chilli and olive oil, if using, and season to taste.

4 Garnish with black olives.

Serve with corn chips or wholewheat pitta bread.

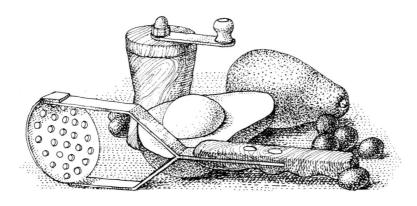

Hummus

50 g (2 oz) chickpeas, soaked for 12
  hours or overnight
1 garlic clove, crushed
30 ml (2 tbsp) lemon juice
good pinch of salt
black pepper
50 ml (2 fl oz) olive oil
100 ml (4 fl oz) water or orange juice
15 ml (1 tbsp) tahini (see p. 50)

Preparation 10 minutes (allow 12 hours
for soaking the chickpeas)
Cooking 2 hours
Serves 2-4

A blender is essential for this recipe. Make sure the chickpeas are thoroughly cooked before liquidizing.

1 Transfer the soaked chickpeas and their liquid to a saucepan. Top up with fresh water, if necessary, to cover the chickpeas. Cover and bring to the boil. Lower the heat and simmer for about 2 hours or until cooked. Drain.

2 Place the garlic, lemon juice, seasoning, oil and water in a blender. Liquidize, then gradually add the chickpeas, blending until smooth.

3 Add the tahini and liquidize, adding a little extra liquid if the mixture is too dry.

Serve as a dip, with a crisp salad and wholewheat rolls.

Kombu Surprise

25 g (1 oz) kombu (see p. 44)
10 ml (2 tsp) soya oil
500 ml (18 fl oz) water
25 ml (5 tsp) honey
100 ml (4 fl oz) tamari

Preparation 5 minutes
Standing 20 minutes
Cooking 35 minutes
Serves 4-6
GF

This traditional kombu dish is served in Japan as a light snack before dinner with _sake_ or rice wine.

1 Put the kombu in a bowl, cover with boiling water and leave to stand for 20 minutes. Pour off the water and cut the kombu into small pieces.

2 Heat the oil in a saucepan. Add the kombu and fry gently for 1-2 minutes.

3 Add the water, honey and tamari and simmer for about 35 minutes with the lid off or until the liquid has reduced to a few tablespoons.

Serve with warm Three-seed Bread (see p. 156).

Leeks Vinaigrette

450 g (1 lb) small leeks, halved
    lengthwise

Vinaigrette
5 ml (1 tsp) whole grain mustard
2.5 ml (½ tsp) apple juice concentrate
    (see p. 51) (optional)
75 ml (3 fl oz) apple cider vinegar
175 ml (6 fl oz) olive oil
salt and black pepper

Preparation 15 minutes
Chilling 2 hours
Serves 4
GF V

Long, thin leeks are best for this recipe. If unobtainable, cut larger, thicker leeks into 1 cm (½ in) thick rounds.

1 Steam the leeks for 5-10 minutes or until tender.

2 Meanwhile, make the dressing: put the ingredients for the vinaigrette in a screw-top jar and shake vigorously.

3 When the leeks are ready, drain well. Transfer to a serving dish and pour over the vinaigrette, while the leeks are still hot (this will help them absorb the dressing more easily).

4 Chill in the refrigerator for at least 2 hours before serving.

Serve with crusty bread or rolls.

Marinated Tofu

500 g (1 lb 2 oz) tofu (see p. 51), cubed
150 ml (5 fl oz) shoyu (see p. 51)
250 ml (9 fl oz) orange juice
15 ml (1 tbsp) soya oil
1 garlic clove, crushed
2.5 ml (½ tsp) grated root ginger
finely chopped fresh basil, to garnish

Preparation 10 minutes
Chilling 30 minutes
Serves 6
GF V

This is a delicious way to eat tofu. The dish is best if prepared well in advance to allow the marinade to soak into the tofu.

1 Put the tofu into a serving bowl.

2 In a separate bowl, mix together the shoyu, orange juice, soya oil, garlic and grated root ginger.

3 Pour the mixture over the tofu and chill in the refrigerator for at least 30 minutes.

4 Sprinkle a little chopped basil over the top before serving.

Serve with hot Sunflower Seed Bread (see p. 155).

Nori & Spinach Rolls

2 l (3½ pt) water
salt
225 g (8 oz) fresh spinach
5 ml (1 tsp) soya oil
2 eggs, beaten
2 sheets nori (see p. 44)
tamari

Sauce
100 ml (4 fl oz) tamari
3 spring onions, finely chopped
¼ tsp grated root ginger

Preparation and Cooking 35 minutes
Serves 4
(GF)

Not an easy recipe to attempt first time round, but it is well worth the effort to learn.

1 Put the water and salt into a large saucepan and bring to the boil.

2 Wash the spinach thoroughly without cutting off the stalks. Put into the boiling water and cook for 3 minutes. Drain and cover with cold water.

3 Pour off the water and squeeze any remaining excess water from the spinach by hand. Divide in two. Take half the spinach, squeeze again and cut off the stalk ends so that the spinach measures the same length as the short side of the nori. Follow the same procedure for the rest of the spinach. Set aside.

4 Heat the oil in a small frying pan and fry the eggs like a small omelette. Set aside.

5 Take the corners of a sheet of nori in your fingertips. Wave the smooth side of the seaweed over an open flame or electric ring until it turns green.

6 Place the nori on a flat surface, and place on top of it, in turn, half the egg, a sprinkling of tamari and half the spinach. Roll up as tightly as possible. Follow the same procedure for the other spinach roll.

7 Make the sauce: put the sauce ingredients in a screw-top jar and shake vigorously.

8 Cut each of the 2 spinach rolls into 4 pieces with a very sharp knife, and leave to cool before serving on individual plates. Serve with sauce handed separately.

Making the nori and spinach rolls

1 Hold the sheet of nori in your fingertips so that the smooth side faces down, and wave gently over the gas flame or electric ring until the seaweed turns green.

2 Trim the spinach so that it is the same length as the short side of the nori.

3 After placing the egg, tamari and spinach on the nori, roll up carefully.

Onion Bhajis with Yogurt Sauce

250 g (9 oz) chickpea flour
150 g (5 oz) semolina
15 ml (1 tbsp) garam masala (see p. 57)
¼ tsp chilli powder
10 ml (2 tsp) ground turmeric
30 ml (2 tbsp) finely chopped fresh
   coriander leaves
salt and black pepper
500 ml (18 fl oz) water
oil for frying
3 large onions, very thinly sliced

Yogurt sauce
275 ml (½ pt) yogurt
30 ml (2 tbsp) finely chopped
   spring onions
15 ml (1 tbsp) finely chopped fresh
   coriander leaves
2.5 ml (½ tsp) ground cumin
salt and black pepper

Preparation 10 minutes
Standing 30 minutes (for the sauce)
Cooking 15 minutes
Serves 6

This yogurt sauce is delicious with hot, spicy dishes or with rice balls, rissoles or savoury loaves. You can also use sheep's or goat's milk yogurt, or fresh mint and parsley instead of the fresh coriander leaves.

1 Make the batter: mix together in a large bowl the chickpea flour, semolina, garam masala, chilli powder, turmeric, coriander leaves and seasoning.

2 Add the water gradually, beating well till the mixture is stiff.

3 Heat the oil in a large frying pan.

4 Mix the slices of onion into the batter. Drop a tablespoon of the mixture into the very hot oil and fry on both sides until golden brown. Drain on kitchen paper to absorb any excess oil.

5 Make the yogurt sauce: put all the sauce ingredients into a bowl and mix well.

Serve with the yogurt sauce handed separately.

Smoked Tofu Appetizer

225 g (8 oz) smoked tofu
   (see p. 51), cubed
1 orange, chopped
4 spring onions, finely chopped
5 ml (1 tsp) brown rice vinegar
15 ml (1 tbsp) sesame oil
5 ml (1 tsp) tamari
50 g (2 oz) alfalfa sprouts
finely chopped fresh parsley or coriander
   leaves, to garnish

Preparation 10 minutes
Serves 4
(GF) (V)

1 Put the tofu into a mixing bowl.

2 Add the orange and spring onions.

3 Pour over the vinegar, sesame oil and tamari.

4 Finally, add the alfalfa sprouts (separate them with your fingers to prevent them from sticking together) and mix well together.

5 Garnish with a little fresh parsley or coriander and serve in individual bowls.

Stuffed Baked Mushrooms

8 field mushrooms

Stuffing
100 g (4 oz) hazelnuts, grated
50 g (2 oz) vegetarian gouda
   cheese, grated
75 g (3 oz) wholewheat breadcrumbs
1 garlic clove, crushed
10 ml (2 tsp) finely chopped fresh dill
   weed or 5 ml (1 tsp) dried

Any nuts can be used for this recipe. Buy them whole if you have a rotary grater or blender; otherwise buy chopped or ground.

1 Heat the oven to 190°C (375°F/Gas 5).

2 Remove stalks from mushrooms. Mince or finely chop the stalks.

3 Combine all the ingredients for the stuffing in a bowl with the minced mushroom stalks. Mix thoroughly.

30 ml (2 tbsp) lemon juice
salt and black pepper

Preparation 10 minutes
Cooking 30-40 minutes
Serves 8

4 Divide into 8 portions and stuff into the mushroom shells.

5 Brush the mushrooms all over with a little olive oil and put them on an oiled baking tray. Cover tightly with aluminium foil.

6 Bake for 30-40 minutes until the mushrooms are cooked.

◆

Tiny Stuffed Tomatoes

8 small tomatoes
¼ cucumber, finely chopped
2 large dill pickles, finely chopped
5 ml (1 tsp) finely chopped fresh
    tarragon or 2.5 ml (½ tsp) dried
15 ml (1 tbsp) finely chopped
    fresh parsley
1 small eating apple
2 garlic cloves, crushed
15 ml (1 tbsp) single cream (optional)
100 g (4 oz) cottage cheese
salt and black pepper
shredded lettuce, to serve

Preparation 15 minutes
Serves 4

Tiny sweet-flavoured tomatoes are best for this recipe. The filling may also be used as a party dip or for stuffing celery or mushrooms.

1 Cut the bottoms off the tomatoes and keep on one side to use as 'lids' for the stuffed tomatoes. (They tend to sit better on their stalk ends, so fill them upside down.) Scoop out the centres and keep for another recipe.

2 Place the tomato shells cut side down, to help drain out any excess moisture, and set aside until needed.

3 Combine the cucumber, pickles, tarragon and parsley in a bowl.

4 Grate the apple and add to the bowl.

5 Add the garlic, cream, if using, and cottage cheese. Season.

6 Fill the tomato shells with the stuffing, replace the 'lids' and serve.

◆

Vegetable Pâté

15 ml (1 tbsp) soya oil
1 onion, chopped
2.5 ml (½ tsp) grated root ginger
5 ml (1 tsp) ground coriander
pinch of chilli powder
2 carrots, finely chopped
a quarter of a cauliflower, finely chopped
100 g (4 oz) mushrooms, thinly sliced
30 ml (2 tbsp) tamari
salt and black pepper
225 g (8 oz) cooked beans or grains
    (for gluten-free grains, see p. 17)
1 garlic clove, crushed
30 ml (2 tbsp) water
finely chopped fresh parsley or lemon
    wedges, to garnish

Preparation 15 minutes (allow extra time if cooking the beans or grains)
Chilling 1 hour
Serves 6

You will need a blender for this recipe.

1 Heat the oil in a saucepan and add the chopped onion, grated root ginger, ground coriander and chilli powder.

2 Add the carrot and cauliflower.

3 Add the mushrooms to the saucepan with the tamari and seasoning and simmer for 5-10 minutes or until the vegetables are tender.

4 Pour the cooked vegetables into a blender with the beans, garlic and water and liquidize until smooth.

5 Put the pâté into a serving bowl or into individual ramekins. Chill in the refrigerator for at least 1 hour before serving, then garnish with a little parsley or lemon wedges.

Serve with buttered toast or wholewheat rolls.

SALADS

◆

Beetroot, Cheese & Peach Salad

400 g (14 oz) cooked beetroots, peeled
225 g (8 oz) soft goat's cheese
3 peaches, sliced
sprigs of fresh tarragon, to garnish

Dressing
30 ml (2 tbsp) lemon juice
60 ml (4 tbsp) soya oil
2.5 ml ($\frac{1}{2}$ tsp) finely chopped fresh
   tarragon or $\frac{1}{4}$ tsp dried
2.5 ml ($\frac{1}{2}$ tsp) apple juice concentrate
   (see p. 51)
salt and black pepper

Preparation 10 minutes
Serves 6
GF

A delicious and decorative summertime salad. Cottage or soft curd cheese can be substituted for the goat cheese, and oranges, clementines or pears can be used instead of peaches.

1 Cut the beetroots into circular pieces.

2 Cut the cheese into similar-sized pieces.

3 Arrange the beetroot, cheese and peaches on a plate.

4 Make the dressing: put all the ingredients for the dressing into a screw-top jar and shake vigorously.

5 Pour over the salad and garnish with fresh tarragon.

Beetroot & Courgette Salad

1.3 kg (3 lb) cooked beetroots, peeled
　and finely chopped
450 g (1 lb) courgettes, thinly sliced
1 small onion or shallot, finely chopped

Dressing
90 ml (6 tbsp) goat's milk yogurt
45 ml (3 tbsp) olive oil
15 ml (1 tbsp) cider vinegar
2.5 ml ($\frac{1}{2}$ tsp) mustard powder
2 garlic cloves
juice of $\frac{1}{2}$ lemon
salt and black pepper

Preparation 10 minutes
Standing 1 hour
Serves 6
(GF)

See page 27 for notes on cooking beetroots and on buying ready-cooked.

1 Put the cooked beetroots into a salad bowl.

2 Add the courgettes and onion.

3 Make the dressing: put all the dressing ingredients into a screw-top jar and shake vigorously.

4 Pour over the vegetables and leave to marinate for at least 1 hour before serving. Chill in the refrigerator, if preferred.

Serve garnished with mustard and cress.

◆

Brown Rice Salad

225 g (8 oz) brown rice
450 ml (16 fl oz) water
1 large carrot, finely chopped
1 small cauliflower, finely chopped
1 green pepper, finely chopped
15 ml (1 tbsp) finely chopped
　fresh parsley
15 ml (1 tbsp) finely chopped fresh dill
　weed or 7.5 ml ($\frac{1}{2}$ tbsp) dried

Dressing
2.5 ml ($\frac{1}{2}$ tsp) mustard powder
2.5 ml ($\frac{1}{2}$ tsp) apple juice concentrate
　(see p. 51)
15 ml (1 tbsp) brown rice vinegar
60 ml (4 tbsp) safflower oil
salt and black pepper

Preparation 10 minutes
Cooking 40-45 minutes
Chilling 1 hour
Serves 6
(GF) (V)

You can substitute whole wheat or barley for the brown rice.

1 Put the rice and water in a large saucepan. Bring to the boil. Lower the heat and simmer, covered, for 45 minutes. Remove from the heat and set aside to cool.

2 Prepare the dressing: put all the dressing ingredients in a screw-top jar and shake vigorously.

3 When the rice has cooled a little, add the vegetables. Pour over the dressing and stir thoroughly. Refrigerate for at least 1 hour before serving.

Buckwheat & Coconut Salad

175 g (6 oz) roasted buckwheat
570 ml (1 pt) water
225 g (8 oz) tomatoes, finely chopped
15 ml (1 tbsp) chopped fresh parsley
25 g (1 oz) desiccated coconut
15 ml (1 tbsp) tamari
5 ml (1 tsp) brown rice vinegar
2 garlic cloves, crushed
salt and black pepper

Preparation 10 minutes
Cooking 20 minutes
Chilling 1 hour
Serves 6
(GF) (V)

1 Put the buckwheat in a medium-sized saucepan. Pour over the water. Bring to the boil, cover and simmer for 20 minutes or until cooked (by this time all the water should be absorbed). Put the cooked buckwheat into a salad bowl.

2 Add the remaining ingredients to the warm buckwheat. Stir together and chill in the refrigerator for at least 1 hour before serving the salad.

Butter Bean Salad

100 g (4 oz) butter beans, soaked for 12 hours or overnight
2 corn on the cobs
1 carrot, finely grated
6 spring onions, thinly sliced
30 ml (2 tbsp) finely chopped fresh parsley

Dressing
5 ml (1 tsp) curry powder (optional)
150 ml ($\frac{1}{4}$ pt) mayonnaise (see p. 96)
salt and black pepper

Preparation 10 minutes (allow 12 hours for soaking the beans)
Cooking 1$\frac{1}{2}$ hours
Serves 4-6
(GF) (V)

This delicious salad tastes just as good with a vinaigrette dressing.

1 Transfer the soaked beans and their liquid to a saucepan. Top up with fresh water, if necessary, to cover the beans. Cover and bring to the boil. Lower the heat and simmer for about 1$\frac{1}{2}$ hours or until cooked. Drain and set aside.

2 Put the corn cobs into a large saucepan of boiling water and cook for 10 minutes until tender. Remove from the heat and leave to cool.

3 Carefully remove the kernels from the cob, using a sharp knife.

4 Put the carrot, onion and parsley into a salad bowl with the beans and sweetcorn.

5 Make the dressing: mix the curry powder, if liked, into the mayonnaise, season to taste and pour over the salad. Mix well.

Curried Coleslaw

400 g (14 oz) white cabbage, shredded
4 carrots, finely grated
1 small green pepper, finely chopped
2 celery sticks, finely chopped
$\frac{1}{4}$ cucumber, finely chopped
1 eating apple
juice and grated rind of 1 lemon
50 g (2 oz) walnut halves
25 g (1 oz) raisins

Dressing
200 ml (7 fl oz) mayonnaise (see p. 96)
5 ml (1 tsp) curry powder

Preparation and Standing 45 minutes
Serves 6
(GF) (V)

1 Put the shredded cabbage into a salad bowl.

2 Add the carrots.

3 Add the green pepper, celery and cucumber.

4 Cut the apple into small pieces and soak in the lemon juice and rind to prevent browning. Add it all to the salad.

5 Add the walnuts and raisins and mix well.

6 Make the dressing: combine the mayonnaise and the curry powder and pour over the salad. Mix thoroughly and leave to stand for 30 minutes before serving to allow the flavours to mingle.

Fennel & Tomato Salad

225 g (8 oz) fennel, sliced into strips
225 g (8 oz) tomatoes, finely chopped
4 large spring onions, thinly sliced
25 g (1 oz) macadamia nuts

Dressing
5 ml (1 tsp) Dijon mustard
15 ml (1 tbsp) cider vinegar
2.5 ml (½ tsp) apple juice concentrate
60 ml (4 tbsp) olive oil
salt and black pepper

Preparation 10 minutes
Standing 30 minutes
Serves 6
GF V

Crisp and crunchy salad ingredients go well with the richness of the macadamia nuts. Try almonds, hazel or cashew nuts if you cannot find macadamias.

1 Put the fennel into a salad bowl.

2 Add the tomatoes, spring onions and nuts.

3 Make the dressing: put all the ingredients for the dressing into a screw-top jar and shake vigorously.

4 Pour the dressing over the salad and mix well. Leave to stand for 30 minutes before serving to allow the flavours to mingle.

Green Salad with Dill Dressing

1 small iceberg lettuce, thinly sliced
½ cucumber, sliced
½ green pepper, sliced
2 celery sticks
1 punnet mustard and cress
15 ml (1 tbsp) chopped fresh parsley
15 ml (1 tbsp) pumpkin seeds

Dressing
2.5 ml (½ tsp) mustard powder
2.5 ml (½ tsp) honey
15 ml (1 tbsp) vinegar
60 ml (4 tbsp) olive oil
2 garlic cloves, crushed
5 ml (1 tsp) finely chopped fresh dill
    weed or 2.5 ml (½ tsp) dried
salt and black pepper

Preparation 10 minutes
Serves 6
GF

You can also use courgette or any other green vegetable in season for this salad.

1 Put the lettuce strips into a salad bowl.

2 Add the cucumber, green pepper and celery.

3 Add the mustard and cress and chopped parsley and mix gently.

4 Make the dressing: put all the ingredients for the dressing in a screw-top jar and shake vigorously.

5 Pour the dressing over the salad just before serving and garnish with the pumpkin seeds.

Melon & Tomato Salad

1 large honeydew melon
225 g (8 oz) tomatoes
15 ml (1 tbsp) finely chopped fresh mint
    or 7.5 ml (½ tbsp) dried
15 ml (1 tbsp) chopped fresh chives
juice of 1 lemon
15 ml (1 tbsp) soya oil
salt and black pepper

Preparation 10 minutes
Serves 6
GF V

1 Slice the melon open and remove the seeds. Cut in quarters over the salad bowl so as to catch the juice, peel off the skin and cut into small cubes.

2 Cut the tomatoes into pieces of a similar size. Add to the melon.

3 Add the mint and chives.

4 Pour the lemon juice and soya oil over the salad. Season to taste and chill in the refrigerator until needed.

Mushroom, Apricot & Chicory Salad

225 g (8 oz) button mushrooms,
  thinly sliced
225 g (8 oz) fresh apricots, stoned
  and quartered
100 g (4 oz) chicory, shredded

Dressing
150 ml (¼ pt) sour cream
15 ml (1 tbsp) finely chopped
  fresh chives
5 ml (1 tsp) apple juice concentrate
  (see p. 51)
salt and black pepper

Preparation 10 minutes
Serves 6

A good summer salad when fresh apricots are in season. Soaked, dried apricots may also be used.

1 Put the mushrooms, apricots and chicory in a salad bowl and mix.

2 Make the dressing: put all the dressing ingredients into a screw-top jar and shake vigorously.

3 Pour over the salad and mix well.

Pineapple Salad

75 g (3 oz) brown rice
175 ml (6 fl oz) water
1 small pineapple, finely chopped
100 g (4 oz) cooked peas
2 celery sticks, finely chopped
75 g (3 oz) roasted sunflower seeds,
  to garnish

Dressing
juice and grated rind of 1 lime
60 ml (4 tbsp) soya oil
30 ml (2 tbsp) finely chopped fresh
  tarragon or 15 ml (1 tbsp) dried
5 ml (1 tsp) whole grain mustard
salt and black pepper

Preparation 10 minutes
Cooking 45 minutes
Serves 6

You can substitute whole wheat or barley for the brown rice. It is preferable to use fresh pineapple, although tins of sugar-free pineapple are now available.

1 Put the rice and water into a large saucepan. Cover and bring to the boil. Lower the heat, simmer for 45 minutes, then leave to cool.

2 Combine the rice and all the salad ingredients in a bowl.

3 Make the dressing: put all the dressing ingredients into a screw-top jar and shake vigorously.

4 Pour the dressing over the salad, mix well and leave to stand for a few minutes.

5 Sprinkle with roasted sunflower seeds before serving.

Red Bean Salad

100 g (4 oz) red kidney beans, soaked
   for 12 hours or overnight
75 g (3 oz) red cabbage, finely chopped
1 small red shallot, finely chopped
4 tomatoes, sliced
1 small yellow pepper, sliced
8 radishes, sliced
15 ml (1 tbsp) finely chopped
   fresh parsley

Dressing
5 ml (1 tsp) whole grain mustard
15 ml (1 tbsp) red wine vinegar
60 ml (4 tbsp) olive oil
2 garlic cloves, crushed
5 ml (1 tsp) finely chopped fresh
   oregano or 2.5 ml ($\frac{1}{2}$ tsp) dried
salt and black pepper

**Preparation 15 minutes (allow 12 hours
for soaking the beans)
Cooking 1$\frac{1}{2}$ hours
Chilling 1 hour
Serves 6**
Ⓖ Ⓥ

1 Transfer the soaked beans and their liquid to a saucepan. Top up with fresh water, if necessary, to cover the beans. Cover and bring to the boil. Cook briskly for 20 minutes, then lower the heat and simmer for about 1 hour until cooked. Drain and leave to cool.

2 Put the cooked and cooled kidney beans in a salad bowl.

3 Add the red cabbage and shallot.

4 Add the tomatoes, pepper and radishes and gently mix into the salad, along with the parsley.

5 Make the dressing: combine all the ingredients in a screw-top jar and shake vigorously.

6 Pour over the salad and allow to marinate in the refrigerator for about 1 hour before serving.

♦

Soya Bean Salad

100 g (4 oz) soya beans, soaked for 12
   hours or overnight
2 tangerines or 1 orange (optional)
225 g (8 oz) cooked beetroot, peeled
   and cubed
$\frac{1}{4}$ cucumber, cubed
4 spring onions, thinly sliced
30 ml (2 tbsp) finely chopped fresh
   coriander leaves, to garnish

Dressing
2.5 ml ($\frac{1}{2}$ tsp) whole-grain mustard
5 ml (1 tsp) apple juice concentrate
   (see p. 51)
5 ml (1 tsp) miso (see p. 50)
30 ml (2 tbsp) tahini (see p. 50)
juice and grated rind of 1 lime
15 ml (1 tbsp) brown rice vinegar
pinch of chilli powder

**Preparation 10 minutes (allow 12 hours
for soaking the beans)
Cooking 2 hours
Serves 6**
Ⓖ Ⓥ

1 Transfer the soaked beans and their liquid to a saucepan. Top up with fresh water, if necessary, to cover the beans. Cover and bring to the boil. Lower the heat and simmer for about 2 hours or until cooked. Drain.

2 Divide the tangerines into segments, if using.

3 Combine all the ingredients in a serving bowl.

4 Make the dressing: put all the dressing ingredients into a small bowl and mix together thoroughly.

5 Pour the dressing over the salad, mix well and garnish with the chopped coriander before serving.

Spinach Salad

100 g (4 oz) spinach, torn into
   small pieces
100 g (4 oz) red cabbage, finely chopped
1 small yellow pepper, finely chopped
$\frac{1}{4}$ cucumber, finely chopped
1 grapefruit, finely chopped
1 eating apple
pumpkin seeds and sliced kiwifruit,
   to garnish

Dressing
200 g (7 oz) medium-fat quark
10 ml (2 tsp) finely chopped fresh dill
   weed or 5 ml (1 tsp) dried
15 ml (1 tbsp) olive oil
2.5 ml ($\frac{1}{2}$ tsp) apple juice concentrate
   (see p. 51)
1 garlic clove, crushed
salt and black pepper

Preparation 15 minutes
Serves 6
(GF)

1 Put the spinach in a salad bowl.

2 Add the remaining vegetables and the grapefruit.

3 Finely chop the apple and add to the salad.

4 Make the dressing: put all the ingredients for the dressing into a screw-top jar and shake vigorously.

5 Pour over the salad vegetables and stir well. Garnish with pumpkin seeds and sliced kiwifruit.

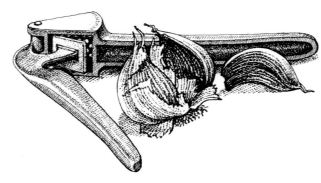

Sprouty Salad

225 g (8 oz) mung bean sprouts
1 small red pepper, finely chopped
$\frac{1}{2}$ cucumber, finely chopped
100 g (4 oz) Chinese cabbage leaves,
   finely chopped
3 celery sticks, finely chopped
4 unsulphured dried apricots
   (see p. 39), soaked for at least 3
   hours, then finely chopped
50 g (2 oz) cashew nuts, to garnish

Dressing
15 ml (1 tbsp) brown rice vinegar
60 ml (4 tbsp) soya oil
$\frac{1}{4}$ tsp grated root ginger
5 ml (1 tsp) tamari
salt and black pepper

Preparation 10 minutes (allow 3 hours
for soaking the apricots)
Serves 4
(GF) (V)

The grated root ginger and brown rice vinegar give this salad an oriental flavour. Any grain, seed or bean sprouts may be used.

1 Put the bean sprouts into a salad bowl.

2 Add the red pepper, cucumber, Chinese cabbage and celery.

3 Add the apricots.

4 Make the dressing: put all the ingredients for the dressing into a screw-top jar and shake vigorously.

5 Pour over the salad, mix well and garnish with the cashew nuts.

Sweetcorn & Mushroom Salad

2 corn on the cobs
100 g (4 oz) button mushrooms, chopped
½ cos lettuce
3 tomatoes, chopped
6 radishes, chopped

Dressing
5 ml (1 tsp) whole grain mustard
15 ml (1 tbsp) white wine vinegar
60 ml (4 tbsp) walnut oil
2 garlic cloves, crushed
2.5 ml (½ tsp) finely chopped fresh basil
  or ¼ tsp dried
salt and black pepper

Preparation 20 minutes
Chilling 20 minutes
Serves 4

Fresh sweetcorn is best for this salad. However, you can now buy fast-frozen sweetcorn kernels which do not contain added salt or sugar.

1 Put the corn cobs in a large saucepan of boiling water. Lower the heat and simmer for 10 minutes until tender. Remove from the heat and leave to cool.

2 When cool, carefully remove the kernels from the cob, using a sharp knife.

3 Put the cooked and cooled sweetcorn in a salad bowl.

4 Add the mushrooms, lettuce, tomatoes and radishes.

5 Make the dressing: put all the ingredients for the dressing into a screw-top jar and shake vigorously.

6 Pour over the salad and allow to marinate for 20 minutes in the refrigerator before serving.

◆

Tabouleh

250 g (9 oz) bulgar
90 ml (6 tbsp) olive oil
juice and grated rind of 3 lemons
3 garlic cloves, crushed
20 ml (4 tsp) finely chopped fresh mint
  or 10 ml (2 tsp) dried
4 tomatoes, finely chopped
1 cucumber, finely chopped
1 green pepper, finely chopped
1 small onion, finely chopped
salt and black pepper
cos lettuce, to serve
12 black olives and a few lemon wedges,
  to garnish

Preparation 10 minutes
Chilling 2 hours
Serves 6
Ⓥ

This traditional Middle Eastern salad can also be made with couscous. However, bulgar is more nutritious.

1 Put the bulgar in a large bowl, cover with boiling water and leave for 5 minutes until it absorbs the water and puffs up.

2 Add the olive oil, lemon juice, rind, garlic and mint and mix well.

3 Add the tomatoes, cucumber, green pepper and onion. Adjust seasoning to taste.

4 Set aside to cool a little or chill in the refrigerator for a minimum of 2 hours.

5 Serve on a bed of cos lettuce. Garnish with olives and a few lemon wedges.

Tabouleh is delicious served with wholewheat pitta bread and Hummus (see p. 83).

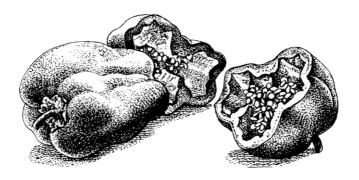

Watercress & Orange Salad

1 bunch watercress
4 carrots, grated
100 g (4 oz) chicory, chopped
2 oranges
15 ml (1 tbsp) finely chopped
   fresh parsley
15 ml (1 tbsp) sunflower seeds,
   to garnish

Dressing
5 ml (1 tsp) honey spiced mustard
15 ml (1 tbsp) cider vinegar
60 ml (4 tbsp) sunflower oil
salt and black pepper

Preparation 10 minutes
Serves 4-6

A nutritious salad that is high in vitamin C. Choose bright, crisp green watercress and avoid any with yellowing or wilting leaves.

1 Break the watercress into small pieces into a salad bowl.

2 Add the carrots.

3 Add the chicory.

4 Using a fine grater, grate the rind off the oranges and set aside for the dressing.

5 Peel off the remaining pith and cut the orange segments into small pieces, adding them to the salad bowl.

6 Mix in the chopped parsley.

7 Make the dressing: put all the ingredients for the dressing into a screw-top jar. Add the orange rind and shake vigorously.

8 Pour over the salad and garnish with sunflower seeds.

Mayonnaise

1 egg
15 ml (1 tbsp) lemon juice
5 ml (1 tsp) vinegar
5 ml (1 tsp) mustard powder
10 ml (2 tsp) finely chopped mixed
   fresh herbs or 5 ml (1 tsp) dried
salt and black pepper
275-325 ml (10-12 fl oz) sunflower oil

Preparation 10 minutes
Makes 425 ml (¾ pt)

This recipe uses dairy products, whilst the next recipe is suitable for a vegan diet. Both recipes may be kept for 4-5 days in an airtight container in the refrigerator. If you do not have a blender, use a wire balloon whisk.

1 Put the egg, lemon juice, vinegar, mustard powder, herbs and seasoning in a blender. Liquidize till smooth.

2 Gradually add the oil with the blender still running until you have a thick consistency. If you add the oil too quickly the mayonnaise may curdle.

Vegan Mayonnaise

100 ml (4 fl oz) soya milk
60 ml (4 tbsp) lemon juice
10 ml (2 tsp) mustard powder
10 ml (2 tsp) finely chopped mixed herbs
   or 5 ml (1 tsp) dried
salt and black pepper
200-300 ml (7-11 fl oz) soya oil

Preparation 10 minutes
Makes 425 ml (¾ pt)

See Mayonnaise recipe above for usage, equipment and storage.

1 Put the soya milk, lemon juice, mustard powder, herbs and seasoning in a blender. Liquidize till smooth.

2 Gradually add the oil with the blender still running until you have a thick consistency.

Starters *(See p. 80)*

Vegetable Pâté (see p. 87) has a soft, spreading consistency. Serve with fingers of warm toast.

Stuffed Baked Mushrooms (see p. 86) are a filling starter with a smoky taste.

Cream Cheese Dip (see p. 82) is flavoured with fresh thyme, basil and marjoram.

Smoked Tofu Appetizer (see p. 86) contains alfalfa and tofu, both very nutritious.

Cottage Cheese Cooler (see p. 82) is a pleasant, light starter with a fresh lemon tang, ideal in summertime.

Citrus Cocktail (see p. 81) is a mixture of grapefruit, oranges, celery and mint.

Leeks Vinaigrette (see p. 84) is particularly delicious if made with tender baby leeks.

Tiny Stuffed Tomatoes (see p. 87) make a decorative starter for a dinner party.

Hummus (see p. 83) is rich in flavour but not heavy.

Egg & Avocado Mayonnaise Dip (see p. 82) also makes a soft and tasty sandwich filling.

Apple & Butter Bean Pâté (see p. 80) has a delicate, slightly sweet flavour.

Guacamole (see p. 83) is a milder version of the traditional Mexican dish.

Aubergine Pâté (se p. 81) has a rich, smoky taste.

Marinated Tofu (see p. 84) is an unusual starter.

Nori & Spinach Rolls (see p. 85) look exciting and yet are easy to prepare.

Onion Bhajis with Yogurt Sauce (see p. 86) are a delicious, spicy starter.

Baked Eggs with Coriander (see p. 81) have a smooth, creamy taste with a bite of fresh coriander.

Kombu Surprise (see p. 84) is a simple seaweed recipe.

Spinach Salad (see p. 94) is nutritious with a sharp, interesting flavour.

Butter Bean Salad (see p. 90) is a fresh, summery salad which is quite light.

Tabouleh (see p. 95) is a Middle Eastern dish, made here with bulgar wheat.

Curried Coleslaw (see p. 90) is a colourful salad with fruit, nuts and raisins.

Mushroom, Apricot & Chicory Salad (see p. 92) has a fresh, fruity flavour.

Fennel & Tomato Salad (see p. 91) is very refreshing.

Crisp and fresh **Green Salad with Dill Dressing** (see p. 91).

Sprouty Salad (see p. 94) includes mung bean sprouts, dried apricots and cashew nuts.

Beetroot, Cheese & Peach Salad (see p. 88) uses goat's cheese for a strong flavour.

Melon & Tomato Salad (see p. 91) is light, sweet and crisp, ideal in summer.

Pineapple Salad (see p. 92) has a tarragon dressing for extra flavour.

Buckwheat & Coconut Salad (see p. 90) is an unusual and delicious combination.

Red Bean Salad (see p. 93) has bright splashes of radish and yellow pepper.

Soya Bean Salad (see p. 93) is a substantial, highly nutritious salad.

Sweetcorn & Mushroom Salad (see p. 95) has a delicious walnut oil dressing.

Beetroot & Courgette Salad (see p. 89) has a vivid colour and an intriguing taste.

Watercress & Orange Salad (see p. 96) has a lovely, slightly tangy flavour.

Brown Rice Salad (see p. 89) is quite filling, with a good contrast of textures.

MAIN COURSES

Artichokes & Tomatoes with Basil

450 g (1 lb) tomatoes
50 g (2 oz) butter
1 large onion, chopped
2 garlic cloves, crushed
5 ml (1 tsp) finely chopped fresh basil, or 2.5 ml (½ tsp) dried
450 g (1 lb) Jerusalem artichokes, chopped
salt and black pepper
finely chopped fresh parsley, to garnish

Preparation 20 minutes
Cooking 10 minutes
Serves 6
Ⓖ︎Ⓕ︎

This quick and simple dish can be made in advance and reheated.

1 Put the tomatoes in a bowl and pour over boiling water. Set aside for 10-15 minutes to allow the skins to soften.

2 Meanwhile, melt the butter in a medium-sized saucepan over a low heat and add the onion, garlic and basil.

3 Add the artichokes, and continue cooking gently.

4 Pour the water off the tomatoes. Drain, peel and break them up with a fork. Add to the artichokes. Season.

5 Simmer for about 10 minutes or until the artichokes are cooked.

6 Serve hot, garnished with the chopped parsley.

Serve with a cooked grain dish and a side salad.

Aubergine & Potato Curry

225 g (8 oz) tomatoes
1 large aubergine, cubed
60 ml (4 tbsp) soya oil
5 ml (1 tsp) cumin seeds
10 ml (2 tsp) coriander seeds
1 large onion, finely chopped
2.5 ml (½ tsp) ground mace
2.5 ml (½ tsp) ground cardamom
2.5 ml (½ tsp) chilli powder
15 ml (1 tbsp) tomato purée
225 g (8 oz) potatoes, finely cubed

Preparation and Cooking 30 minutes
Serves 4
(GF) (V)

This is a 'dry' curry, so make sure you stir frequently to prevent the mixture sticking.

1 Put the tomatoes in a bowl. Pour over boiling water and set aside for 10-15 minutes to allow the skins to soften.

2 Meanwhile, prepare the aubergine as necessary (see p. 27).

3 Heat the oil in a medium-sized saucepan. Add the cumin and coriander seeds and cook gently for a few minutes until the cumin seeds pop.

4 Add the onion, mace, cardamom, chilli powder and tomato purée. Cook gently for a further 5 minutes.

5 Add the potatoes and stir well to prevent sticking.

6 Add the aubergine.

7 Pour the water off the tomatoes, drain and peel them and add to the saucepan.

8 Cook gently for a further 10-15 minutes, stirring frequently, until the vegetables are cooked.

Serve with brown rice, a slightly 'wetter' vegetable dish and a selection of chutneys and other traditional curry accompaniments.

Baked Avocado with Stilton & Walnuts

30 ml (2 tbsp) soya oil or
   25 g (1 oz) butter
1 onion, thinly sliced
100 g (4 oz) mushrooms, thinly sliced
30 ml (2 tbsp) low-fat quark or a mixture
   of 15 ml (1 tbsp) quark and 15 ml
   (1 tbsp) port
75 g (3 oz) Stilton cheese
25 g (1 oz) walnut halves
salt and black pepper
2 large avocados

Preparation 15 minutes
Cooking 10 minutes
Serves 4
(GF)

This is included as a main course as it is both substantial and rich. However, smaller avocados could be used for a starter. Any combination of nuts and cheese can be used. For a vegan diet substitute tofu (see p. 51) for the cheese.

1 Heat the oven to 150°C (300°F/Gas 2).

2 Heat the oil in a medium-sized saucepan, and sauté the onion and mushrooms for about 5 minutes until soft.

3 Add the quark, crumble in the Stilton and add the walnuts and seasoning. Stir well and remove from heat.

4 Halve the avocados and scoop out most of the flesh, leaving a small amount close to the skins.

5 Mash the avocado flesh, add it to the onion mixture and adjust the seasoning to taste.

6 Pile the mixture into the avocado shells and bake for 10 minutes, or until warmed through.

Serve with a light salad or steamed vegetables.

Barley, Fruit & Vegetable Pollo

225 g (8 oz) whole pot barley
700 ml (1¼ pt) water
30 ml (2 tbsp) tahini (see p. 50)
50 g (2 oz) butter or 30 ml (2 tbsp)
  soya oil
1 large onion, chopped
1 green pepper, chopped
2 carrots, chopped
100 g (4 oz) peas
30 ml (2 tbsp) finely chopped fresh
  coriander leaves
salt and black pepper
25 g (1 oz) sultanas
50 g (2 oz) unsulphured dried apricots
  (see p. 39)
50 g (2 oz) cashew nuts
30 ml (2 tbsp) orange juice
15 ml (1 tbsp) tamari
100 ml (4 fl oz) boiling water

Preparation 15 minutes
Cooking 1 hour 10 minutes
Serves 4

1 Put the whole barley in a saucepan, add the water and bring to the boil. Lower the heat and simmer, covered, for 45 minutes or until cooked and tender.

2 Heat the oven to 180°C (350°F/Gas 4).

3 Remove barley from heat and mix in the tahini.

4 Melt half the butter in a large pan. Add the onion, pepper and carrots and cook gently for 5 minutes till soft.

5 Add the peas and coriander and mix well. Season and put aside.

6 Melt the remaining butter in a small pan. Add the sultanas, apricots and cashews. Cook for a few minutes.

7 Stir in the orange juice and tamari and set aside.

8 Spread half the barley over the bottom of an ovenproof dish.

9 Cover with the vegetable mixture.

10 Spread over half the remaining barley and then the fruit mixture.

11 Put the rest of the barley on top. Pour over the boiling water and cover with a tightly fitting lid.

12 Bake for 20-25 minutes or until the vegetables are cooked.

Serve with leafy green vegetables and a fresh salad.

Beanburgers

100 g (4 oz) black-eyed beans, soaked
  for 12 hours or overnight
150 g (5 oz) brown rice
275 ml (½ pt) water
1 small onion, finely chopped
½ red pepper, finely chopped
15 ml (1 tbsp) chopped fresh parsley
5 ml (1 tsp) ground cumin
2.5 ml (½ tsp) ground coriander
¼ tsp chilli powder
10 ml (2 tsp) finely chopped fresh basil
  or 5 ml (1 tsp) dried
15 ml (1 tbsp) tomato purée
15 ml (1 tbsp) tamari
10 ml (2 tsp) desiccated coconut
25 g (1 oz) raisins (optional)
salt and black pepper
mixture of wholewheat flour and a few
  sesame seeds, for rolling
a little oil, for shallow- or deep-frying

Preparation 10 minutes (allow 12 hours
for soaking the beans)
Cooking 1 hour 20 minutes
Makes 8 burgers

ⓥ

1 Transfer the soaked beans and their liquid to a saucepan. Top up with fresh water, if necessary, to cover the beans. Cover and bring to the boil. Lower the heat and simmer, covered, for 1 hour or until cooked and tender.

2 Meanwhile, put the rice in a saucepan with the water. Bring to the boil. Lower the heat and simmer for 45 minutes or until cooked.

3 Combine the beans, rice and remaining ingredients except the flour, sesame seeds and oil in a food processor or large bowl and mix thoroughly until the mixture holds together well.

4 Using an ice cream scoop or your hands, form the rice and bean mixture into smaller burger shapes. Roll them in the flour and sesame seeds till well covered.

5 Heat enough oil for deep- or shallow-frying and when very hot gently lower the beanburgers into the oil and fry for 3-4 minutes on each side till golden brown.

6 Drain on absorbent kitchen paper.

Serve warm or cold or sandwiched between a wholewheat granary-style bap with mayonnaise, tomato, cucumber and mustard and cress.

Black Bean Chilli

200 g (7 oz) black kidney beans, soaked
   for 12 hours or overnight
900 g (2 lb) tomatoes
30 ml (2 tbsp) groundnut oil
1 large onion, thinly sliced
1 large green pepper, thinly sliced
$\frac{1}{4}$ tsp ground cinnamon
5 ml (1 tsp) ground coriander
$\frac{1}{4}$-$\frac{1}{2}$ tsp chilli powder
$\frac{1}{4}$ tsp ground anise (optional)
350 g (12 oz) courgettes, grated
60 ml (4 tbsp) tomato purée
salt and black pepper
175 g (6 oz) strong cheese, grated

**Preparation 15 minutes (allow 12 hours
for soaking the beans)
Cooking 1 hour 45 minutes
Serves 6**
(GF)

**This chilli dish is traditionally made with red kidney beans but
black beans make an attractive change.**

1 Transfer the soaked beans and their liquid to a saucepan. Top up
with fresh water, if necessary, to cover the beans. Cover and bring to
the boil. Lower the heat and simmer, covered, for $1\frac{1}{2}$ hours until
tender. Drain and set aside and leave to cool.

2 Meanwhile, put the tomatoes in a bowl. Pour boiling water over
them and set aside for 10-15 minutes to allow the skins to soften.

3 Heat the oil in a large saucepan. Add the onion, green pepper and
spices. Cook gently for 5 minutes or until the onion is soft.

4 Add the courgettes to the saucepan. Stir well and continue
cooking gently.

5 By now the tomatoes should be ready to peel. Pour off the water,
drain, peel and chop the tomatoes coarsely, taking care not to lose
their juices.

6 Add the chopped tomatoes and the tomato purée to the mixture
in the saucepan, stir well and continue cooking.

7 Add the cooked and cooled beans, season to taste and cook for a
further 5-10 minutes or until the beans are heated through.

8 Stir the cheese into the chilli just before serving.

Serve on a bed of brown rice or other grain if preferred.

Brown Rice Risotto

2 onions, sliced into rings
50 g (2 oz) butter or 30 ml (2 tbsp)
   soya oil
3 carrots, chopped
4 celery sticks, chopped
100 g (4 oz) broccoli, chopped
10 ml (2 tsp) finely chopped fresh basil
   or 5 ml (1 tsp) dried
15 ml (1 tbsp) ground turmeric
salt and black pepper
225 g (8 oz) brown rice
50 ml (2 fl oz) tamari
825 ml ($1\frac{1}{2}$ pt) vegetable stock or water
100 g (4 oz) shelled pistachio nuts,
   to garnish

**Preparation 15 minutes
Cooking 1$\frac{1}{2}$ hours
Serves 6-8**
(GF) (V)

**You can also use a mixture of brown rice and rye grain in this
delicious risotto.**

1 Heat the oven to 200°C (400°F/Gas 6).

2 Sauté the onions in the butter in a saucepan for 5 minutes until
soft and tender.

3 Add the carrots, celery and broccoli to the onions, together with
the basil, turmeric and seasoning.

4 Stir in the brown rice and mix well. Simmer for 3-4 minutes,
stirring occasionally.

5 Pour the tamari and stock over the mixture and transfer to an
ovenproof dish.

6 Bake, covered, for 1$\frac{1}{2}$ hours or until the rice is completely cooked.

7 Sprinkle with the pistachio nuts before serving.

Serve with Ratatouille (see p. 110) and a crisp salad.

Buckwheat Pancakes with Tomato Sauce

Pancakes
175 g (6 oz) buckwheat flour
175 g (6 oz) wholewheat flour
10 ml (2 tsp) baking powder
5 ml (1 tsp) finely chopped fresh dill
    weed or 2.5 ml (½ tsp) dried
225 ml (8 fl oz) milk
100 ml (4 fl oz) water
100 g (4 oz) Greek-style yogurt
3 eggs, beaten
salt and black pepper (optional)
a little butter or oil, for frying

Sauce
675 g (1½ lb) tomatoes
30 ml (2 tbsp) soya oil
1 large onion, finely chopped
1 large red pepper, finely chopped
3 bay leaves
10 ml (2 tsp) finely chopped fresh
    marjoram or 5 ml (1 tsp) dried
2.5 ml (½ tsp) grated nutmeg
pinch of chilli powder (optional)
45 ml (3 tbsp) tomato purée
10 ml (2 tsp) apple juice concentrate
    (see p. 51)
salt and black pepper
finely chopped fresh parsley and grated
    cheese, to garnish

Preparation 20 minutes
Cooking 15 minutes
Makes 16-20 pancakes

To prepare the batter in advance, make up as directed but do not add the baking powder until just before cooking. The sauce can also be made in advance and reheated when needed. If you do not have a blender, use a potato masher.

1 First make the pancake batter: combine all the dry ingredients in a bowl. Then, in a jug, mix the milk, water, yogurt and eggs.

2 Pour the liquid into the flour and mix together gently, stirring, until there are no lumps. Add a little salt and pepper, if wished, and set aside.

3 Next, make the sauce: put the tomatoes in a bowl and pour over boiling water. Leave to stand for 10-15 minutes to allow the skins to soften.

4 Meanwhile, heat the oil in a medium-sized saucepan and add the onion, red pepper, bay leaves, marjoram, nutmeg and chilli, if using. Cook gently for 5 minutes or until the vegetables are soft.

5 Pour the water off the tomatoes and peel off their skins. Chop coarsely and add to the saucepan with the tomato purée and apple juice concentrate. Simmer for a further 2-3 minutes.

6 Put the mixture into a blender and liquidize till smooth. Pour back into the saucepan. Season to taste and set aside.

7 Now you are ready to make the pancakes: put about 10 ml (2 tsp) oil into a small frying pan over a high heat. When the oil is hot, carefully spoon 30 ml (2 tbsp) of the mixture into the pan. (The pancake should be about 15 cm (6 in) in diameter.)

8 Turn the heat down a little and cook for 3-4 minutes until little bubbles appear on the surface. Turn the pancake and cook the other side.

9 Remove the pancake from the pan, drain on some absorbent kitchen paper and keep warm while you are cooking the remaining pancakes. Repeat the process till all the pancakes are cooked.

10 Before serving, reheat the tomato sauce and serve either separately or poured over the pancakes. Decorate with a sprinkling of chopped parsley and grated cheese.

Serve with a green salad or a green leafy vegetable.

Buckwheat Spaghetti with Mushrooms, Dill & Sour Cream

about 1 l (1¾ pt) water
250 g (9 oz) 100% buckwheat
    spaghetti (soba)
50 g (2 oz) butter
2 large onions, sliced
2 garlic cloves, crushed
10 ml (2 tsp) finely chopped fresh dill
    weed or 5 ml (1 tsp) dried
350 g (12 oz) mushrooms, sliced
150 ml (¼ pt) sour cream or
    Greek-style yogurt
salt and black pepper
a little fresh parsley, to garnish

**Preparation and Cooking 30 minutes
Serves 4**
(GF)

1 Pour the water into a medium-sized saucepan and bring to the boil. Add the spaghetti. Stir a few times to prevent sticking and simmer for about 20 minutes or until cooked.

2 Meanwhile, melt the butter in a large frying pan and add the sliced onions, garlic and dill. Cook for 5 minutes, stirring occasionally, until the onions are soft.

3 Add the mushrooms and cook for a further 5 minutes.

4 Finally, add the sour cream, a little salt, if liked, and a generous helping of freshly ground black pepper.

5 By now the spaghetti should be ready. Drain well, put in a serving dish, pour over the mushroom sauce and sprinkle liberally with the freshly chopped parsley.

Try serving with a fresh salad, baby carrots or petits pois.

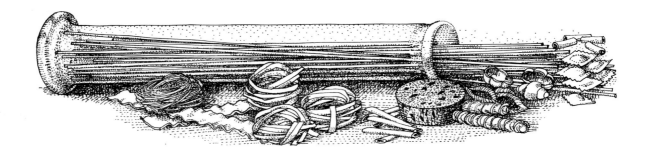

Caribbean Stew

30 ml (2 tbsp) groundnut oil
1 large onion, finely chopped
1 red pepper, finely chopped
5 ml (1 tsp) grated root ginger
4 garlic cloves, crushed
1 small swede, cubed
1 small parsnip, cubed
1 large sweet potato, cubed
570 ml (1 pt) pineapple juice
30 ml (2 tbsp) tomato purée
60 ml (4 tbsp) creamed coconut
2.5-5 ml (½-1 tsp) chilli powder
salt and black pepper

**Preparation 15 minutes
Cooking 20 minutes
Serves 6-8**
(GF) (V)

Quick and simple to make, the creamed coconut and root ginger give this stew a truly Caribbean flavour.

1 Heat the oil in a medium-sized saucepan. Add the onion, red pepper, grated root ginger and crushed garlic. Sauté for 5 minutes, stirring occasionally, until the onion is soft.

2 Add the swede, parsnip and sweet potato to the saucepan and sauté for a further 3 minutes to seal in the flavours.

3 Add the pineapple juice, tomato purée, coconut, chilli powder and seasoning and simmer for 20 minutes or until the vegetables are cooked and tender.

Serve on a bed of brown rice with Red Bean Salad (see p. 93).

Cauliflower & Carrots with Spicy Hazelnut Sauce

1 large cauliflower
2 carrots, sliced
50 g (2 oz) butter, ghee (see p. 47) or vegetable oil
1 red pepper, finely chopped
2.5 ml ($\frac{1}{2}$ tsp) grated root ginger
$\frac{1}{4}$ tsp chilli powder
1 bunch spring onions, finely chopped
100 g (4 oz) hazelnut butter (see p. 50)
200 ml (7 fl oz) boiling water
30 ml (2 tbsp) shoyu (see p. 51)

Preparation and Cooking 15 minutes
Serves 4-6
(GF) (V)

You can substitute peanut, cashew or almond butter for the hazelnut butter.

1 Break the cauliflower into florets and cut the stem and leaves into similar-sized pieces.

2 Steam the cauliflower and carrots for 5-10 minutes or until tender.

3 Meanwhile, melt the butter in a saucepan. Add the red pepper, root ginger and chilli and cook gently. Add the spring onions.

4 Put the hazelnut butter into a bowl. Pour on the boiling water and shoyu and mix to a smooth paste.

5 Add to the red pepper mixture, mix well and season.

6 By now the cauliflower and carrots will be cooked. Transfer to a serving dish, pour over the hazelnut sauce and serve immediately.

Serve with cooked grains and a side salad.

Cheesy Stuffed Peppers with Creamed Mushroom Sauce

2 large red peppers

Stuffing
100 g (4 oz) fresh wholewheat breadcrumbs
100 g (4 oz) cheese, grated
1 parsnip, finely grated
50 g (2 oz) cashew nut pieces
15 ml (1 tbsp) sugar-free tomato sauce
pinch of chilli powder
120 ml (4$\frac{1}{2}$ fl oz) vegetable stock or the same quantity of water plus 15 ml (1 tbsp) tamari
salt and pepper

Sauce
1 large onion, sliced
50 g (2 oz) butter
2 garlic cloves, crushed
$\frac{1}{4}$ tsp grated nutmeg
225 g (8 oz) mushrooms
100 ml (4 fl oz) single cream
salt and black pepper

Preparation 20 minutes
Cooking 40 minutes
Serves 4

For a vegan diet, substitute tofu (see p. 51) for the cheese and serve with tomato sauce (see p. 115).

1 Heat the oven to 190°C (375°F/Gas 5).

2 Cut the peppers in half lengthwise. Remove the stalk and seeds. Put the pepper halves in a large saucepan, and cover with cold water. Cover and bring to the boil, then remove from heat, pour off the water and turn face down to drain away any excess liquid.

3 Prepare the stuffing: in a large mixing bowl, put the breadcrumbs, grated cheese, grated parsnip, cashew nuts, tomato sauce, chilli powder and stock.

4 Mix together until you have a soft pliable mixture, adding more liquid if necessary. Season to taste.

5 Fill the peppers with the stuffing, place in an ovenproof dish and cook for 30 minutes or until the peppers are cooked.

6 Meanwhile, make the sauce: sauté the sliced onion in the butter.

7 Next, add the garlic, nutmeg and mushrooms. Cook for a further 5 minutes and remove from heat. Add the cream. Mix and season.

8 Remove the peppers from the oven when cooked. Pour the mushroom sauce over the top, return to the oven for 10 minutes and serve immediately.

Serve with a salad, grain or potato dish.

Chestnut & Prune Roast

ıts, soaked for

soaked for
ernight
, oz) wholewheat breadcrumbs
100 g (4 oz) curd cheese
1 egg, beaten
10 ml (2 tsp) finely chopped fresh
    tarragon or 5 ml (1 tsp) dried
10 ml (2 tsp) finely chopped fresh sage
    or 5 ml (1 tsp) dried
salt and black pepper

**Preparation 15 minutes (allow 12 hours
for soaking the chestnuts and prunes)
Cooking 2 hours
Serves 6**

**For a vegan diet, substitute crumbled tofu (see p. 51) for the
curd cheese and 15 ml (1 tbsp) of tahini for the egg.**

1 Top up the water on the chestnuts to cover, if necessary, and boil
in a saucepan for about 1½ hours or until tender.

2 Reserve a little of the cooking liquid and set aside.

3 Heat the oven to 180°C (350°F/Gas 4).

4 Purée the chestnuts by pressing through a sieve or using a blender.

5 Remove the stones from the prunes and purée the flesh using a
sieve or blender. Retain a little of the soaking liquid.

6 In a large bowl, combine the chestnut and prune purées and add
the breadcrumbs, curd cheese, egg, tarragon, sage and seasoning.
(You want a fairly moist mixture so add a little of the reserved
liquid if necessary.)

7 Spoon the mixture into an ovenproof casserole dish and bake,
covered, for 35-40 minutes until the roast is set and browned on top.

Serve with buttered Brussels sprouts, carrots or a crisp green salad.

Chestnut Roast

250 g (9 oz) dried chestnuts, soaked for
    12 hours or overnight
30 ml (2 tbsp) cider vinegar
150 g (5 oz) parsnips, finely chopped
150 g (5 oz) swedes, finely chopped
100 g (4 oz) Brussels sprouts,
    finely chopped
15 ml (1 tbsp) sesame oil
1 onion, chopped
3 garlic cloves, crushed
30 ml (2 tbsp) tamari
100 g (4 oz) mushrooms
juice and grated rind of 1 orange
400 g (14 oz) wholewheat breadcrumbs
about 275 ml (½ pt) vegetable stock
    or water
sprigs of fresh parsley and orange
    slices, to garnish

**Preparation 15 minutes (allow 12 hours
for soaking the chestnuts)
Cooking 2 hours
Serves 6**

This is a delicious dish for a vegetarian Christmas dinner.

1 Top up the water on the chestnuts to cover, if necessary, and boil
in a saucepan with the cider vinegar for about 1½ hours or till tender.

2 Heat the oven to 170°C (325°F/Gas 3).

3 Meanwhile, steam the parsnips, swedes and sprouts for 8-10
minutes until tender. Leave to cool and set aside.

4 When the chestnuts are cooked, pour off the water and chop them
coarsely. Put into a large mixing bowl.

5 Put the oil in a small saucepan and add the chopped onion and
garlic. Cook gently.

6 Add the tamari and mushrooms and continue cooking for a
further 5 minutes.

7 Remove from heat and add to the chestnuts. Add the vegetables.

8 Add the orange juice and rind, together with the breadcrumbs.

9 Mix vigorously and gradually add the stock or water until the
mixture has the consistency of a thick paste.

10 Press into a well-greased ovenproof dish and bake for 30 minutes
or until cooked through. Cool and turn out on to a board.

11 Garnish with parsley and thin slices of orange.

Country Vegetable Pie

450 g (1 lb) parsnips, finely chopped
450 g (1 lb) carrots, finely chopped
30 ml (2 tbsp) sunflower oil
1 large onion, sliced
450 g (1 lb) leeks, sliced
1 red pepper, thinly sliced
10 ml (2 tsp) finely chopped fresh herbs
    of your choice or 5 ml (1 tsp) dried
2 garlic cloves, crushed
225 g (8 oz) mushrooms, sliced
salt and black pepper
50 g (2 oz) butter
$\frac{1}{4}$ tsp grated nutmeg

Preparation 30 minutes
Cooking 20 minutes
Serves 6
(GF)

Parsnips and carrots make an interesting change from potatoes as a topping. Sweet potatoes and turnips can also be used.

1 Heat the oven to 180°C (350°F/Gas 4).

2 In a saucepan, boil the parsnips and carrots for 10-15 minutes or until tender.

3 Meanwhile, heat the oil in a medium-sized saucepan. Add the sliced onion and cook gently.

4 Add the leeks and red pepper.

5 Add the mixed herbs and garlic. Stir well.

6 Add the sliced mushrooms, simmer for 2-3 minutes, season to taste and remove from the heat.

7 By now the parsnips and carrots should be ready. Drain well and set aside.

8 Add the butter and grated nutmeg to the leek mixture. Blend into a smooth purée with a food processor or potato masher. Season with salt and pepper to taste.

9 Put the vegetable mixture into an ovenproof dish and spread the parsnips and carrots over the top.

10 Cook in the oven for 20 minutes.

Serve immediately with steamed green vegetables or a crisp salad.

Fresh Coriander Dhal

25 g (1 oz) ghee (see p. 47) or butter
2 large onions, thinly sliced
4 garlic cloves, thinly sliced
350 g (12 oz) tinned tomatoes
30 ml (2 tbsp) garam masala (see p. 57)
15 ml (1 tbsp) grated root ginger
pinch of grated asafoetida (see p. 56)
pinch of grated nutmeg
75 ml (5 tbsp) finely chopped fresh
    coriander leaves
2.5-5 ml ($\frac{1}{2}$-1 tsp) chilli powder
500 g (1 lb 2 oz) lentils or split peas
2.2 l (4 pt) water

Garnish
1 large onion, sliced into rings
finely chopped fresh coriander leaves
lemon slices

Preparation 10 minutes
Cooking 35 minutes
Serves 6-8
(GF)

1 Heat the ghee in a large saucepan and sauté the onions and garlic for 5 minutes until soft.

2 Add the rest of the ingredients except for the water and stir-fry for a few minutes.

3 Add the water, bring to the boil and simmer for 35 minutes or until cooked.

4 Prepare the garnish: in a frying pan, fry the onion for the garnish in a little ghee until crispy brown.

5 When the dhal is cooked, pour into a serving dish and garnish with the fried onion, coriander and lemon slices.

Serve with brown rice and steamed vegetables.

Fresh Vegetable Curry

oo ...) groundnut oil
10 ml (2 tsp) grated root ginger
3 garlic cloves, crushed
5 ml (1 tsp) coriander seeds
5 ml (1 tsp) ground cumin
2.5 ml (½ tsp) ground cardamom
10 ml (2 tsp) cayenne
2.5 ml (½ tsp) chilli powder
1 large onion, finely chopped
1 kohlrabi, finely chopped
1 large green pepper, finely chopped
2 large carrots, finely chopped
1 large parsnip, finely chopped
200 ml (7 fl oz) orange juice
1 large cooking apple
15 ml (1 tbsp) raisins (optional)
salt and black pepper

Preparation and Cooking 30 minutes
Serves 6

This quick and simple curry can be made in advance and reheated later without spoiling its flavour.

1 Heat the oil in a large frying pan and add the spices and onion.

2 Add the kohlrabi.

3 Add the green pepper, carrots and parsnip.

4 Pour over the orange juice. Finely chop the apple, and add to the pan with the raisins, if using, and cook for about 15 minutes or until the vegetables are tender. Season to taste.

Serve with brown rice, tamari, roasted peanuts and a selection of chutneys and other traditional curry accompaniments.

Fried Tempeh with Orange Sesame Sauce

30 ml (2 tbsp) groundnut or sesame oil
225 g (8 oz) tempeh (see p. 51), thawed if frozen, cubed
¼ tsp grated root ginger

Sauce
15 ml (1 tbsp) miso (see p. 50)
45 ml (3 tbsp) tahini (see p. 50)
juice and grated rind of 1 orange or 1 lemon
150 ml (¼ pt) water

Preparation and Cooking 10 minutes
Serves 4

1 Heat the oil gently in a small frying pan.

2 Add the tempeh and ginger and shallow-fry for about 5 minutes, turning occasionally, until the pieces are evenly browned. Turn on to some absorbent kitchen paper to drain.

3 Make the sauce: put the miso and tahini into a bowl and add the grated orange or lemon rind and squeezed juice.

4 Now add the water and mix the sauce ingredients together into a smooth paste.

Serve with the sauce handed separately, and with brown rice and stir-fried vegetables.

Gado-gado

225 g (8 oz) potatoes
225 g (8 oz) carrots
225 g (8 oz) green beans
15 ml (1 tbsp) groundnut oil
1 large onion, finely sliced
100 g (4 oz) tempeh (see p. 51), cubed
1 cucumber, coarsely chopped
1 small Chinese cabbage, shredded
100 g (4 oz) bean sprouts
100 g (4 oz) tofu (see p. 51), cubed
2 eggs, hard-boiled and sliced

1 Boil the potatoes for about 20 minutes until tender. Drain and leave to cool, then cut into bite-sized pieces and set aside.

2 Meanwhile, steam the carrots and green beans together for 8-10 minutes and drain. Slice into bite-sized pieces and set aside.

3 Make the sauce: heat the oil in a small saucepan and add the onion, chilli and garlic. Cook for 5 minutes, stirring occasionally, until the onion is soft.

4 Add the peanut butter, coconut, honey, lemon juice, rind and water. Simmer gently until the sauce is smooth and thick. Set aside.

Sauce
30 ml (2 tbsp) groundnut oil
1 onion, chopped
2 green chilli peppers, chopped, or
  5 ml (1 tsp) chilli powder
3 garlic cloves, crushed
225 g (8 oz) peanut butter
50 g (2 oz) creamed coconut, grated
5 ml (1 tsp) honey
juice and grated rind of 1 lemon
570 ml (1 pt) water

Preparation 10 minutes
Cooking 25 minutes
Serves 6
(GF)

5 Heat the groundnut oil in a frying pan and add the onion and tempeh. Fry for 5 minutes, turning the tempeh until golden brown. Drain on absorbent kitchen paper.

6 Arrange the cooked vegetables together with the remaining, raw, vegetables and tofu on a serving platter. Top with the sliced hard-boiled eggs, and serve with the peanut sauce handed separately.

Serve with a tomato salad.

Homestyle Baked Beans

100 g (4 oz) haricot beans, soaked for
  12 hours or overnight

Sauce
450 g (1 lb) tomatoes
30 ml (2 tbsp) soya oil or 25 g (1 oz)
  butter
1 large onion, chopped
10 ml (2 tsp) finely chopped fresh
  marjoram or 5 ml (1 tsp) dried
45 ml (3 tbsp) tomato purée
salt and black pepper
15 ml (1 tbsp) apple juice concentrate
  (see p. 51)

Preparation 20 minutes (allow 12 hours
for soaking the beans)
Cooking 2½ hours
Serves 4
(GF) (V)

This is a healthier alternative to the tinned varieties: a good recipe for young children.

1 Transfer the soaked beans and their liquid to a saucepan. Top up with fresh water, if necessary, to cover the beans. Cover and bring to the boil. Lower the heat and simmer for 1½ hours or until tender.

2 While the beans are cooking, make the sauce: first put the tomatoes in a bowl and pour over boiling water. Cover and set aside for 10-15 minutes to allow the skins to soften.

3 Meanwhile, heat the oil in a saucepan. Add the onion and marjoram, and fry gently for 5 minutes.

4 Pour the water off the tomatoes. Drain, peel and chop coarsely, and add to the saucepan.

5 Add the tomato purée, seasoning and apple juice concentrate. Bring to the boil and simmer for 5 minutes.

6 Put the mixture in a blender and liquidize till smooth, or mix together well, using a potato masher.

7 Heat the oven to 180°C (350°F/Gas 4).

8 When the beans are cooked, drain well, reserving 100 ml (4 fl oz) of the cooking liquid. Add the beans and the liquid to the tomato sauce.

9 Mix well and pour into a casserole dish.

10 Put the bean mixture in the oven and bake, covered, for 1 hour. Serve on toast and with steamed vegetables.

Joey's Egg Curry

50 ml (2 tbsp) soya oil
5 ml (1 tbsp) poppy seeds
¼ tsp fennel seeds
1 large onion, chopped
15 ml (1 tbsp) Madras curry powder
1 green pepper, chopped
2 garlic cloves, crushed
400 ml (14 fl oz) Greek-style yogurt
50 g (2 oz) creamed coconut
100 ml (4 fl oz) orange juice
4 eggs, hard-boiled and shelled
salt and black pepper

Preparation and Cooking 20 minutes
Serves 4-6

1 Put the oil in a medium-sized saucepan. Add the poppy seeds and fennel seeds and cook over a medium heat, stirring occasionally.

2 Add the onion and curry powder. Stir well.

3 Add the green pepper and garlic and continue cooking for a further 5 minutes.

4 Mix in the yogurt, coconut and orange juice. Simmer gently for 5 minutes until the coconut has melted and you have a smooth sauce.

5 Add the eggs to the curry sauce. Season and serve immediately.

Serve with brown rice and a selection of chutneys and other traditional curry accompaniments.

Macaroni Cheese

25 g (1 oz) butter
1 onion, finely chopped
1 red pepper, thinly sliced
30 ml (2 tbsp) wholewheat flour
275 ml (½ pt) milk
175 g (6 oz) strong cheese, grated
¼ tsp grated nutmeg
salt and black pepper
175 g (6 oz) wholewheat macaroni
15 ml (1 tbsp) coarsely chopped
    fresh parsley

Preparation and Cooking 20 minutes
Serves 4

1 Melt the butter in a medium-sized saucepan and sauté the onion.

2 Add the red pepper and cook for 3-4 minutes.

3 Remove from the heat and stir in the wholewheat flour. Gradually add the milk, a little at a time.

4 Return to the stove and bring to the boil, stirring continuously. When the sauce begins to thicken, add the grated cheese, nutmeg and seasoning. Set aside.

5 Bring a saucepan half-full of water to the boil, add the macaroni and simmer for 10 minutes or until tender. Drain well.

6 Reheat the sauce till it bubbles. Add the macaroni and the chopped parsley. Stir through and serve immediately.

Millet Casserole

30 ml (2 tbsp) soya oil
1 small onion, chopped
50 g (2 oz) celeriac, chopped
100 g (4 oz) carrots, chopped
1 small green pepper, thinly sliced
100 g (4 oz) leeks, cut into rings
100 g (4 oz) whole millet
1 l (1¾ pt) water
5 ml (1 tsp) yeast extract
salt and black pepper
100 g (4 oz) cheese, grated
3 eggs, separated

Preparation 20 minutes
Cooking 30 minutes
Serves 4
GF

1 Heat the oven to 180°C (350°F/Gas 4).

2 Heat the oil in a medium-sized saucepan and sauté the onion, celeriac and carrots. Add the pepper and leeks.

3 Add the millet and stir-fry for 1 minute. Pour over the water and add the yeast extract and seasoning. Bring to the boil.

4 Add half the grated cheese and the egg yolks to the saucepan. Stir well.

5 Stiffly whip the egg whites and fold into the millet mixture.

7 Transfer to an ovenproof dish. Sprinkle the remaining cheese on top and bake for 30 minutes or until browned.

Mung Bean Casserole

100 g (4 oz) mung beans, soaked for
  4 hours
15 ml (1 tbsp) corn oil
1 large onion, chopped
1 red pepper, chopped
2.5 ml (½ tsp) mixed herbs
300 g (11 oz) broccoli, coarsely chopped
275 ml (½ pt) carrot juice
salt and black pepper
15 ml (1 tbsp) cashew nuts, to garnish

**Preparation 15 minutes (allow 4 hours
for soaking the beans)
Cooking 1 hour 5 minutes
Serves 4**
(GF) (V)

If you have a juicer, make your own carrot juice. Otherwise, bottled juice is fine.

1 Transfer the soaked beans and their liquid to a saucepan. Top up with fresh water, if necessary, to cover the beans. Cover, bring to the boil and then lower the heat and simmer for 45 minutes.

2 Meanwhile, heat the oil in a medium-sized saucepan, and add the chopped onion and red pepper. Add the mixed herbs and cook gently for 5 minutes.

3 Add the broccoli.

4 Pour over the carrot juice and simmer for 15 minutes.

5 Add the drained and cooked beans and season to taste.

6 Serve immediately, garnished with cashews.

Serve on a bed of bulgar, brown rice or couscous.

Pinto, Courgette & Mushroom Bake

75 g (3 oz) pinto beans, soaked for
  12 hours or overnight
50 g (2 oz) butter
1 large onion, finely chopped
15 ml (1 tbsp) tomato purée
10 ml (2 tsp) finely chopped fresh basil
  or 5 ml (1 tsp) dried
225 g (8 oz) courgettes, thinly sliced
225 g (8 oz) mushrooms, finely chopped
2 garlic cloves, crushed
salt and black pepper
4 tomatoes, sliced

Sauce
50 g (2 oz) butter
30 ml (2 tbsp) wholewheat flour
570 ml (1 pt) milk
150 g (5 oz) cheese, grated
salt and black pepper
2.5 ml (½ tsp) grated nutmeg
1 egg, beaten
15 ml (1 tbsp) finely chopped fresh
  parsley, to garnish

**Preparation 30 minutes (allow 12 hours
for soaking the beans)
Cooking 2 hours 20 minutes
Serves 6**

Flageolet or cannellini beans can be used instead of pinto beans.

1 Transfer the soaked beans and their liquid to a saucepan. Top up with fresh water, if necessary, to cover the beans. Cover and bring to the boil. Lower the heat and **simmer** for 1½ hours until tender. Drain and set aside.

2 Meanwhile, melt the first 50 g (2 oz) butter in a saucepan.

3 Add the onion and cook gently.

4 Stir in the tomato purée and basil.

5 Add the courgettes and mushrooms.

6 Add the garlic. Mix well and leave the vegetables to simmer on a low heat, covered, for 20 minutes.

7 Meanwhile, make the white sauce: melt 50 g (2 oz) butter. Remove from heat and stir in the wholewheat flour.

8 Gradually add the milk and return to the stove.

9 Heat gently, stirring continuously until the sauce thickens.

10 Pour half of the sauce into a jug and add the grated cheese to the remaining half in the saucepan. Cook for 1 minute, remove from heat and season if liked.

11 Add the cooked pinto beans, mix thoroughly and pour into a large ovenproof serving dish.

12 Heat the oven to 190°C (375°F/Gas 5).

13 Season the vegetables and pour over the beans.

Continued, page 110.

Pinto, Courgette & Mushroom Bake, continued from page 109.

14 Lay the tomatoes down the two longest sides of the dish, leaving a space so that the vegetables show in the middle.

15 To the remaining white sauce, add the nutmeg and a good sprinkling of black pepper.

16 Add the beaten egg to the sauce and carefully pour it over the vegetables, trying not to cover the tomatoes.

17 Bake for about 50 minutes or until the top is golden brown.

18 Serve garnished with chopped parsley.

Serve with a grain dish and a salad.

Ratatouille

1 large aubergine, chopped
30 ml (2 tbsp) olive oil
1 large onion, sliced
1 red pepper, thinly sliced
450 g (1 lb) courgettes, thinly sliced
45 ml (3 tbsp) tomato purée
450 g (1 lb) tomatoes, peeled and
   coarsely chopped
100 g (4 oz) mushrooms, thinly sliced
3 garlic cloves, crushed
salt and black pepper
finely chopped fresh parsley or
   coriander, to garnish

Preparation 30 minutes
Cooking 45 minutes-1 hour
Serves 4
(GF) (V)

1 Prepare the aubergine as necessary (see p. 27).

2 Heat the olive oil in a large saucepan. Add the onion and red pepper. Cook gently for 4-5 minutes.

3 Add the courgettes.

4 Add the aubergine with the tomato purée. Stir well.

5 Add the tomatoes and mushrooms.

6 Finally, add the garlic, season to taste, turn the heat down low and simmer gently for 45 minutes-1 hour, stirring occasionally, but taking care not to break up the vegetables too much. (You should not have to add any extra liquid if the vegetables are cooked gently.)

7 Before serving, sprinkle liberally with a garnish of chopped fresh parsley or coriander.

Serve with brown rice.

Red Pepper & Broccoli Quiche

Pastry
300 g (11 oz) fine wholewheat flour
2.5 ml (½ tsp) salt
50 ml (2 fl oz) soya oil
200 ml (7 fl oz) cold water

Filling
50 g (2 oz) butter
1 large onion, chopped
1 large red pepper, chopped
450 g (1 lb) broccoli, chopped
salt and black pepper
8 eggs
825 ml (1½ pt) milk
7.5 ml (1½ tsp) grated nutmeg
salt and black pepper
225 g (8 oz) cheese, grated

Preparation 30 minutes
Cooking 45 minutes
Serves 8-10

1 Heat the oven to 200°C (400°F/Gas 6).

2 Grease a 30 cm × 25 cm (12 in × 10 in) quiche dish. Sprinkle with a little of the wholewheat flour.

3 Make the pastry: put the flour and salt in a large mixing bowl or food processor. Add the oil and mix in thoroughly.

4 Slowly add the water. Stop mixing in the water as soon as the pastry holds together. Do not overbeat the mixture, or it will become rubbery.

5 Put the pastry dough on a flat floured surface and roll out to a thickness of 0.5 cm (¼ in). Line the quiche dish and flute the edges of the pastry. Prick the bottom and sides of the case with a fork and put in the oven for 10-15 minutes. Remove from the oven and put to one side.

6 Meanwhile, prepare the filling: melt the butter in a medium-sized saucepan and sauté the onion and pepper.

7 Add the broccoli to the other vegetables with some salt and pepper. Simmer gently for 10 minutes.

8 Break the eggs into a mixing bowl and beat them vigorously. Add the milk, grated nutmeg and seasoning.

9 Put the cooked vegetables in the bottom of the cooked pastry case. Sprinkle over the grated cheese, then pour over the sauce.

10 Bake for 45 minutes until golden brown on top. Remove from oven and leave to stand for 5 minutes before cutting.

Serve with steamed vegetables and a bean salad.

Preparing the quiche pastry

1 To line the quiche dish: roll the pastry on to the floured rolling pin so that it can be moved easily on to the dish.

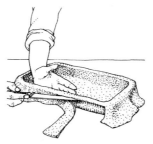

2 Trim the excess pastry away with a sharp knife, just under the rim of the quiche dish.

3 Flute the edges of the pastry for decoration, squeezing between your forefinger and thumb.

4 Prick the base of the pastry with a fork before putting in the oven.

Rice Balls

225 g (8 oz) brown rice
450 ml (16 fl oz) water
1 small onion, finely chopped
15 ml (1 tbsp) finely chopped
   fresh parsley
5 ml (1 tsp) grated root ginger
15 ml (1 tbsp) tahini (see p. 50)
15 ml (1 tbsp) tamari
15 ml (1 tbsp) sunflower seeds
1-2 garlic cloves, crushed
2.5 ml (½ tsp) coriander seeds (optional)
salt and black pepper
a little wholewheat flour and a few
   sesame seeds, for rolling
a little oil, for frying

Preparation 5-10 minutes
Cooking 50 minutes
Makes 8 rice balls

1 Put the rice and water in a large saucepan. Bring to the boil. Lower the heat and simmer, covered, for 45 minutes until the rice is cooked. Leave to cool and set aside.

2 Combine all the ingredients except the flour, sesame seeds and oil in a large bowl or food processor and mix together thoroughly for 3-4 minutes until the mixture holds together easily.

3 Sprinkle the wholewheat flour and sesame seeds on to a plate and mix together with your fingertips.

4 Using an ice cream scoop or your hands, form the rice mixture into small balls. Roll the balls in the flour and sesame seeds until well covered.

5 Heat enough oil for deep- or shallow-frying and when very hot gently lower the rice balls into the oil and fry for 2-3 minutes until golden brown.

6 Drain on absorbent kitchen paper.

Serve warm or cold with a vegetable dish or salad.

Savoury Kombu & Carrots

15 g (½ oz) kombu (see p. 44)
15 ml (1 tbsp) groundnut oil
1 onion, sliced into rings
225 g (8 oz) carrots, cut in
   thin matchsticks
275 ml (½ pt) water
30 ml (2 tbsp) tamari

Preparation 20-30 minutes
Cooking 20 minutes
Serves 4

This seaweed has a strong flavour. Try serving with a sprinkling of gomashio (see p. 50).

1 Put the kombu into a bowl and cover with boiling water. Leave for 20 minutes.

2 Heat the oil in a saucepan. Add the onion and carrots and sauté for 5 minutes or until the onion is soft.

3 Drain the kombu, cut into thin strips and add to the saucepan.

4 Pour over the water and tamari and simmer, without a cover, for 20 minutes.

Serve with a cooked grain and steamed vegetables.

Seaweed Rolls

225 g (8 oz) brown rice
450 ml (16 fl oz) water
¼ tsp grated root ginger
5 ml (1 tsp) tahini (see p. 50)
salt and black pepper
3 sheets of nori (see p. 44)
a little tamari
1 large carrot, cut into long thin strips
¼ cucumber, cut into long thin strips
3 umeboshi plums (see p. 51)

Preparation 15-20 minutes
Cooking 40-45 minutes
Chilling 1 hour
Serves 6
(GF) (V)

1 Put the rice and water in a large saucepan. Bring to the boil, lower the heat and simmer, covered, for 40-45 minutes until cooked.

2 Transfer the cooked and drained rice to a mixing bowl. Add the grated root ginger, tahini and seasoning and mix well.

3 Wave the smooth side of the nori over a gas flame or electric ring until it turns green.

4 Now you are ready to make the rolls: lay 1 slice of the nori on a dry, flat surface. Brush with a little tamari.

5 Divide the rice mixture into 3. Take one third of the rice in damp hands, squeeze together and roll into a sausage shape to fit the length of the seaweed. Press it down securely along the short side of the seaweed, flattening it with your hand.

6 Lay a strip of carrot and cucumber in the middle of the rice. Put an umeboshi plum in the middle. Roll up the seaweed. Make up the other seaweed rolls in a similar way.

7 Cut each roll in half. Refrigerate for about 1 hour before serving.

Serve with shoyu (see p. 51) or tamari.

Making the seaweed rolls

1 Wave the sheet of nori over the heat until the seaweed turns green.

2 Place the rice mixture, carrot, cucumber and umeboshi on the nori.

3 Roll up the nori carefully, starting from the side nearest to you.

Seitan with Hiziki

15 g (½ oz) hiziki (see p. 44)
30 ml (2 tbsp) soya oil
1 onion, finely chopped
5 ml (1 tsp) grated root ginger
1 courgette, finely chopped
15 ml (1 tbsp) tamari
1 garlic clove, crushed
275 ml (½ pt) water
225 g (8 oz) seitan (see p. 50)
5 ml (1 tsp) gomashio (see p. 50)

Preparation 20 minutes
Cooking 30 minutes
Serves 4-6

1 Pour boiling water over the hiziki and soak for 20 minutes.

2 Meanwhile, put the oil into a medium-sized saucepan and add the onion and ginger. Cook gently for about 5 minutes.

3 Add the courgette to the saucepan with the tamari and garlic.

4 Drain the hiziki, squeezing out excess water, and add to the pan.

5 Pour over the 275 ml (½ pt) water, then break the seitan into small pieces and add to the saucepan.

6 Simmer, covered, for 30 minutes. Garnish with gomashio.

Serve on a bed of brown rice with steamed vegetables.

Sesame Roast Parsnips

225 ml (8 fl oz) soya oil
50 g (2 oz) sesame seeds
50 ml (2 fl oz) tamari
900 g (2 lb) parsnips, sliced into strips

Preparation 5 minutes
Cooking 10 minutes
Serves 4

1 Heat the oven to 220°C (425°F/Gas 7).

2 Pour the oil into a baking dish and heat for a few minutes in the oven.

3 Add the sesame seeds and tamari and mix well.

4 Finally, add the parsnips and roast for about 10 minutes until brown on the outside and soft inside.

Serve with cooked grains and steamed vegetables.

Spinach & Mushroom Lasagne

550 g (1¼ lb) fresh spinach
¼ tsp grated nutmeg
salt and black pepper
225 g (8 oz) spinach wholewheat
   lasagne
grated cheese, to garnish

Mushroom sauce
25 g (1 oz) butter
2 large onions, thinly sliced
225 g (8 oz) mushrooms, thinly sliced
4 garlic cloves, crushed
10 ml (2 tsp) finely chopped fresh
   oregano or 5 ml (1 tsp) dried
5 ml (1 tsp) finely chopped fresh basil or
   2.5 ml (½ tsp) dried
60 ml (4 tbsp) tomato purée
400 g (14 oz) tin of tomatoes
15 ml (1 tbsp) tamari
5 ml (1 tsp) honey
salt and black pepper

Cheese sauce
75 g (3 oz) butter
60 ml (4 tbsp) fine wholewheat flour
570 ml (1 pt) milk
225 g (8 oz) strong cheese, grated
salt and black pepper

Preparation 30 minutes
Cooking 40 minutes
Serves 6-8

Use fresh spinach where possible. If not available, you can substitute frozen spinach.

1 Heat the oven to 180°C (350°F/Gas 4).

2 First make the mushroom sauce: melt the butter in a saucepan. Add the onions and sauté.

3 Add the mushrooms to the onions with the crushed garlic, oregano, basil and tomato purée.

4 Put the tinned tomatoes in a bowl and roughly break them up with a fork. Add to the sauce with the tamari, honey and seasoning and simmer for 10 minutes.

5 Now make the cheese sauce: melt the butter in another saucepan. Add the flour and cook over a high heat, stirring continuously for about 3 minutes.

6 Add the milk slowly, keeping the pan on a low heat and stirring throughout. Bring to the boil and simmer for 3 minutes. Remove from the heat and add the grated cheese and seasoning. Set aside.

7 Pack the spinach into a pan without any water. Place over a high heat for 1-2 minutes. Add the nutmeg and seasoning. Lower the heat and simmer for another 5 minutes.

8 Put a large pan of water on to boil and parboil the spinach lasagne by boiling for 8 minutes. Drain well.

9 Grease a large ovenproof dish. Line the bottom and sides with some of the parboiled lasagne. Proceed with alternate layers of cheese sauce, spinach, mushroom sauce and lasagne, finishing with a layer of cheese sauce. Sprinkle a little grated cheese on top.

10 Bake for 40 minutes or until browned on top.

Serve immediately with assorted steamed vegetables and salad.

Stir-fry Swiss Chard & Mushrooms

15 ml (1 tbsp) soya oil or 25 g (1 oz)
   butter
225 g (8 oz) Swiss chard, cut into strips
225 g (8 oz) mushrooms, thinly sliced
$\frac{1}{4}$ tsp grated nutmeg
10 ml (2 tsp) tamari
5 ml (1 tsp) roasted sesame seeds,
   to garnish

Preparation 5 minutes
Cooking 10 minutes
Serves 4
(GF) (V)

Any green leafy vegetable such as spinach or seakale can be used instead of the Swiss chard.

1 Heat the oil in a wok or large saucepan. Add the chard and cook over a high heat, stirring continuously for 3-4 minutes or until the chard begins to shrink in size.

2 Add the mushrooms, grated nutmeg and tamari and stir-fry for a further 5 minutes or until the mushrooms and chard are cooked.

3 Sprinkle over roasted sesame seeds and serve immediately.

Serve with brown rice, buckwheat or millet.

Stuffed Aubergines with Tomato Sauce

3 large aubergines
olive oil, for brushing
15 ml (1 tbsp) finely chopped fresh
   parsley or pecan nuts, to garnish

Sauce
450 g (1 lb) tomatoes
50 g (2 oz) butter
1 large onion, finely chopped
10 ml (2 tsp) finely chopped fresh
   oregano or 5 ml (1 tsp) dried
3 garlic cloves, crushed
salt and black pepper

Stuffing
75 g (3 oz) dried chestnuts, soaked for
   12 hours or overnight
100 g (4 oz) pecan nuts
100 ml (4 fl oz) fresh orange juice
100 g (4 oz) wholewheat breadcrumbs

Preparation 20 minutes (allow 12 hours for soaking the chestnuts)
Cooking 2 hours 15 minutes
Serves 6

You will need a blender for this recipe.

1 Begin to prepare the stuffing: put the chestnuts in a saucepan and cover with water. Bring to the boil, then lower the heat and simmer for $1\frac{1}{2}$ hours or until tender.

2 Meanwhile, cut the aubergines in half lengthwise, and scoop out the middles, leaving about 0.5 cm ($\frac{1}{4}$ in) all the way round. (Keep aubergine flesh for another recipe.) Salt inside of shell as necessary (see p. 27).

3 Make the sauce: put the tomatoes in a bowl, cover with boiling water and leave to stand for 10-15 minutes for the skins to soften.

4 Melt the butter in a saucepan and add the onion, oregano and garlic. Continue cooking for 5 minutes or until the onion is soft.

5 Pour the water off the tomatoes. Drain and peel the tomatoes, break them up and add to the onion. Cook for a further 5 minutes, season with black pepper and salt and set aside.

6 Heat the oven to 180°C (350°F/Gas 4).

7 Now you are ready to make the stuffing: put the pecans, orange juice and drained chestnuts in a blender. Liquidize till smooth.

8 Put the mixture into a bowl, add the breadcrumbs and mix well.

9 Divide the stuffing into 6 equal portions and fill the centres of the aubergines. Brush with olive oil and put in an ovenproof dish, covered with foil.

10 Bake for 45 minutes or until the aubergines are cooked.

11 Just before the aubergines are ready, reheat the tomato sauce and pour over the top. Garnish with chopped parsley or a sprinkling of pecan nuts.

Serve with a fresh salad and a grain dish.

Summer Okra Casserole

90 ml (6 tbsp) soya oil
2 onions, finely chopped
450 g (1 lb) potatoes, cubed
675 g (1½ lb) okra, topped, tailed and
    thinly sliced
400 g (14 oz) tinned tomatoes
2 green peppers, thinly sliced
salt and black pepper
30 ml (2 tbsp) finely chopped fresh
    oregano or 15 ml (1 tbsp) dried
4 garlic cloves, crushed

Preparation 20 minutes
Cooking 20 minutes
Serves 6
 GF V

Buy young, tender okra, as the large ones can be very tough and stringy. Okra can also have a rather slimy texture, which can be reduced by soaking the cut pieces in water beforehand.

1 Heat 45 ml (3 tbsp) of the oil in a large saucepan and sauté the onions for 5 minutes until soft.

2 Add the potatoes and cook for about 10 minutes until browned, stirring frequently to prevent sticking.

3 Heat the remaining oil in another large saucepan and add the okra. Sauté gently, stirring occasionally, for about 5 minutes, or until the okra is tender but still firm.

4 Add the tomatoes and green peppers and cook for a further 5 minutes.

5 When the potatoes are browned, add to the okra and mix well. Simmer gently for 10 minutes over a low heat. Season to taste.

6 A few minutes before serving, add the fresh oregano and crushed garlic.

Serve with brown rice, bulgar or any other grain.

Swede & Orange Pie

30 ml (2 tbsp) soya oil
1 large onion, finely chopped
1 large red pepper, finely chopped
2 small turnips, finely chopped
2.5 ml (½ tsp) ground cinnamon
15 ml (1 tbsp) tomato purée
15 ml (1 tbsp) tamari
450 g (1 lb) courgettes, finely chopped
100 g (4 oz) mushrooms, finely chopped
salt and black pepper

Topping
1 kg (2 lb 3 oz) swedes, chopped
50 ml (2 fl oz) soya oil or 50 g (2 oz)
    butter
juice and grated rind of 1 orange
50 g (2 oz) desiccated coconut
salt and black pepper

Preparation 15 minutes
Cooking 20 minutes
Serves 6
GF V

Puréed swedes with a hint of orange and coconut make this an unusual dish.

1 Heat the oven to 200°C (400°F/Gas 6).

2 First boil the swedes for the topping for 10 minutes or steam them for 15 minutes, until tender.

3 Meanwhile, heat 30 ml (2 tbsp) oil in a medium-sized saucepan and add the onion, red pepper and turnips.

4 Add the cinnamon, tomato purée and tamari and cook gently.

5 Add the courgettes and mushrooms to the saucepan. Cook for a further 8-10 minutes or until the vegetables are tender. Season to taste.

6 By now the swedes should be ready. Drain well.

7 Make the rest of the topping: add the oil, orange juice and rind and coconut to the swedes and blend to a smooth purée in a blender or with a potato masher. Season to taste.

8 Put the vegetables into an ovenproof dish and spread the swedes over the top.

9 Bake for 20 minutes until cooked through.

Serve immediately with a crisp green salad.

Tofu & Mushroom Flan

Pastry
225 g (8 oz) fine wholewheat flour
¼ tsp salt
5 ml (1 tsp) chopped dill leaves
50 ml (2 fl oz) soya oil
150 ml (¼ pt) cold water

Filling
15 ml (1 tbsp) olive oil
1 onion, finely chopped
1 garlic clove, crushed
225 g (8 oz) mushrooms, thinly sliced
30 ml (2 tbsp) shoyu (see p. 51)
¼ tsp black pepper
250 g (9 oz) tofu (see p. 51)
juice of 1 lemon

Preparation 20 minutes
Cooking 40 minutes
Serves 4-6
Ⓥ

1 Heat the oven to 200°C (400°F/Gas 6).

2 Grease a 23 cm (9 in) pie dish.

3 Put the wholewheat flour, salt and dill into a mixing bowl or food processor. Mix the soya oil in thoroughly.

4 Slowly mix in the water. Stop mixing in the water as soon as the pastry holds together. Do not overbeat, or the pastry will become tough and rubbery.

5 Put the pastry dough on a flat, floured surface. Roll out to a thickness of 0·5 cm (¼ in) and line the pie dish. Cut off the excess pastry round the edge, prick the bottom and the sides of the case with a fork and bake for 10 minutes or until the base is cooked. Remove from oven and set aside.

6 Meanwhile, make the filling: heat the olive oil in a frying pan and sauté the onion and garlic.

7 Add the mushrooms to the onion with the shoyu and black pepper. Cook gently for 5 minutes or until the onion is soft.

8 Meanwhile, put the tofu in a bowl. Add the lemon juice and mash well with a potato masher.

9 When the mushroom mixture is ready, remove from heat and stir in the tofu mixture.

10 Spoon the mushroom and tofu mixture into the precooked pastry case, return to the oven and bake for 30 minutes until the topping has set.

Serve warm or cold with a grain and salad dish.

◆

Unroasted Buckwheat Casserole

30 ml (2 tbsp) groundnut oil
150 g (5 oz) whole raw buckwheat
1 large onion, thinly sliced
1 green pepper, thinly sliced
2 carrots, thinly sliced
2.5 ml (½ tsp) caraway seeds
100 g (4 oz) mushrooms, thinly sliced
salt and black pepper
400 ml (14 fl oz) water
15 ml (1 tbsp) tamari
finely chopped fresh parsley, to garnish

Preparation 10 minutes
Cooking 20 minutes
Serves 4
Ⓖ🄵 Ⓥ

1 Heat the oil in a medium-sized saucepan. Add the buckwheat and gently sauté for 2-3 minutes until slightly browned. Add the green pepper, carrots and caraway seeds. Fry gently for 2-3 minutes.

2 Add the mushrooms to the saucepan and season.

3 Add the water and tamari. Bring to the boil. Lower heat and simmer for 20 minutes until the buckwheat is cooked. Remove from heat and serve, garnished with a sprinkling of parsley.

Serve with some steamed vegetables with a cheese sauce (see p. 114).

Vegetable Loaf with Couscous

100 g (4 oz) couscous
5 ml (1 tsp) soya grits (optional)
15 ml (1 tbsp) sesame oil
1 onion, thinly sliced into rings
4 celery sticks, thinly sliced
10 ml (2 tsp) finely chopped fresh basil
    or 5 ml (1 tsp) dried
15 ml (1 tbsp) tomato purée
100 g (4 oz) mushrooms, thinly sliced
15 ml (1 tbsp) tamari
salt and black pepper
6 slices of tomato
5 ml (1 tsp) gomashio (see p. 50)

Preparation 25 minutes
Chilling 4 hours (minimum)
Serves 4-6

(v)

This easy dish can look quite spectacular if the top and sides are decorated with slices of vegetables and/or nuts.

1 Put the couscous and soya grits, if using, in separate bowls. Cover both with boiling water and set aside for about 10 minutes until they puff up.

2 Meanwhile, heat the oil in a frying pan and sauté the onion and celery with the basil and tomato purée. Cook gently for 5 minutes.

3 Add the mushrooms, tamari and drained soya grits, if using. Cook for a further 5 minutes or until the vegetables are tender.

4 Add the drained couscous to the vegetables. Mix well and season to taste.

5 Grease a 15 cm × 9 cm × 7.5 cm (6 in × 3½ in × 3 in) loaf tin, line with a layer of greaseproof paper and grease again.

6 Put the tomato slices on the bottom of the loaf tin. Sprinkle with gomashio.

7 Pour the vegetables and couscous mixture into the loaf tin and press down well.

8 Chill in the refrigerator for at least 4 hours or overnight. Remove from refrigerator just before serving.

9 To serve, gently slide a knife between the sides of the tin and the paper. Turn out on to a serving dish and cut into slices.

Try serving with a tomato sauce (see p. 115) or yogurt sauce (see p. 86).

Preparing the tin and turning out the vegetable loaf

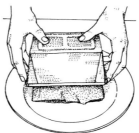

1 Place 6 tomato slices in the lined loaf tin and sprinkle gomashio over the top.

2 To turn out the cooked loaf, turn upside down on a plate, tap firmly and gently pull off the tin.

3 Peel off the greaseproof paper and the loaf is ready for slicing.

Wakame

40 g (1½ oz) wakame (see p. 44)
1 cucumber, thinly sliced

Dressing
50 g (2 oz) seasame seeds
15 ml (1 tbsp) soya oil
5 ml (1 tsp) mustard powder
75 ml (3 fl oz) brown rice vinegar
100 ml (4 fl oz) shoyu (see p. 51)

Preparation 20 minutes
Cooking 30 minutes
Serves 6-8

1 Put the wakame in a saucepan. Cover with boiling water and leave to stand for 20 minutes. Bring back to the boil and simmer for 30 minutes until the wakame is cooked.

2 Meanwhile, prepare the dressing: put the sesame seeds on a chopping board and chop them roughly with a large sharp knife to bring out their flavour.

3 Heat the oil in a small frying pan and add the sesame seeds. Stir-fry for 5-8 minutes or until the seeds are a golden brown colour. Remove from heat.

4 Mix together the mustard powder, rice vinegar and shoyu in a bowl or jug.

5 By now the wakame will be ready. Drain well and cut into small pieces. Arrange on a serving plate.

6 Add the cucumber.

7 Pour the dressing over the top and sprinkle with the sesame seeds.

Serve with brown rice and a side dish of vegetables.

Wholewheat Pizza

Dough
25 g (1 oz) fresh yeast
275 ml (½ pt) warm water
600 g (1 lb 5 oz) wholewheat flour
2.5 ml (½ tsp) salt

Sauce
400 g (14 oz) tinned tomatoes
10 ml (2 tsp) finely chopped fresh
    oregano or 5 ml (1 tsp) dried
3 garlic cloves
pinch of chilli powder
salt and black pepper

Topping
1 onion, thinly sliced
175 g (6 oz) mushrooms, sliced
250 g (9 oz) cheese, grated
1 green pepper, sliced
3 tomatoes, sliced in rings
12 black olives

Preparation 20 minutes (allow 1 hour proving time)
Cooking 15 minutes
Serves 6

1 Make the dough: crumble the yeast into the warm water and stir in 350 g (12 oz) of the flour to make a thick batter. Cover and leave in a warm place to rise for about 30 minutes.

2 Add the salt and work in the remaining flour until the dough holds together. Turn on to a lightly oiled surface and knead. The dough should be strong and elastic and not stick to your hands. Return to the bowl when smooth and leave in a warm place to rise for another 30 minutes.

3 Punch down, divide into 2 and roll out each piece on a lightly floured board.

4 Grease two 30 cm × 20 cm (12 in × 8 in) baking trays and line with the dough, pushing it well into the sides.

5 Heat the oven to 250°C (500°F/Gas 10).

6 Make the sauce: put all the ingredients into a blender and mix thoroughly. Alternatively mash thoroughly with a potato masher. Spread the sauce over the dough.

7 Make the topping: sprinkle over the chopped onion and mushrooms. Cover with cheese and decorate with the green pepper, tomatoes and olives.

8 Bake for about 15 minutes or until the base is cooked and the cheese and vegetables are slightly browned.

Serve with a selection of salads.

PUDDINGS

Note: Cashew Cream is a delicious substitute for cream or
yogurt to serve with puddings.

◆

Apple, Soya & Almond Pudding

675 g (1½ lb) cooking apples,
  finely chopped
150 ml (¼ pt) boiling water
100 g (4 oz) butter
50 ml (2 fl oz) honey
1 egg, beaten
juice and grated rind of 1 lemon
75 g (3 oz) ground almonds
25 g (1 oz) soya flour
¼ tsp vanilla essence
2.5 ml (½ tsp) baking powder (use
  appropriate baking powder for
  recipe, see p. 133)

Preparation 15 minutes
Cooking 30-40 minutes
Serves 4
Ⓖ Ⓕ

**You can substitute fresh plums or peaches for the apples, when
they are in season.**

1 Heat the oven to 180°C (350°F/Gas 4).

2 Put the apples into a medium-sized saucepan, add the water and
stew gently for 5 minutes.

3 In a bowl, cream together the butter and honey. Add the egg to
the creamed mixture and mix well.

4 Add the lemon juice and rind.

5 Add the almonds, soya flour, vanilla essence and baking powder
and beat together until you have a smooth mixture.

6 Put the apples in an ovenproof dish.

7 Spread the cake mixture over the top and bake for 30-40 minutes
or until golden brown on top.

Serve immediately with yogurt or cream.

Apricot & Orange Sago Cream

225 g (8 oz) dried apricots, soaked
    for 12 hours or overnight
juice and grated rind of 1 orange
570 ml (1 pt) milk
100 g (4 oz) sago
2 eggs, separated

**Preparation 20 minutes (allow 12 hours
for soaking the apricots)
Cooking 20 minutes
Chilling 2 hours minimum
Serves 4**

You will need a blender for this recipe.

1 Drain the apricots and reserve 4 for decoration. Purée the rest, together with the orange juice, in a blender and set aside.

2 Put the milk, sago and orange rind in a medium-sized saucepan and simmer gently for 15 minutes or until the sago is cooked. Stir occasionally to prevent sticking.

3 Add the egg yolks and heat gently for a further 5 minutes.

4 Remove from the heat and stir in the puréed apricots. Cool.

5 Whip the egg whites stiffly and fold into the cooled sago mixture.

6 Pour into 4 individual dishes and chill in the refrigerator for at least 2 hours before serving. Decorate with the reserved apricots.

Baked Apples

6 large cooking apples, cored

Stuffing
175 g (6 oz) mixed dried fruit,
    finely chopped
30 ml (2 tbsp) honey or apple juice
    concentrate (see p. 51)
5 ml (1 tsp) mixed spice
2.5 ml ($\frac{1}{2}$ tsp) ground cloves
75 g (3 oz) regular oats

**Preparation 10 minutes
Cooking 30 minutes
Serves 6**

The dried fruit needs to be chopped very finely, to ensure thorough cooking.

1 Heat the oven to 220°C (425°F/Gas 7).

2 Place the apples on a greased baking tray.

3 Make the stuffing: mix together the mixed dried fruit, honey, mixed spice, cloves and oats.

4 Using a teaspoon, fill the centres of the apples with the stuffing.

5 Bake in the oven for 30 minutes or until the apples are soft.

Serve warm with whipped cream, yogurt or custard.

Baked Bananas with Yogurt Sauce

15 ml (1 tbsp) honey
75 g (3 oz) butter
5 ml (1 tsp) mixed spice
6 bananas

Sauce
425 ml ($\frac{3}{4}$ pt) Greek-style yogurt
75 ml (3 fl oz) single cream
$\frac{1}{4}$ tsp ground cardamom
5 ml (1 tsp) grated nutmeg
15 ml (1 tbsp) honey
juice and grated rind of 1 orange or
    1 lemon

**Preparation 10 minutes
Cooking 20 minutes
Serves 6**

1 Heat the oven to 180°C (350°F/Gas 4).

2 Gently melt the honey and butter in a small saucepan and add the mixed spice.

3 Coat the bananas in the mixture and place on an oiled baking tray.

4 Bake for 20 minutes or until the bananas are soft.

5 Meanwhile, make the yogurt sauce: mix all the sauce ingredients together. Pour over the hot bananas and serve immediately.

Banana Frozen Yogurt

3 bananas
275 ml (½ pt) Greek-style yogurt
30 ml (2 tbsp) maple syrup
juice and grated rind of ½ lemon
   (optional)

Preparation 5 minutes
Freezing 5 hours minimum
Chilling 45 minutes
Serves 4
(GF)

You will need a blender for this recipe.

1 Put all the ingredients into a blender and liquidize till smooth.

2 Pour into a serving bowl or freezer container and put in the freezer for about 3 hours or until almost set.

3 Remove from the freezer and whip again with a hand whisk or electric food mixer.

4 Return to the freezer for about 2 hours or until completely set.

5 Refrigerate for about 45 minutes to soften slightly before serving.

Carob & Sunflower Mousse

250 g (9 oz) sunflower seeds
300 ml (11 fl oz) water
30 ml (2 tbsp) carob powder
15 ml (1 tbsp) pear and apple spread
   (see p. 51)
15 ml (1 tbsp) brandy (optional)

Preparation 5 minutes
Chilling 1 hour minimum
Serves 6
(GF) (V)

This very rich mousse should be served in small quantities. For a lighter, non-vegan mousse, fold in 2 whipped egg whites.
   You will need a blender for this recipe.

1 Put all the ingredients into a blender. Liquidize until smooth.

2 Pour into 6 individual dishes or a serving bowl and chill in the refrigerator for 1 hour before serving.

Cheesecake

Base
30 ml (2 tbsp) honey
25 g (1 oz) butter
75 g (3 oz) fine wholewheat flour
2.5 ml (½ tsp) baking powder

Topping
100 ml (4 fl oz) honey
100 g (4 oz) butter
60 ml (4 tbsp) potato flour
4 eggs, separated
juice and grated rind of 1 lemon or
   1 orange
500 ml (18 fl oz) yogurt
500 g (1 lb 2 oz) low-fat quark

Preparation 20 minutes
Cooking 1½ hours
Cooling 1 hour
Serves 8

1 Heat the oven to 170°C (325°F/Gas 3).

2 Grease and line a 23 cm (9 in) shallow cake tin.

3 Make the base: cream together the honey and butter in a bowl.

4 Add the flour and baking powder, to make a fairly crumbly dough.

5 Place the mixture in the prepared tin, press down well and bake for 15 minutes or until lightly browned. Remove from the oven. Turn the oven down to 150°C (300°F/Gas 2).

6 Make the topping: cream together the honey and butter.

7 Add the potato flour and mix it in.

8 Add the rest of the ingredients, apart from the egg whites, and mix thoroughly.

9 Beat the egg whites until stiff and carefully fold into the mixture. Pour over the precooked base.

10 Bake for 1¼ hours or until set.

11 Turn the oven off and leave for another hour so it can cool down slowly. Remove from the oven and serve chilled, if wished.

Cherry Pie

Pastry
225 g (8 oz) fine wholewheat flour
100 g (4 oz) butter or margarine
30 ml (2 tbsp) water
15 ml (1 tbsp) apple juice concentrate
(see p. 51)

Filling
675 g (1½ lb) cherries, unstoned
570 ml (1 pt) water
15 ml (1 tbsp) apple juice concentrate
(see p. 51)
20 ml (4 tsp) kuzu (see p. 50), crushed
grated rind of 1 lemon

Preparation 30 minutes
Cooking 10 minutes
Serves 8
Ⓥ

This pie is delicious hot or cold. A little vegetable oil can be substituted for the butter, if preferred.

1 Heat the oven to 200°C (400°F/Gas 6).

2 Grease a 23 cm (9 in) pie dish.

3 Put the cherries in a medium-sized saucepan and add the water. Bring to the boil and simmer for about 30 minutes or until cooked.

4 Meanwhile, prepare the pastry: put the wholewheat flour in a large mixing bowl. Rub in the butter with your fingers until the mixture resembles fine breadcrumbs.

5 Add the 30 ml (2 tbsp) water and 15 ml (1 tbsp) apple juice concentrate, and mix in with a knife or metal spoon until the pastry sticks together.

6 Roll out the pastry as thinly as possible on a lightly floured surface and line the prepared pie dish. Prick the base and sides of the pastry with a fork.

7 Bake for 10-15 minutes or until the pastry is cooked.

8 While the pastry is cooking, remove the cherries from the heat, reserving the cooking liquid. Set the cherries aside to cool for a few minutes, then take out the stones. Put the cherries in a bowl and set aside.

9 Pour the reserved cooking liquid into a measuring jug. Add 15 ml (1 tbsp) apple juice concentrate and top up with water to make 275 ml (½ pt) liquid.

10 Sprinkle the crushed kuzu into the saucepan in which the cherries were cooked and gradually add the liquid, taking care not to form any lumps.

11 Heat gently, stirring continuously, and cook for about 2 minutes until the sauce thickens. Remove from heat.

12 Stir in the lemon rind and cherries.

13 By now the pastry will be cooked. Pour the cherry mixture into the pastry case and set aside until needed.

Serve hot or cold. To reheat, cover with aluminium foil and heat gently at 170°C (325°F/Gas 3).

Christmas Puddings

250 ml (9 fl oz) soya oil
7.5 ml (1½ tsp) mixed spice
2.5 ml (½ tsp) grated nutmeg
5 ml (1 tsp) cinnamon
175 g (6 oz) fine wholewheat flour
800 g (1 lb 12 oz) honey
350 g (12 oz) sultanas
350 g (12 oz) raisins
350 g (12 oz) currants
75 g (3 oz) chopped almonds
juice and grated rind of 2 oranges
juice and grated rind of 2 lemons
1 large cooking apple, grated
6 eggs, beaten
250 ml (9 fl oz) stout
100 ml (4 fl oz) brandy

Preparation 30 minutes
Cooking 5 hours
Makes 4 × 900 g (2 lb) puddings

This recipe makes 4 good-sized puddings. Do not make more than 2 months in advance.

1 Mix all the ingredients together in a large bowl.

2 Grease four 900 g (2 lb) pudding bowls. Cut out 4 circles of greaseproof paper to fit the tops.

3 Weigh out 900 g (2 lb) of the mixture into each of the prepared pudding bowls and cover with greaseproof paper.

4 Steam each pudding for 3 hours or pressure-cook for 1 hour according to manufacturer's instructions.

5 Leave to cool. Wrap each pudding in calico, then store for between 2 weeks and 2 months in a cool place.

6 On the day on which the pudding is to be eaten, steam for 2 hours or pressure-cook for 45 minutes to 1 hour.

Serve with brandy butter and whipped cream or Cashew Cream (see p. 132).

Crustless Cheesecake

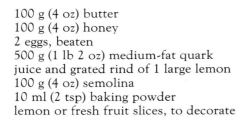

100 g (4 oz) butter
100 g (4 oz) honey
2 eggs, beaten
500 g (1 lb 2 oz) medium-fat quark
juice and grated rind of 1 large lemon
100 g (4 oz) semolina
10 ml (2 tsp) baking powder
lemon or fresh fruit slices, to decorate

Preparation 10 minutes
Cooking 1 hour
Serves 6-8

1 Heat the oven to 180°C (350°F/Gas 4).

2 Grease a 20 cm (8 in) loose-bottomed cake tin.

3 Cream together the butter and honey.

4 Gradually add the eggs and quark, mixing in alternately.

5 Mix in the lemon juice and rind.

6 Carefully mix in the semolina and baking powder. Pour the mixture into the prepared tin and bake on the bottom shelf of the oven for 1 hour or until set.

7 Remove from oven and leave to cool completely before removing from tin. Decorate with slices of lemon or other fresh fruit.

Fresh Fruit Flan

Base
50 g (2 oz) butter
100 g (4 oz) honey
150 g (5 oz) fine wholewheat flour
5 ml (1 tsp) baking powder

Topping
a mixture of fresh fruit (e.g. strawberries, peaches, apricots, etc.), sliced
100 ml (4 fl oz) black grape juice
10 ml (2 tsp) potato flour

Preparation 15 minutes
Cooking 25 minutes
Cooling 1 hour minimum
Serves 6-8

This flan is ideal for a dinner party, as it can be made in advance.

1 Heat the oven to 170°C (325°F/Gas 3).

2 Grease a 23 cm (9 in) tin and line with greased greaseproof paper.

3 Make the base: cream together the butter and honey in a bowl.

4 Add the flour and the baking powder and mix in. Press the dough into the base of the prepared tin and prick with a fork.

5 Bake for 20-25 minutes or until golden brown. Remove from the oven and leave to cool.

6 Prepare the topping: arrange the fresh fruit over the base.

7 Put the grape juice and potato flour into a small saucepan. Bring to the boil, stirring continuously, and simmer for 30 seconds.

8 Remove from heat and carefully spread over the top of the flan with a tablespoon.

9 Leave to cool for at least 1 hour before serving.

Gooseberry Fool

900 g (2 lb) gooseberries
275 ml (½ pt) water
30 ml (2 tbsp) honey
10 ml (2 tsp) kuzu (see p. 50)
150 ml (¼ pt) double cream
2 egg whites (optional)

Preparation 30 minutes
Chilling 2 hours
Serves 4
(GF)

1 Put the gooseberries in a medium-sized saucepan with the water. Boil gently for 5 minutes or until the gooseberries are soft.

2 Add the honey and kuzu and cook for a further 5 minutes. Cool.

3 Meanwhile, whip the cream and egg whites (if using) until stiff, in separate bowls.

4 Mix the cream into the gooseberry mixture, then gently fold in the egg white.

5 Put into individual serving glasses and chill in the refrigerator for 2 hours before serving.

Hunza Cream

250 g (9 oz) hunza apricots (see p. 39), soaked for 12 hours or overnight
250 g (9 oz) Greek-style sheep's milk yogurt
2 egg whites
grated rind of 1 lemon

Preparation 10 minutes (allow 12 hours for soaking the apricots)
Chilling 30 minutes minimum
Serves 4-5

You will need a blender for this recipe.

1 Take the stones out of the apricots and put the diced flesh into a blender.

2 Add the yogurt and blend till smooth. Pour into a bowl.

3 Whip the egg whites until stiff and fold them into the apricot and yogurt mixture.

4 Add the grated lemon rind and pour the mixture into a serving bowl or individual dishes and chill for at least 30 minutes before serving the cream.

Peach & Brandy Ice Cream

675 g (1½ lb) fresh peaches
4 egg yolks
275 ml (½ pt) single cream
30 ml (2 tbsp) acacia honey
30 ml (2 tbsp) brandy

Preparation 20 minutes
Freezing 5 hours
Chilling 45 minutes
(GF)

You will need a blender for this recipe.

1 Put the peaches into a large bowl and pour over boiling water. Set aside for about 10 minutes to allow the skins to soften.

2 Put the egg yolks and cream into the top of a double boiler, or into a bowl over a pan of boiling water and cook gently until the mixture thickens.

3 Pour the water off the peaches. Drain, peel and stone the peaches.

4 Put the peach flesh, honey and brandy into a blender and liquidize till smooth.

5 Add the cream and egg yolks, liquidize and check for sweetness. (Remember, the mixture will not taste as sweet when frozen.)

6 Pour into a bowl or freezer container and put into the freezer for about 3 hours or until almost set.

7 Remove from the freezer and whip thoroughly with a hand whisk or electric food mixer.

8 Return to the freezer for about 2 hours or until completely set.

9 Chill in the refrigerator for about 45 minutes to soften slightly before serving.

Peach Custard Tart

Base
225 g (8 oz) cake crumbs
30 ml (3 tbsp) brandy or water

Custard
2 peaches
5 ml (1 tsp) vanilla essence
275 ml (½ pt) single cream
15 ml (1 tbsp) maple syrup
3 eggs

Topping
4 peaches
10 ml (2 tsp) maple syrup
5 ml (1 tsp) kuzu (see p. 50)

Preparation 25 minutes
Cooking 55 minutes
Chilling 3 hours minimum
Serves 6

1 Heat the oven to 220°C (425°F/Gas 7).

2 Grease a 23 cm (9 in) circular cake tin.

3 Put the 6 peaches for the custard and the topping in a large bowl. Pour over boiling water. Set aside for about 10 minutes to allow the skins to soften.

4 Meanwhile, in another bowl, combine the cake crumbs and brandy. Press the mixture on to the base of the prepared cake tin.

5 Bake for 10 minutes until the base is firm.

6 While the base is cooking, prepare the custard: remove the skins and stones from 2 of the peaches and put the flesh into a blender.

7 Add the vanilla essence, cream, maple syrup and eggs and liquidize until the custard is smooth.

8 When the base is ready, remove it from oven and turn the heat down to 200°C (400°F/Gas 6).

9 Pour the custard over the base and put the tart into the oven. Cook for another 40-45 minutes or until the custard has set.

10 While the custard is cooking, make the topping: remove the skins and stones from 2 more peaches. With a fork or in a blender, liquidize the peaches. Transfer the purée into a small saucepan.

11 Add the maple syrup to the peach purée and heat the mixture gently. Sprinkle the kuzu on top and cook gently until thickened. Set aside.

12 Cut the remaining 2 peaches into thin slices.

13 When the custard has set, remove base from oven and set aside for at least 10 minutes to allow the cake to cool a little. When cooled, arrange the peach slices along the edges on top of the cake and pour the peach purée into the space in the middle. Using a small pastry brush, lightly coat the outsides of the peach slices with the purée.

Chill for at least 3 hours before serving.

Peach & Pear Crumble

4 peaches
2 pears
30 ml (2 tbsp) apple juice concentrate
(see p. 51)

Crumble topping
100 g (4 oz) regular oats
100 g (4 oz) fine wholewheat flour
2.5 ml (½ tsp) ground ginger
30 ml (2 tbsp) soya oil
30 ml (2 tbsp) apple juice concentrate
(see p. 51)

**Preparation 15 minutes
Cooking 1 hour
Serves 4**
Ⓥ

A few sesame or sunflower seeds can be added to the crumble for a nuttier flavour and texture.

1 Heat the oven to 180°C (350°F/Gas 4).

2 Put the peaches in a bowl and pour over boiling water. Set aside for about 10 minutes to allow the skins to soften.

3 Meanwhile, cut the pears into quarters. Remove the cores, and peel if tough. Cut into slices and put in an ovenproof dish.

4 To make the crumble: put the oats, flour and ginger in a mixing bowl.

5 Add the oil and 30 ml (2 tbsp) apple juice concentrate and mix in with a spoon or your fingertips.

6 Pour the water off the peaches. Drain, peel and remove the stones. Cut into slices and add to the ovenproof dish with the pears and 30 ml (2 tbsp) apple juice concentrate.

7 Sprinkle the crumble mixture over the top and bake on the bottom shelf of the oven for 1 hour or until the topping is golden brown.

Serve with whipped cream, custard or yogurt.

Polenta Pudding with Seasonal Fruit

570 ml (1 pt) milk
100 g (4 oz) polenta
100 g (4 oz) raisins
5 ml (1 tsp) vanilla essence
25 g (1 oz) butter
15 ml (1 tbsp) honey
juice and grated rind of 1 lemon
    (optional)
75 g (3 oz) pecan nuts, broken into
    small pieces
sliced fresh seasonal fruit, to decorate

Preparation 10 minutes
Chilling 2 hours minimum
Serves 8
(GF)

Instead of seasonal fruit, try spreading a fruit purée over the top. Dried apricots are particularly delicious, or puréed rhubarb or apple thickened and sweetened with a little kuzu (see p. 50) and honey.

1 Put the milk in a medium-sized saucepan and warm till just below boiling. Put the polenta into a bowl. Pour over the warm milk slowly. Mix thoroughly and return to saucepan.

2 Bring to the boil, stirring all the time. Simmer for 5 minutes: the mixture should be rather stiff.

3 Remove from heat. Add the raisins, vanilla essence, butter and honey. Mix in well.

4 Add the lemon juice and rind to the mixture.

5 Stir in the pecans. Set aside.

6 Grease and line a 30 cm × 20 cm (12 in × 8 in) baking tray. Press the mixture into the tray, smoothing down the surface with a flat spatula. Leave to cool for at least 2 hours. The polenta will have set hard by this time.

7 Cut the polenta into slices and decorate each with the fresh fruit.

Serve with fresh whipped cream or yogurt.

◆

Prune & Raspberry Whip

225 g (8 oz) dried prunes, soaked for
    12 hours or overnight
275 ml ($\frac{1}{2}$ pt) prune juice (water from
    soaked prunes)
250 g (9 oz) tofu (see p. 51)
30 ml (2 tbsp) maple syrup
juice and grated rind of 1 lemon
175 g (6 oz) fresh raspberries or
    strawberries

Preparation 5 minutes (allow 12 hours for soaking the prunes)
Chilling 1 hour minimum
Serves 4-6
(V)

You will need a blender for this recipe.

1 Remove the stones from the prunes.

2 Put the prune flesh, prune juice, tofu, maple syrup, lemon juice and rind into a blender. Reserve a few raspberries for decoration and add the rest to the blender.

3 Liquidize till smooth. Pour into a serving bowl or individual dishes and chill for at least 1 hour before serving. Decorate with the reserved raspberries.

Main Courses (See p. 97)

From top, clockwise: **Tofu & Mushroom Flan** (see p. 117), **Swede & Orange Pie** (see p. 116), **Red Pepper & Broccoli Quiche** (see p. 111), **Wholewheat Pizza** (see p. 119).

Rice Balls (see p. 112) on a bed of watercress leaves.

Wakame (see p. 119) combines seaweed and sesame seeds.

Joey's Egg Curry (see p. 108) on rice and chickpeas.

Deliciously spicy **Aubergine & Potato Curry** (see p. 98).

Savoury Kombu & Carrots (see p. 112) is light and tasty.

Cauliflower & Carrots with Spicy Hazelnut Sauce (see p. 103).

Baked Avocado with Stilton & Walnuts (see p. 98).

Summer Okra Casserole (see p. 116) includes oregano.

Seitan with Hiziki (see p. 113) is high in protein.

Black Bean Chilli (see p. 100) is succulent and very spicy.

Cashew Cream (see p. 132) is a delicious topping.

Rhubarb & Banana Crumble (see p. 129) is a crunchy, high-fibre pudding.

Tropical Fruit Salad (see p. 132) is a lovely combination of flavours.

This **Christmas Pudding** (see p. 124) is packed with fruit, nuts and spices.

Use **natural yogurt** (see p. 47) instead of cream.

Apricot & Orange Sago Cream (see p. 121) is a rich but sugar-free dessert.

Rice Pudding (see p. 130) is made with brown rice for texture and flavour.

Peach & Brandy Ice Cream (see p. 126) has a smooth, luxurious taste.

Baked Bananas with Yogurt Sauce (see p. 121) has a coating of rich caramel.

You can use any fruit to top **Polenta Pudding with Seasonal Fruit** (see p. 128).

Gooseberry Fool (see p. 125) is a light dessert, sweet with a hint of sharpness.

Hunza Cream (see p. 125) is a low-fat dessert made from dried hunza apricots.

Strawberries and lychees are the topping for **Fresh Fruit Flan** (see p. 125).

Apple, Soya & Almond Pudding (see p. 120) is a warming winter pudding.

Strawberry Mousse (see p. 130) uses soya milk for an unusual, creamy flavour.

Carob & Sunflower Mousse (see p. 122) uses carob as a substitute for chocolate.

Prune & Raspberry Whip (see p. 128) is sweetened naturally with maple syrup.

Rhubarb & Almond Mousse (see p. 129) is light and fluffy, with a nutty taste.

Redcurrant & Raspberry Summer Pudding

450 g (1 lb) redcurrants
450 g (1 lb) raspberries
45 ml (3 tbsp) agar-agar flakes (see p. 43)
15-30 ml (1-2 tbsp) honey or maple syrup
6-8 slices wholewheat bread, crusts removed

Preparation 20 minutes
Chilling 3 hours minimum
Serves 6
(V)

This traditional recipe uses redcurrants and raspberries, but any combination of berry fruits can be used, as available.

1 Put the redcurrants and raspberries in a heavy-bottomed saucepan with no added water. Heat gently and simmer for 5 minutes.

2 Sprinkle on the agar-agar and simmer for another 5 minutes.

3 Remove from heat and stir in the honey to taste.

4 Line a 900 g (2 lb) pudding bowl with slices of wholewheat bread, making sure there are no gaps between the slices.

5 Pour the fruit mixture into the lined bowl and chill for at least 3 hours, or preferably overnight.

6 Just before serving, loosen the pudding round the edges with a knife and turn it out on to a plate.

Serve with whipped cream or yogurt.

Rhubarb & Almond Mousse

570 ml (1 pt) unsweetened soya milk
15 ml (1 tbsp) agar-agar flakes (see p. 43)
225 g (8 oz) stewed rhubarb
30 ml (2 tbsp) apple juice concentrate (see p. 51)
50 g (2 oz) ground almonds
1 small banana (optional)

Preparation 15 minutes
Chilling 2 hours minimum
Serves 4
(GF) (V)

You will need a blender for this recipe.

1 Pour the soya milk into a saucepan and add the agar-agar flakes.

2 Bring to the boil and simmer for 5 minutes, stirring occasionally.

3 Remove the milk from the heat and pour into a blender.

4 Add the stewed rhubarb, apple juice concentrate, ground almonds and banana, if using.

5 Liquidize for 2-3 minutes till smooth.

6 Pour the mousse into a serving dish or individual dishes and chill for at least 2 hours.

Rhubarb & Banana Crumble

900 g (2 lb) rhubarb, finely chopped
3 bananas
juice and grated rind of 1 orange
45 ml (3 tbsp) honey
100 g (4 oz) millet flakes
175 g (6 oz) 85% self-raising wholewheat flour
15 ml (1 tbsp) sunflower seeds
15 ml (1 tsp) ground giner
75 g (3 oz) butter

Millet flakes are used in this crumble topping, but any other grain could be added.

1 Heat the oven to 190°C (375°F/Gas 5).

2 Put the rhubarb in an ovenproof dish. Slice the bananas and put on top.

3 Pour the orange juice over the rhubarb and bananas.

Continued, page 130 *Continued, page 130*

Rhubarb & Banana Crumble, continued from page 129.

Preparation 15 minutes
Cooking 40 minutes
Serves 6

4 Pour 30 ml (2 tbsp) honey over the top. If your honey is set and not runny, first heat gently in a pan until soft.

5 Put the millet flakes, wholewheat flour, sunflower seeds, ginger and orange rind in a mixing bowl.

6 Melt the butter and remaining honey together. Pour over the dry ingredients and mix thoroughly.

7 Cover the rhubarb with the crumble and bake for 40 minutes or until golden brown.

Serve with yogurt or cream.

Rice Pudding

200 g (7 oz) brown rice
good pinch of salt
60 ml (4 tbsp) honey
50 g (2 oz) butter
200 ml (7 fl oz) water
1 l (1¾ pt) milk

Preparation 10 minutes
Cooking 3-3½ hours
Serves 6
(GF)

1 Heat the oven to 150°C (300°F/Gas 2).

2 Wash the rice and put in a large ovenproof dish with the salt, honey and butter.

3 Boil the water and pour over the rice. Heat the milk to just below boiling and pour over the rice. Mix together well.

4 Bake, uncovered, for 3-3½ hours, stirring the skin in every 30 minutes. When cooked, the grains of the rice should be soft and the texture of the pudding thick but moist.

Serve warm or cold on its own, with cream or yogurt.

Strawberry Mousse

570 ml (1 pt) unsweetened soya milk
15 ml (1 tbsp) agar-agar flakes
   (see p. 43)
about 225 g (8 oz) strawberries, hulled
15 ml (1 tbsp) maple syrup

Preparation 10 minutes
Chilling 4 hours minimum
Serves 4
(GF) (V)

This mousse is made without eggs or dairy products, but is wonderfully rich and creamy.
  You will need a blender for this recipe.

1 Pour the soya milk into a saucepan and add the agar-agar flakes.

2 Bring to the boil and simmer for 5 minutes, stirring occasionally.

3 Pour the soya milk and agar-agar into a blender. Add the strawberries and the maple syrup and blend for 2-3 minutes until smooth.

4 Pour the mousse into a serving bowl or individual dishes and chill in the refrigerator for at least 4 hours.

5 Decorate with fresh strawberries before serving.

Sweet Potato Pie

Pastry
225 g (8 oz) fine wholewheat flour
100 g (4 oz) butter
30 ml (2 tbsp) water
15 ml (1 tbsp) apple juice concentrate
(see p. 51)

Filling
450 g (1 lb) sweet potatoes, peeled and
  cut into small pieces
25 g (1 oz) butter
30 ml (2 tbsp) honey
2.5 ml ($\frac{1}{2}$ tsp) ground cinnamon
$\frac{1}{4}$ tsp ground ginger
pinch of salt

Glaze
juice and grated rind of $\frac{1}{2}$ lemon
15 ml (1 tbsp) honey

Preparation 25 minutes
Cooking 15 minutes
Chilling 1 hour
Serves 6-8

For a special occasion, lay slices of fresh fruit over the sweet potato mixture before adding the glaze. Peaches or nectarines are particularly delicious when in season.

1 Heat the oven to 200°C (400°F/Gas 6).

2 Boil or steam the potatoes for 10-15 minutes.

3 Grease a 23 cm (9 in) pie dish.

4 Make the pastry: put the wholewheat flour into a mixing bowl. Rub in the butter with your fingers until the mixture resembles fine breadcrumbs.

5 Add the water and apple juice concentrate. Mix in with a knife or metal spoon until the mixture holds together.

6 Roll the pastry out on a lightly floured board as thinly as possible and line the prepared pie dish. Prick the sides and base of the pastry with a fork.

7 Bake for about 15 minutes or until the pie crust is cooked.

8 When the sweet potatoes are cooked, drain well and add the butter, honey, cinnamon, ginger and salt. Mash well with a potato masher or in a food processor.

9 Remove the cooked pastry case from the oven and spoon in the sweet potato mixture. Smooth down evenly.

10 Make the glaze: mix the lemon juice and rind with the honey. Then, using a pastry brush or the back of a spoon, spread the glaze over the pie and chill in the refrigerator for 1 hour before serving.

Serve with whipped cream or yogurt.

Tapioca & Lime Soufflés

50 g (2 oz) tapioca
570 ml (1 pt) milk
25 ml (5 tsp) honey
2.5 ml ($\frac{1}{2}$ tsp) vanilla essence
grated rind of 1-2 small limes
2 egg whites
20 g ($\frac{3}{4}$ oz) butter

Preparation 20 minutes
Cooking 15 minutes
Makes 8

These individual soufflés need to be served immediately they are cooked and ready.

1 Heat the oven to 180°C (350°F/Gas 4).

2 Put the tapioca, milk, honey, vanilla essence and grated lime rind into a saucepan. Bring to the boil and simmer gently for 15 minutes, stirring occasionally.

3 Whip the egg whites until stiff. Set aside.

4 Remove the tapioca from the stove and mix in the butter.

5 Fold in the whipped egg whites and pour the mixture into 8 buttered ramekin dishes.

6 Bake for 10-15 minutes or until soufflés are well risen and browned on top. Serve immediately.

Traditional Apple Crumble

675 g (1½ lb) cooking apples
150 ml (¼ pt) water
50 ml (2 fl oz) apple juice concentrate
  (see p. 51)
5 ml (1 tsp) ground cinnamon
225 g (8 oz) fine wholewheat flour
100 g (4 oz) butter
50 ml (2 fl oz) honey
5 ml (1 tsp) grated lemon rind

Preparation 15 minutes
Cooking 45-50 minutes
Serves 6

1 Heat the oven to 180°C (350°F/Gas 4).

2 Cut the apples into very small pieces. Put into an ovenproof dish.

3 Pour the water, apple juice concentrate and cinnamon into a mixing jug. Mix together and pour over the apples.

4 Put the flour in a mixing bowl. Gently rub in the butter with your fingertips.

5 Add the honey and grated lemon rind: stir in carefully with a metal spoon.

6 Pour the crumble topping over the apple and bake at the bottom of the oven for 45-50 minutes or until the topping is browned.

Serve immediately with whipped cream or yogurt.

Tropical Fruit Salad

1 large mango
1 papaya
1 pineapple
2 ripe bananas
1 ripe avocado
2 granadillas (see p. 35)
juice and grated rind of 1 lime
15 ml (1 tbsp) desiccated coconut
2 kiwifruits, sliced, to decorate

Preparation 10 minutes
Serves 4
(GF) (V)

1 Cut the mango, papaya, pineapple, bananas and avocado into small pieces in a large serving bowl.

2 Scoop out the granadillas and add to the bowl.

3 Add the lime juice and rind to the salad together with the desiccated coconut. Mix well.

4 Decorate the top with sliced kiwifruit.

Serve with a creamy Greek-style yogurt or Cashew Cream (see next recipe).

Cashew Cream

250 g (9 oz) cashew nuts
300 ml (11 fl oz) water
15 ml (1 tbsp) apple juice concentrate
  (see p. 51)

Preparation 5 minutes
Serves 10
(GF) (V)

This makes a delicious substitute for cream on cakes, puddings and pastries.
  You will need a blender for this recipe.

1 Put all the ingredients into a blender.

2 Liquidize for 3-4 minutes until a smooth thick paste is formed. Transfer to a serving bowl.

CAKES, PASTRIES, BISCUITS & SCONES

Introduction to making cakes

The light, delicate texture which characterises a sponge cake is achieved by techniques that are in many ways opposite to those used when making bread (see p. 147). Unlike bread, once the flour has been added to the wet ingredients, the barest mixing is sufficient or else the cake will have a tough, bread-like consistency. For the best results, you can use a hand whisk. Again, cakes are generally risen with a swiftly acting chemical raising agent, usually baking powder, rather than with yeast which requires time to work.

Baking powder is a mixture of an alkali (bicarbonate of soda or 'baking soda') and an acid (cream of tartar) in a base of wheat flour. When the liquid is added, the alkali and acid elements form a chemical reaction which releases gases that aerate the sponge. Baking powder only works until this reaction is exhausted, so it is vital to get a cake into the oven as quickly as possible once the liquid ingredients have been added. Some recipes include acid ingredients such as sour milk or lemon and therefore only require the use of bicarbonate of soda; however as a general rule baking powder and baking soda are not interchangeable.

Rather than adding baking powder to plain flour, many people prefer to use self-raising flour, where a proportion of baking powder has been premixed with the flour. The main advantages are convenience and a consistent rise for cakes and scones. However, different cake recipes call for different proportions of baking powder to flour, so you will probably get better results if you buy plain flour and add your own baking powder. Baking powder usually consists of sodium bicarbonate and wheat flour. A low-sodium, gluten-free baking powder is also now available, consisting of potassium bicarbonate and potato flour.

Cake tins

Cake tins with a non-stick finish do not as a rule need greasing, but you should follow manufacturer's instructions where applicable. All other tins will need greasing: oil, margarine or butter may be used.

For the following recipes, you should line the cake tins: use good quality greaseproof paper lightly brushed with oil or rubbed with margarine or butter. If wished, the greased tins can be sprinkled with a little flour to avoid sticking.

To line a cake tin, you will need to cut a circle of greaseproof paper for the base and a long strip to go round the sides. Cut the strip of paper about 5 cm (2 in) longer than the circumference of the cake tin, and about 2.5 cm (1 in) wider for an overlap. To fit it into the tin, make a few small cuts along the length on one side, so that the paper can bend at the base.

To test whether a cake is cooked

To test whether a cake is fully cooked, insert a skewer which should come out clean, or press the top of the cake gently with your finger – the sponge should spring back up when pressure is released. Always remove a cake from the oven gently and carefully: if you bang it down, it is likely to sink. After removing the cake from the oven, leave it in the tin for 10 minutes. By leaving the cakes to cool in this way they will shrink from the sides of the tin, making them easier to turn out. A round-bladed knife can be used to ease the cake out if necessary. Turn it out on to a wire rack and peel off the greaseproof paper.

Apple Sauce Cake

100 ml (4 fl oz) soya oil
100 ml (4 fl oz) honey or maple syrup
150 ml (5 fl oz) apple purée (not
  too runny)
75 g (3 oz) raisins or sultanas
225 g (8 oz) fine wholewheat flour
5 ml (1 tsp) ground cinnamon
¼ tsp ground allspice
5 ml (1 tsp) baking soda
pinch of salt (optional)
water or fruit juice, if necessary

Preparation 10 minutes
Cooking 1-1¼ hours
Makes 18 cm (7 in) round cake
Ⓥ

1 Heat the oven to 170°C (325°F/Gas 3).

2 Grease an 18 cm (7 in) deep round cake tin and line with greaseproof paper.

3 In a food processor or large mixing bowl combine the oil, honey and apple purée.

4 In another bowl, combine all the dry ingredients, mixing well.

5 Add the dry ingredients to the oil, honey and apple purée. Mix in gently but thoroughly. (You should be able to pour the mixture into the cake tin: if it is too stiff, add a little water or fruit juice.)

6 Pour the mixture into the prepared cake tin and bake for about 1 hour until golden brown, or until a skewer inserted into the cake comes out clean.

7 Remove from the oven and leave to cool before turning out.

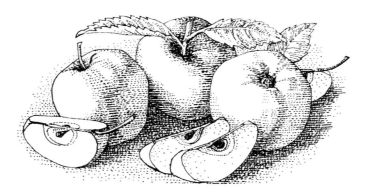

Bakewell Tart

Base
30 ml (2 tbsp) honey
25 g (1 oz) butter
75 g (3 oz) fine wholewheat flour
2.5 ml (½ tsp) baking powder
200 g (7 oz) sugar-free raspberry jam
  (see p. 52)

Topping
100 g (4 oz) butter
100 g (4 oz) honey
2 eggs, beaten
5 ml (1 tsp) almond essence
100 g (4 oz) soya flour, sifted
10 ml (2 tsp) baking powder, sifted

Preparation 20 minutes
Cooking 1 hour 50 minutes
Makes 23 cm (9 in) round cake

This delicious tea-time cake can also be eaten warm as a pudding.

1 Heat the oven to 170°C (325°F/Gas 3).

2 Grease a 23 cm (9 in) shallow round cake tin and line with greaseproof paper.

3 For the base: cream together the honey and butter in a bowl.

4 Add the flour and baking powder, to make a fairly crumbly dough. Line the base of the prepared tin with the dough and bake for 15 minutes or until lightly browned. Turn the oven down to 150°C (300°F/Gas 2).

5 Spread the jam over the precooked base.

6 For the topping: cream together the butter, honey and eggs in a bowl.

7 Add the almond essence. Mix in the soya flour and baking powder.

8 Spread the topping over the jam, taking care not to squeeze all the jam to the outside. (To counteract this, try putting little dots of topping on the jam, spreading each very carefully.)

9 Bake in the centre of the oven for 1-1½ hours, until set and golden brown or until a skewer inserted into the cake comes out clean.

10 Remove from oven and leave to cool before turning out.

Making the bakewell tart

1 Press the base mixture into the lined cake tin with a spatula.

2 After the jam has been spooned over the base, spoon the topping over the jam in large blobs, then spread into each other with a spatula.

Banana Cream Cake

This cake can also be served as an attractive pudding, decorated with chopped bananas and nuts.

Base
700 g (1 lb 5 oz) cake crumbs
200 ml (7 fl oz) fruit juice

Topping
400 g (14 oz) bananas
50 ml (2 fl oz) honey
¼ tsp grated nutmeg
6 eggs
juice and grated rind of 1 lemon
570 ml (1 pt) milk

Preparation 15 minutes
Cooking 20 minutes
Serves 12

1 Heat the oven to 180° C (350°F/Gas 4).

2 Grease a 25 cm × 30 cm (10 in × 12 in) shallow cake tin and line with greaseproof paper.

3 Make the base: put the cake crumbs and fruit juice into a large bowl and beat together thoroughly. Press into the bottom of the tin, making sure the mixture reaches right into the corners, and bake for about 10 minutes while you make the topping.

4 Make the topping: put the bananas into a mixing bowl and beat till smooth.

5 Add the honey, nutmeg, eggs, juice and rind and beat again.

6 Add the milk and mix thoroughly.

7 Remove the base from the oven and pour over the banana cream mixture.

8 Return to the middle of the oven and cook for 20 minutes or until the banana cream has set.

9 Remove from oven and leave to cool before cutting.

Banana Nut Cake

225 g (8 oz) bananas
75 ml (3 fl oz) soya oil
75 ml (3 fl oz) honey
2 eggs, beaten
juice and grated rind of 1 lemon
100 g (4 oz) raisins
50 g (2 oz) hazelnuts
350 g (12 oz) fine wholewheat flour
2.5 ml ($\frac{1}{2}$ tsp) baking soda
25 g (1 oz) broken cashew nuts

Preparation 10 minutes
Cooking 1 hour 20 minutes
Makes 800 g (1 lb 12 oz) loaf cake

1 Heat the oven to 170°C (325°F/Gas 3).

2 Grease an 18 cm × 11.5 cm × 8.5 cm (7$\frac{1}{4}$ in × 4$\frac{1}{2}$ in × 3$\frac{1}{2}$ in) loaf tin. Line with greaseproof paper.

3 Put the bananas into a large bowl and beat till smooth.

4 Mix in the oil, honey, eggs, lemon juice and rind.

5 Add the raisins and hazelnuts and mix in gently.

6 Fold in the flour and baking soda carefully, taking care not to overbeat the mixture.

7 Pour into the loaf tin, sprinkle the cashew nuts on top, and bake for about 1 hour and 20 minutes until golden brown, or until a skewer inserted into the cake comes out clean.

8 Remove from oven and leave to cool.

Basic Wholewheat Sponge Cake

125 ml (5 fl oz) soya or other oil
175 ml (6 fl oz) honey
2 eggs
pinch of salt
5 ml (1 tsp) baking powder
150 g (5 oz) wholewheat flour

Preparation 10 minutes
Cooking 35-40 minutes
Makes 20 cm (8 in) round cake

This is an easy and extremely versatile recipe. To vary the recipe, add fresh or cooked fruit, nuts and spices, and sherry or custard. If dry ingredients are added, you may need to use less flour; if wet, add slightly more flour. For a richer sponge, substitute butter or milk for the oil.

1 Heat the oven to 170°C (325°F/Gas 3).

2 Put the oil, honey and eggs into a large bowl and beat them all together till smooth.

3 Mix the salt and baking powder with the flour before adding to the liquid ingredients. Beat the mix just enough to achieve a smooth consistency.

4 Grease a 20 cm (8 in) round cake tin and line carefully with greaseproof paper.

5 Pour the mixture into the tin and bake for 35-40 minutes until a skewer inserted into the centre of the cake comes out clean.

Note: For a sandwich cake, you can double all the quantities given, and use 2 tins.

Brandy Fruit Cake

50 g (2 oz) butter
50 ml (2 fl oz) honey
25 ml (1 fl oz) soya oil
2 eggs, separated
100 g (4 oz) fine wholewheat flour

Fruit mix
250 g (9 oz) raisins
200 g (7 oz) currants
50 g (2 oz) dried figs, finely chopped
50 g (2 oz) dried apricots, finely chopped
juice and grated rind of 1 orange
juice and grated rind of 1 lemon
50 ml (2 fl oz) brandy
100 ml (4 fl oz) cider

Preparation 10 minutes (allow 12 hours for soaking the fruit mix)
Cooking 1 hour 45 minutes
Makes 800 g (1 lb 12 oz) loaf cake

1 First prepare the fruit mix. Mix all the ingredients together well and marinate for 12 hours or overnight in a container with a tightly fitting lid.

2 Heat the oven to 150°C (300°F/Gas 2).

3 Grease an 18 cm × 11.5 cm × 8.5 cm (7$\frac{1}{4}$ in × 4$\frac{1}{2}$ in × 3$\frac{1}{2}$ in) loaf tin. Line with greaseproof paper.

4 In a large bowl or food processor, combine the butter and honey. Add the oil and mix well.

5 Add the egg yolks to the mixing bowl. Pour in the prepared fruit mix and mix thoroughly but gently.

6 Gradually mix in the flour, taking care not to break up the fruit. The resulting mixture should have a soft consistency: neither too stiff nor too runny. Add a little extra liquid or flour if necessary.

7 Whip the egg whites until stiff and fold into the cake mixture.

8 Pour into the prepared cake tin and smooth down the surface with the back of your hand, dipped in water.

9 Put on the bottom shelf of the oven and bake for 1 hour and 45 minutes until brown, or until a skewer inserted into the centre of the cake comes out clean.

10 Remove from oven and leave to cool before removing from tin.

◆

Bran Muffins

50 g (2 oz) bran
150 g (5 oz) wholewheat flour
5 ml (1 tsp) baking soda
pinch of salt
100 g (4 oz) raisins
1 egg, beaten
50 ml (2 fl oz) soya oil
25 ml (1 fl oz) molasses
25 ml (1 fl oz) honey
250 ml (9 fl oz) milk
juice and grated rind of 1 orange
orange slices, to decorate
mixture of 5 ml (1 tsp) honey and 5 ml
   (1 tsp) lemon juice, to glaze (optional)

Preparation 10 minutes
Cooking 10-15 minutes
Makes 12 muffins

1 Heat the oven to 180°C (350°F/Gas 4).

2 Put the bran, wholewheat flour, baking soda, salt and raisins into a mixing bowl. Mix together with a wooden spoon.

3 In another bowl or a measuring jug, mix together the egg, oil, molasses, honey, milk, orange juice and rind.

4 Make a well in the centre of the dry ingredients and pour in the wet mixture.

5 Mix together gently, taking care not to overbeat the mixture.

6 Place 12 paper cases into a patty tin. Put about a dessertspoonful of the mixture into each case and press a small slice of orange on top of each. Bake at the top of the oven for 10-15 minutes or until brown. Remove from oven.

7 Spoon over the glaze, if liked, and leave to cool.

Brioche Whirls

Filling
500 g (1 lb 2 oz) puréed dates or other
   dried fruit
150 g (5 oz) dried apricots, soaked for
   12 hours or overnight
50 g (2 oz) raisins, soaked for 12 hours
   or overnight
50 g (2 oz) chopped mixed nuts
5 ml (1 tsp) ground cinnamon

Dough
15 ml (1 tbsp) honey
150 ml ($\frac{1}{4}$ pt) milk
20 g ($\frac{3}{4}$ oz) fresh yeast or 5 ml (1 tsp)
   dried
350 g (12 oz) fine wholewheat flour
50 g (2 oz) butter
pinch of salt
1 egg
mixture of 5 ml (1 tsp) honey and 5 ml
   (1 tsp) lemon juice, to glaze

**Preparation 2 hours (allow 12 hours for
soaking the fruit)
Cooking 15 minutes
Makes 12 brioches**

**These delicious pastries will reward the little extra time and effort
required to make them.**

1 Prepare the dough: stir the honey with the milk and then crumble
in the yeast and allow it to dissolve.

2 Put all but a handful of the flour into a large mixing bowl. Rub
the butter into the flour with your fingertips. Mix in the salt.

3 Make a well in the middle of the flour and break the egg into it.
With a spoon, work the flour from around the edges into the centre,
gradually adding the yeasted milk and honey until you have
achieved a sticky dough.

4 With your hands work in the remaining flour and set aside. The
dough should be slack but not wet.

5 Cover the bowl and set aside for 30 minutes in a warm place
in order to rise.

6 Remove the dough from the bowl and place on a flat, lightly
floured surface. Scrape the bowl clean, grease and set aside.

7 Gently knead the dough into a smooth, compact mass and replace
in the oiled bowl. Cover and set aside for another 30 minutes in a
warm place until the dough has almost doubled in size.

8 Meanwhile, make the filling: put the ingredients except the
apricots into a bowl and mix well.

9 Knead the dough again, flour it on both sides and carefully roll it
out into a sheet measuring 45 cm × 30 cm (18 in × 12 in).

10 Spread the filling thinly and evenly over the entire surface
except for a strip 2.5 cm (1 in) wide along the side nearest to you.

11 Arrange a row of the soaked apricots along the side farthest
from you. Then, reaching to the far side of the dough, with both
hands roll it up towards you, using the row of apricots as a core.
Keep the roll as tight as you can, taking care not to tear it.

12 Just before you finish rolling, brush the bare strip of dough with
milk and seal the end of the brioche.

13 Gently smooth out the sausage of dough and cut the ends off.

14 Heat the oven to 230°C (450°F/Gas 8).

15 Line 2 large baking trays with greased greaseproof paper.

16 Cut the dough into approximately 12 slices about 4 cm (1$\frac{1}{2}$ in)
wide. Carefully lay the flat slices on the trays. Gently press them
down and shape them into circles about 10 cm (4 in) across. Leave at
least 2.5 cm (1 in) between each brioche.

17 Brush the upper surfaces with milk and leave to rise for about
10 minutes.

18 Bake for 12-15 minutes or until golden brown.

19 Remove from oven and brush with the honey and lemon glaze. Leave to cool before eating.

Making the brioche whirls

1 Spread the filling over the rolled-out oblong of dough and place the soaked apricots in a neat line along the edge of the dough farthest away from you. Press down gently.

2 Starting from the far edge, and using the line of soaked apricots as a core, roll up the brioche tightly towards you.

3 Holding the brioche roll tightly in one hand, carefully cut off thick slices. These can then be slightly flattened with your hand to make them larger and rounder.

Carob Brownies

These delicious cakes can be served plain or iced. Decorate with nuts for special occasions.

275 ml (10 fl oz) soya oil
225 ml (8 fl oz) honey
4 eggs, beaten
75 g (3 oz) carob powder (see p. 51), sifted
225 g (8 oz) fine wholewheat flour
5 ml (1 tsp) baking powder

Icing (optional)
15 ml (1 tbsp) carob powder (see p. 51)
300 g (11 oz) cream cheese
5 ml (1 tsp) vanilla essence
15 ml (1 tbsp) honey

Preparation 10 minutes
Cooking 25 minutes
Makes 12 brownies

1 Heat the oven to 180°C (350°F/Gas 4).

2 Grease a 25 cm × 30 cm (10 in × 12 in) shallow cake tin and line with greaseproof paper.

3 In a bowl or food processor, combine the oil, honey and eggs.

4 Carefully add the carob powder, wholewheat flour and baking powder and mix in thoroughly but gently.

5 Pour the cake mixture into the prepared tin and bake for 25 minutes, until dark brown or until a skewer inserted into the cake comes out clean. Remove from oven and leave to cool before cutting.

6 If making the icing, sift the carob powder into the cream cheese. Add the vanilla essence and honey. Mix thoroughly and spread over top of cake before cutting.

Carrot & Coconut Cake

150 ml (5 fl oz) soya oil
100 ml (4 fl oz) honey
2 large eggs
225 g (8 oz) carrots, grated
75 g (3 oz) raisins
50 g (2 oz) desiccated coconut
200 g (7 oz) fine wholewheat flour
5 ml (1 tsp) baking powder
5 ml (1 tsp) ground cinnamon
¼ tsp grated nutmeg
¼ tsp ground mixed spice

Preparation 10 minutes
Cooking 1 hour 20 minutes
Makes 800 g (1 lb 12 oz) loaf cake

1 Heat the oven to 170°C (325°F/Gas 3).

2 Grease an 18 cm × 11.5 cm × 8.5 cm (7¼ in × 4½ in × 3½ in) loaf tin and line with greaseproof paper.

3 Put the oil, honey and eggs into a large bowl or food processor and beat together till smooth.

4 Add the grated carrot, raisins and coconut and mix in gently.

5 Fold in the flour, baking powder, cinnamon, nutmeg and mixed spice, taking care not to overbeat the mixture. (This would hinder the action of the baking powder and break up the fruit.)

6 Pour into the loaf tin and bake for 1 hour and 20 minutes until brown, or until a skewer inserted into the cake comes out clean.

7 Remove from oven and leave to cool before removing from tin.

Cheese Scones

100 g (4 oz) butter
450 g (1 lb) fine wholewheat flour
15 ml (1 tbsp) baking powder
5 ml (1 tsp) salt
5 ml (1 tsp) mustard powder
10 ml (2 tsp) finely chopped fresh herbs
  or 5 ml (1 tsp) dried
2.5 ml (½ tsp) black pepper or pinch of
  chilli powder
250 g (9 oz) cheese, grated
100 ml (4 fl oz) milk
mixture of 1 beaten egg and a little milk,
  to glaze
grated cheese, to garnish

Preparation 15 minutes
Cooking 15 minutes
Makes 12 scones

Fresh dill or basil is particularly delicious in these scones.

1 Heat the oven to 220°C (425°F/Gas 7).

2 In a large mixing bowl, rub the fat into the flour.

3 Add the rest of the dry ingredients.

4 Pour in the milk and mix together gently to form a soft dough.

5 On a lightly floured surface, roll out the dough to a thickness of about 4 cm (1½ in) and cut out scones with a 5 cm (2 in) cutter.

6 Brush each scone with the egg glaze and top with a little grated cheese to garnish.

7 Set the scones on a floured baking tray and bake for about 15 minutes or until golden brown.

8 Remove from oven and leave to cool before serving.

Couscous Cake

250 g (9 oz) mixed dried fruit
400 g (14 oz) couscous
50 g (2 oz) sesame seeds
juice and grated rind of 1 lemon
50 ml (2 fl oz) maple syrup or apple juice concentrate (see p. 51) (optional)

Preparation 15 minutes (allow 1 hour for soaking the fruit)
Chilling 6 hours minimum
Makes 15 cm (6 in) round cake
Ⓥ

This unusual cake requires thorough chilling before serving.

1 Cover the dried fruit with boiling water and leave to stand for at least 1 hour, until the fruit has absorbed some of the liquid.

2 Grease a 15 cm (6 in) round cake tin and carefully line with greaseproof paper.

3 Gently squeeze the fruit and pour off the liquid into a separate jug. Top up the liquid with boiling water to make 700 ml (1¼ pt).

4 Cut the fruit into small pieces.

5 Put the couscous in a bowl and pour over the liquid made up from the reserved fruit juice and boiling water.

6 Add the chopped fruit, sesame seeds, juice and rind of the lemon and maple syrup, if using, and leave to stand for 15 minutes or until the couscous absorbs some of the liquid and puffs up.

7 Press the mixture down into the tin and chill in the refrigerator for at least 6 hours until the mixture has set.

Date & Oat Bars

500 g (1 lb 2 oz) stoned dried dates
200 g (7 oz) jumbo oats
200 g (7 oz) regular oats
200 g (7 oz) wholewheat flour
2.5 ml (½ tsp) salt
175 ml (6 fl oz) malt extract
175 ml (6 fl oz) soya oil
50 g (2 oz) desiccated coconut

Preparation 10 minutes (allow extra time for soaking and cooking the dates, if necessary)
Cooking 30-40 minutes
Makes 16 bars
Ⓥ

1 Heat the oven to 180°C (350°F/Gas 4).

2 Grease a 25 cm × 30 cm (10 in × 12 in) cake tin and line with greaseproof paper.

3 Put the dates in a medium-sized saucepan. Cover with water. Bring to the boil, then lower the heat and simmer, covered, for 10-15 minutes until the dates have softened. Stir well when cooked and leave to cool.

4 Put the jumbo oats, regular oats, flour and salt into a bowl or food processor.

5 Pour the malt into the dry mixture and mix as fast as possible for 2-3 minutes.

6 Mixing more slowly, gradually pour in the oil, to end up with a light crumbly mixture.

7 Spread three-quarters of this mixture into the bottom of the prepared cake tin, packing it down well with your hands.

8 Spread the dates over the top.

9 Add the coconut to the remaining oat mixture and sprinkle this on top of the dates.

10 Bake for 30-40 minutes until golden brown.

11 Remove from oven and leave to cool before cutting.

Flapjacks

100 g (4 oz) fine wholewheat flour
75 g (3 oz) regular oats
100 g (4 oz) peanuts
100 g (4 oz) chopped mixed nuts
100 g (4 oz) raisins
100 g (4 oz) butter, melted
100 ml (4 fl oz) molasses
7.5 ml (3 fl oz) honey
150 ml (5 fl oz) soya oil

Preparation 10 minutes
Cooking 45 minutes
Serves 12

1 Heat the oven to 180°C (350°F/Gas 4).

2 Grease a 25 cm × 30 cm (10 in × 12 in) cake tin and line with greaseproof paper.

3 Put all the ingredients into a large bowl and mix thoroughly with a wooden spoon.

4 Pour into the cake tin, making sure the mixture reaches right into the corners and the surface is smooth.

5 Bake for 45 minutes or until dark brown.

6 Remove from oven and leave to cool before cutting.

Fruit Scones

450 g (1 lb) fine wholewheat flour
100 g (4 oz) butter
10 ml (2 tsp) mixed spice
15 ml (1 tbsp) baking powder
100 g (4 oz) raisins
100 ml (4 fl oz) honey
100 ml (4 fl oz) milk
1 egg, beaten
nuts, to decorate

Preparation 10 minutes
Cooking 15-20 minutes
Makes 20 scones

These can be served plain or with butter, jam and/or honey.

1 Heat the oven to 230°C (450°F/Gas 8).

2 Mix the flour and the butter together in a large bowl or in a food processor.

3 Add the mixed spice, baking powder and raisins.

4 In a jug, mix the honey and milk together and pour on to the dry ingredients. Mix together to form a soft dough.

5 On a lightly floured surface, roll out the dough to a thickness of 4 cm (1½ in) and cut the scones into squares or circles as desired.

6 Brush the top with beaten egg and decorate each scone with a nut.

7 Cook on a baking tray for about 15 minutes or until browned.

Ginger Cake

225 g (8 oz) fine wholewheat flour
30 ml (2 tbsp) ground ginger
15 ml (1 tbsp) mustard powder
15 ml (1 tbsp) ground cinnamon
15 ml (1 tbsp) baking powder
200 ml (7 fl oz) soya oil
75 ml (3 fl oz) molasses
75 ml (3 fl oz) malt extract
50 ml (2 fl oz) honey
2 eggs
100 ml (4 floz) milk or water

Preparation 10 minutes
Cooking 1¼-1½ hours
Makes 800 g (1 lb 12 oz) loaf cake

A rich, spicy but not too sweet loaf.

1 Heat the oven to 150°C (300° F/Gas 2).

2 Grease an 18 cm × 11.5 cm × 8.5 cm (7¼ in × 4½ in × 3½ in) loaf tin and line with greaseproof paper.

3 Mix together the flour, ginger, mustard powder, ground cinnamon and baking powder. Set aside.

4 In another bowl, beat together the oil, molasses, malt, honey, eggs and milk.

5 Fold in the dry ingredients.

6 Pour in the prepared cake tin. Bake on the bottom shelf of the oven for 1¼-1½ hours, or until a skewer inserted into the cake comes out clean. Remove from oven and leave to cool before serving.

Macaroon Cake

225 ml (8 fl oz) soya oil
200 ml (7 fl oz) honey
3 eggs
5 ml (1 tsp) vanilla essence
275 g (10 oz) fine wholewheat flour
10 ml (2 tsp) baking powder

Topping
5 eggs, separated
300 g (11 oz) desiccated coconut
100 ml (4 fl oz) honey
2.5 ml (½ tsp) almond essence
175 g (6 oz) sugar-free jam (see p. 52),
   or fruit purée

Preparation 30 minutes
Cooking 45 minutes
Makes 1·3 kg (2 lb 14 oz) cake

This cake can also be eaten warm with custard as a pudding.

1 Heat the oven to 180°C (350°F/Gas 4).

2 Grease a 25 cm × 30 cm (10 in × 12 in) cake tin and line with greaseproof paper.

3 In a food processor or large bowl, combine the oil, honey, eggs and vanilla essence.

4 Add the wholewheat flour and baking powder and mix in thoroughly but gently.

5 Pour the cake mixture into the prepared tin and bake for about 25-30 minutes.

6 Meanwhile, make the topping: put the egg yolks in a bowl with the coconut, honey and almond essence. Mix well.

7 Whip the egg whites until stiff and gently fold into the coconut mixture. Set aside.

8 When the cake is cooked, remove from the oven and leave to cool for a few minutes.

9 Spread the sugar-free jam or fruit purée over the cake and spread the coconut mixture on top.

10 Return to the oven and cook for a further 30 minutes or until the top is golden brown.

11 Remove from the oven and leave to cool before cutting.

Oat & Raisin Biscuits

100 g (4 oz) raisins
300 ml (11 fl oz) boiling water
350 g (12 oz) regular oats
100 g (4 oz) jumbo oats
100 g (4 oz) fine wholewheat flour
25 g (1 oz) sunflower seeds
good pinch of salt
150 ml (5 fl oz) soya oil

Preparation 10 minutes (allow 30 minutes for soaking the raisins)
Cooking 20 minutes
Makes 24 biscuits
Ⓥ

1 Put the raisins in a bowl, pour over the boiling water and leave to stand for 20-30 minutes until the fruit has absorbed some of the liquid. Reserve the soaking liquid.

2 Heat the oven to 190°C (375°F/Gas 5).

3 In a food processor or large bowl, mix the dry ingredients.

4 Add the oil. Then add the raisins and 200 ml (7 fl oz) of their soaking liquid. Mix together well and add a little more liquid if necessary, to form a soft, pliable dough.

5 On a lightly floured surface, roll out the dough to a thickness of about 1.5 cm (½ in). Cut the biscuits out with a 7 cm (3 in) cutter.

6 Put them on a floured baking tray and cook for 20 minutes or until golden brown.

7 Remove from the oven and leave to cool. (The biscuits will harden a little as they cool.)

Orange Sesame Cake

100 ml (4 fl oz) soya oil
150 ml (5 fl oz) honey
2 eggs, beaten
juice and grated rind of 1 large orange
50 ml (2 fl oz) water
100 g (4 oz) sesame seeds
300 g (11 oz) fine wholewheat flour
15 ml (1 tbsp) baking powder

Filling
300 g (11 oz) cream cheese
15 ml (1 tbsp) honey
1 orange

Preparation 20 minutes
Cooking 35 minutes
Makes 20 cm (8 in) round cake

1 Heat the oven to 180°C (350°F/Gas 4).

2 Grease two 20 cm (8 in) cake tins.

3 Put the oil and honey in a food processor or large mixing bowl, and mix together till smooth. Stir the eggs into the mixture.

4 Add the orange juice and rind to the mixing bowl with the water and sesame seeds.

5 Add the flour and baking powder. Mix thoroughly and divide the mixture between the 2 cake tins.

6 Bake for 30-35 minutes, until golden brown or until a skewer inserted into the cake comes out clean. Remove from oven and leave to cool before turning out.

7 For the filling: mix the cream cheese and honey together in a bowl. Grate the orange, using the finest part of the grater, and add to the cream cheese mixture. Cut the orange into decorative strips.

8 Spread half the mixture over one cake and put the other cake on top. Put the rest of the cream cheese icing on top and decorate with slices of orange.

Peanut Butter Cookies

100 ml (4 fl oz) soya oil
100 ml (4 fl oz) honey or maple syrup
250 g (9 oz) peanut butter
150 g (5 oz) regular oats
250 g (9 oz) fine wholewheat flour
5 ml (1 tsp) baking powder
2.5 ml ($\frac{1}{2}$ tsp) ground cinnamon
2.5 ml ($\frac{1}{2}$ tsp) ground cloves
2.5 ml ($\frac{1}{2}$ tsp) ground nutmeg
2.5 ml ($\frac{1}{2}$ tsp) salt
75 g (3 oz) raisins

Preparation 15 minutes
Cooking 8-10 minutes
Makes 25 cookies
(v)

1 Heat the oven to 230°C (450°F/Gas 8).

2 In a food processor or large bowl, beat together the oil, honey and peanut butter.

3 In a separate bowl, combine all the remaining dry ingredients and mix thoroughly.

4 Mix the dry ingredients with the peanut butter mixture to make a fairly stiff dough.

5 On a lightly floured surface, roll out the dough to a thickness of 1.5 cm ($\frac{1}{2}$ in) and cut out into 7.5 cm (3 in) circles.

6 Bake the cookies on a lined or floured baking tray for 8-10 minutes or until golden brown.

7 Remove from oven and leave to cool before eating.

Cakes, Pastries, Biscuits & Scones (See p. 133)

Ginger Cake (see p. 142) is rich and succulent, with a spicy flavour.

Banana Nut Cake (see p. 136) is a delicious mixture of nuts, banana, honey and raisins.

Carrot & Coconut Cake (see p. 140) is moist and chewy, a lovely cake for tea-time.

Brandy Fruit Cake (see p. 137) is packed with dried fruit, nutritious and tasty.

Vegan Fruit Bars (see p. 146) are made without animal or dairy products.

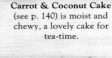

Date & Oat Bars (see p. 141) contain coconut and malt extract for added flavour.

These **Flapjacks** (see p. 142) are dark and rich because of the molasses and honey.

Sesame Honey Bars (see p. 145) have a deliciously sweet, nutty taste.

Carob Brownies (see p. 139) use carob as a nutritious alternative to chocolate.

Banana Cream Cake (see p. 135) is succulent and moist, good as a dessert.

Orange Sesame Cake (see p. 144) has a sponge base flavoured with sesame seeds and orange, topped with honey cream cheese.

Cheese Scones (see p. 140) make a good savoury snack.

Unusual **Tofu Cake** (see p. 146) consists of a spicy tofu cream on a malted oat base.

Sunflower Bars (see p. 145) are rich and chewy, with a nutty texture.

Macaroon Cake (see p. 143) is a honey sponge with a melt-in-the-mouth topping.

Brioche Whirls (see p. 138) are rich fruity pastries.

Fruit Scones (see p. 142) have a moist, chewy texture.

Bran Muffins (see p. 137) contain orange rind and juice for an extra tang.

Peanut Butter Cookies (see p. 144) are nutty biscuits popular with children.

Oat & Raisin Biscuits (see p. 143) have sunflower seeds for crunch and taste.

Breads *(See p. 147)*

The standard **Basic Whole-wheat Bread** (see p. 149).

Cheese & Herb Bread (see p. 152) is full of flavour.

Three-seed Bread (see p. 156), unusual and rich.

Nutritious **Sunflower Seed Bread** (see p. 155).

Sourdough bread (see p. 147) has a sharp flavour.

Rye bread (see p. 154) is dark and moist.

Wholewheat rolls (see p. 149).

Rolls with sesame seeds.

Dervish Barley Bread (see p. 152) is unleavened.

Wholewheat bread dough can be shaped in many ways. Here, it is patted into a large round before baking.

A **wholewheat cottage loaf** is easily made with basic wholewheat dough (see the diagrams on p. 149).

Fruit & Malt Bread (see p. 153) is rich and sweet.

A **wholewheat French stick** made from wholewheat dough (see p. 149).

A **wholewheat plait** is an interesting variation (see p. 149 for method).

Basic White Bread (see p. 150) is a lighter loaf.

Granary-style Bread (see p. 153) with poppy seeds.

Sesame Honey Bars

Base
225 g (8 oz) butter
175 ml (6 fl oz) honey
250 g (9 oz) fine wholewheat flour

Topping
3 eggs, beaten
250 ml (9 fl oz) honey
100 g (4 oz) desiccated coconut
150 g (5 oz) sesame seeds
5 ml (1 tsp) baking powder

Preparation 10 minutes
Cooking 30-40 minutes
Makes 20 bars

1 Heat the oven to 180°C (350°F/Gas 4).

2 Grease a 25 cm × 30 cm (10 in × 12 in) cake tin and line with greased greaseproof paper.

3 Make the base: in a food processor or large bowl, combine the butter, honey and wholewheat flour.

4 Spread this mixture over the bottom of the prepared cake tin. Smooth down with a damp spatula or the dampened back of your hand and prick the surface all over with a fork.

5 Bake for 15-20 minutes or until golden brown.

6 While the base is cooking, make the topping: in a large bowl combine the beaten eggs, honey, coconut and sesame seeds and mix thoroughly. Set aside. Just before you take the cake tin out of the oven, add the baking powder and mix well.

7 Pour the topping over the cooked base and return to the oven for a further 15 minutes or until the top is golden brown.

8 Remove from oven. Cut into pieces while still hot and leave to cool before removing from the cake tin.

Sunflower Bars

75 g (3 oz) hazelnut or cashew nut
   butter (see p. 50)
75 ml (3 fl oz) apple juice concentrate
   (see p. 51) or maple syrup
2.5 ml (½ tsp) vanilla essence
2.5 ml (½ tsp) salt
425 g (15 oz) sunflower seeds
150 g (5 oz) desiccated coconut

Preparation 10 minutes
Cooking 20 minutes
Makes 10-12 bars
Ⓖ𝐅 Ⓥ

1 Heat the oven to 180°C (350°F/Gas 4).

2 Grease a 30 cm × 20 cm (12 in × 8 in) Swiss roll tin or baking tray.

3 In a food processor or large bowl, combine all the ingredients.

4 Press down into the prepared tin and bake for 35 minutes or until golden brown.

5 Remove from oven. Cut while still warm and leave to cool completely before removing from baking tray.

Tofu Cake

Base
100 g (4 oz) fine wholewheat flour
100 g (4 oz) regular oats
pinch of salt
50 ml (2 fl oz) malt extract
50 ml (2 fl oz) soya oil

Topping
350 g (12 oz) tofu (see p. 51)
75 ml (3 fl oz) apple juice concentrate
   (see p. 51)
200 ml (7 fl oz) water
45 ml (3 tbsp) puréed dates
5 ml (1 tsp) tahini (see p. 50)
juice and grated rind of 1 lemon
pinch each of grated nutmeg, ground
   cinnamon and mixed spice
fresh fruit slices, to decorate

Preparation 15 minutes
Cooking 35 minutes
Makes 20 cm (8 in) round cake
Ⓥ

Similar to a cheesecake, this recipe substitutes tofu for the more fattening and less nutritious cream cheese.
You will need a blender for this recipe.

1 Heat the oven to 170°C (325°F/Gas 3).

2 Make the base: put the flour, oats and salt into a food processor or large bowl. Add the malt and mix thoroughly till evenly distributed. Add the oil and mix again.

3 Grease a 20 cm (8 in) loose-bottomed round cake tin. Press the oat mixture firmly into the base of the tin and bake for 10-15 minutes or until browned.

4 Make the topping: put all the ingredients for the topping in a blender and liquidize till smooth.

5 Pour the mixture over the partially cooked base and bake for 25 minutes until the tofu is set. Remove from oven and cool.

6 Carefully remove from the cake tin and decorate with slices of fresh fruit before serving.

Vegan Fruit Bars

300 g (11 oz) dried whole apricots,
   soaked for 12 hours or overnight
100 g (4 oz) dried apricot halves,
   soaked for 12 hours or overnight
200 g (7 oz) raisins, soaked for 12 hours
   or overnight
200 g (7 oz) mixed nuts
150 g (5 oz) desiccated coconut
100 g (4 oz) wholewheat flour
100 g (4 oz) regular oats
75 ml (3 fl oz) soya oil
75 ml (3 fl oz) apple juice concentrate
   (see p. 51)
5 ml (1 tsp) almond essence
50 g (2 oz) pumpkin seeds

Preparation 10 minutes (allow 12 hours
for soaking the fruit)
Cooking 30-40 minutes
Makes 18 slices
Ⓥ

1 Heat oven to 150°C (300°F/Gas 2).

2 Grease a 25 cm × 30 cm (10 in × 12 in) cake tin and line with greaseproof paper.

3 Mix all the ingredients together by hand in a large mixing bowl until you have a soft pliable mixture. You may need to add a little more liquid as some brands of oats and flours are more absorbent than others.

4 Pour into the cake tin, making sure that the mixture reaches right into the corners. Flatten with the back of your dampened hand or with a damp spatula and bake in the bottom of the oven for 30-40 minutes, or until browned.

5 Remove from oven and leave to cool before cutting.

BREADS

Introduction to making bread

Making good bread is as much an art as a science and strict adherence to a recipe will therefore not always produce the best results. There are many factors to take into account, such as the temperature in your kitchen, the type of oven you use, and so on. So do not give up if your first attempt is disappointing. The following notes may be useful.

Using yeast

Yeasts are not chemicals, but living organisms that are all around us in different forms: in the air, on the leaves and fruit of plants and even on our own skins. In moist, warm conditions, such as in a mass of dough, yeast cells will reproduce rapidly, feeding on the sugary starch from the grain and releasing carbon dioxide and alcohol.

Fresh yeast for baking is usually grey and crumbly in texture. It is increasingly available in health food stores, or even from supermarkets or your local baker. It will keep for 2-3 months in the freezer or 2-3 weeks in the refrigerator. Dried yeast is also available and can be kept for as long as 3 years. It acts exactly like fresh yeast when dissolved in water and produces the same results. As a rough guide, 30 g (1 oz) fresh yeast is equal to 7.5 ml (1½ level tsp) dried yeast. The nutritional supplement, Brewer's Yeast, however, is not suitable for making bread rise.

In particularly cold weather, you may need to use slightly more yeast, but in general you should not try to hurry bread-making by using extra yeast. A dough that has not had time to mature and strengthen will tend to collapse, however much yeast is used. It is far better to use less yeast, and allow longer proving times.

In order to scale a recipe up or down, you will need to alter the proportion of yeast to other ingredients. If the quantities of flour and water in a recipe are doubled, then only one and a half times the amount of yeast will be required. If the quantities of flour and water are halved, then two thirds the amount of yeast should be used. It is quite unnecessary to use sugar or any other sweetener to activate the yeast: the flour itself contains enough sugars to keep the yeast fed and active.

Spontaneous leaven and sourdough

Although compressed baker's yeast is now most commonly used, you can make your own yeast leaveners. Natural or 'spontaneous' leavens are made by mixing a thick porridge of wholewheat flour and warm water, about 570 ml (1 pt) water to every 450 g (1 lb) flour. Leave the porridge to stand in a warm place for up to 20 hours, during which time the yeasts in the atmosphere and in the flour itself start a spontaneous ferment. Loaves made with this dough will rise less and more slowly than those made from a normal yeasted dough. Salt is not normally added, since this inhibits the action of the leaven.

The sourdough method provides a stronger rise. Here, a naturally leavened dough is made as above and part of it is kept back as a starter, about 6 oz (175 g). Then, it is put in a plastic bag and refrigerated until needed. For a couple of days before baking the starter is kept at room temperature and fed once every 24-48 hours with about 100 ml (4 fl oz) water and a handful of flour. To make the bread, work another 450 g (1 lb) flour and 225 ml (8 fl oz) warm water into the dough, knead gently and bake as for Basic Wholewheat Bread (see p. 149). Keep a lump of this dough back as a starter for the next bake. It should get stronger with each bake.

Proving or rising

It is important to have a warm, draught-free place in which to 'prove' or rise a yeasted dough. An airing cupboard with a hot-water tank is ideal or you can warm an ordinary cupboard with a small heater. A kitchen range such as an Aga or Rayburn with a warming compartment is also ideal. In summer, a draught-free spot inside a sunny window works well.

Kneading

Unlike cakes and scones, bread dough has to be mixed and kneaded over a period of several hours. The moistened flour needs time to release its gluten (see p. 17) and must be kneaded vigorously to bind the strands of gluten into a strong dough to obtain the elasticity which enables bread to rise and hold together successfully.

The dough should be kneaded on a smooth, lightly floured surface such as Formica, marble or stainless steel, although any kitchen table-top will do. Start to knead as soon as you can remove the dough from the bowl without it sticking to your hands. Push the dough down and away from you with the heels of your hands, and fold it back towards you with your fingers. Do this a few times, then turn the dough through 90 degrees and repeat. Turn and repeat, turn and repeat. If the dough sticks, scrape the surface clean and lightly flour it again. Try not to work in more flour than the dough can easily absorb, or it will become dry and hard. Try not to tear the dough: steady pressure in the kneading action is better than fierce strength. For the final kneading and moulding of the loaves, you may find it better to oil the surface and your hands slightly, rather than flouring them.

Finishing the loaves

For a neater finish, always make sure that the last fold in the moulded dough is at the bottom of your loaf. To prevent the top crust from drying out in the final proving, brush it with warm water. Make a cut in the top of the loaf to help prevent the crust from cracking as the bread rises.

After the final proving, be gentle when transferring the tins to the oven: just a knock can cause the bread to subside and become heavy.

Bread tins

The bread tins most commonly available are 'large', designed to take about 800 g (1 lb 12 oz) dough, and 'small', for 400 g (14 oz) dough, though intermediate sizes may also be found. Good quality double-thickness bread tins with reinforced corners can be bought fairly cheaply.

All bread tins should be very thoroughly oiled the first couple of times they are used, and should not be used for other types of baking. Your bread tins should last a lifetime, and will gradually season to give you evenly baked loaves which slip easily from the tin every time with only the lightest oiling. Avoid non-stick tins: they are more expensive and the surface will eventually break up, leaving bits of the 'magic' coating in the crusts of the loaves.

Ovens

Modern domestic ovens (except in ranges such as Agas or Rayburns) generally bake by heating and circulating the air inside the oven, rather than by all-round heat from floor, walls and roof which is better for breadmaking. To improve results, you should stand the tins on a metal tray preheated in the oven, rather than on the rails of the oven shelves, and place an ovenproof dish of water on the bottom of the oven to create a moist atmosphere. Loaves should always be baked in the middle of the oven; rolls are better at the top where the oven is hottest. To brown off the bottom of your loaves, you may need to turn them upside down in their tins for the last 5 minutes of baking.

One final point: you should never open the oven door until just before you expect bread (or cakes) to be done. The longer the oven temperature is maintained, the better bread will bake. The bread will sound hollow when tapped, if cooked.

Measurements

It is particularly important in baking to follow the exact measurements given in the recipes, even though conversions may vary from those used elsewhere in the book. In all the bread recipes, 30 g rather than the more usual 25 g is given as the equivalent of 1 oz. When following the imperial conversions for dried yeast, please note that the 1½ level teaspoons used throughout refers to 5 ml teaspoons. If you do not have a 5 ml spoon, use 1½ heaped teaspoons.

Making bread

1 In a bowl, thoroughly mix a little over half the flour into the water and dissolved yeast with a hand whisk. It should have a smooth, soupy or porridge-like consistency.

2 After proving, work in the salt and the remaining flour with your hand to form a dough.

3 It is easiest to knead the dough while still in the bowl. Use one hand to knead and the other to turn the bowl. The first movement involves pulling the dough up and over towards you with your fingers so that it folds over.

4 The second kneading movement involves pushing the folded dough down into the bowl with your fist. Then, push the dough away from you, pick up the edge and begin the movements again. The process is a smooth continuous one, and the bowl should be rotated all the time to ensure even kneading of the dough.

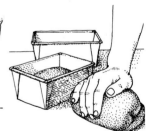

5 Divide the dough into 2 halves and pat each into a loaf shape. Place into the prepared loaf tins.

Basic Wholewheat Bread

30 g (1 oz) fresh yeast or 7.5 ml (1½ tsp) dried
570 ml (1 pt) warm water
1 kg (2 lb 3 oz) wholewheat flour
10 ml (2 tsp) salt

Preparation 20 minutes (allow 2 hours proving time)
Cooking 40-45 minutes
Makes 2 × 800 g (1 lb 12 oz) loaves or 4 × 400 g (14 oz) loaves

1 In a large bowl, dissolve the yeast in the water.

2 Stir in a little over half the flour until the mixture has a porridge-like consistency.

3 Mix thoroughly with a hand whisk, then cover and stand to prove in a warm, draught-free place for 30-45 minutes until the mixture has risen visibly.

4 Stir in the salt with a wooden spoon, then gradually work in more flour until you have a dough that you can knead.

5 Knead thoroughly and methodically until a smooth texture is achieved.

6 Cover and stand to prove in a warm, draught-free place for 30-45 minutes, until the dough has doubled in size.

7 Knead again, then divide and mould into 2 individual loaves.

8 Oil two 18 cm × 11.5 cm × 8.5 cm (7¼ in × 4½ in × 3½ in) loaf tins or four 15 cm × 9 cm × 7.5 cm (6 in × 3½ in × 3 in) loaf tins. Place the loaves in the tins. Stand to prove for a further 30 minutes. or until they have doubled in size, rising to fill the tins.

9 Meanwhile, heat the oven to 220°C (425°F/Gas 7).

10 Bake for 40-45 minutes until the loaves sound hollow when tapped. Remove from tins and stand on a rack to cool.

Shaping different loaves

Making a cottage loaf
1 Pat the dough into shape, cut off a third and roll into two balls.

2 Press the small ball into the large ball with your thumb.

Making a plait
1 Roll out 3 long tubes, press together at one end and plait.

2 Tuck the ends under the loaf and press together securely.

Making a French stick
1 Roll out the dough into a long thick tube with your hands.

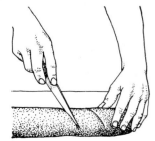

2 Round the edges and make evenly spaced diagonal cuts with a sharp knife for decoration.

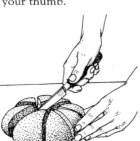

Making rolls
1 To make 8 rolls, cut the dough into even segments. Pull apart and pat each into a round.

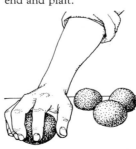

2 Knead each roll with the palm of your hand on a flat surface, rolling and folding.

Making a mouse
1 You need: an egg-shaped body, 2 ears, a tail, a nose and 2 raisins for eyes.

2 Put the pieces together, using a spot of water to seal. Press the ears on to the body with a chopstick.

Basic White Bread

20 g (¾ oz) fresh yeast or 5 ml (1 tsp)
  dried
425 ml (15 fl oz) warm water
625 g (1 lb 6 oz) strong white flour
7.5 ml (1½ tsp) salt

Preparation 20 minutes (allow 1½ hours proving time)
Cooking 40-45 minutes
Makes 3 × 400 g (14 oz) loaves

1 In a large bowl, dissolve the yeast in the water.

2 Stir in a little over half the flour until the mixture has a porridge-like consistency.

3 Mix thoroughly with a hand whisk, then cover and stand to prove in a warm draught-free place for 30 minutes until the mixture has risen visibly.

4 Stir in the salt with a wooden spoon, then gradually work in more flour until you have a dough you can knead.

5 Knead the dough thoroughly and methodically until a smooth texture is achieved.

6 Cover and stand to prove in a warm, draught-free place for 30-45 minutes until the mixture has doubled in size.

7 Knead again, then divide and mould into 3 individual loaves.

8 Oil three 15 cm × 9 cm × 7.5 cm (6 in × 3½ in × 3 in) loaf tins. Place the loaves in the tins. Stand to prove for a further 20 minutes, until they have approximately doubled in size, rising to fill the tins.

9 Meanwhile, heat the oven to 220°C (425°F/Gas 7).

10 Bake for 40 minutes, until the loaves sound hollow when tapped.

11 Remove from tins and leave to cool on a rack.

Cheese Croissants with Mushrooms

Filling
50 g (2 oz) butter
225 g (8 oz) mushrooms, thinly sliced
15 ml (1 tbsp) tamari
3 garlic cloves, crushed
2.5 ml (½ tsp) grated ginger root
5 ml (1 tsp) finely chopped fresh basil or
  2.5 ml (½ tsp) dried
250 g (9 oz) cheese, grated

Dough
30 g (1 oz) fresh yeast or 7.5 ml (1½ tsp)
  dried
275 ml (½ pt) milk
600 g (1 lb 5 oz) fine wholewheat flour
100 g (4 oz) butter
2.5 ml (½ tsp) salt
2 eggs

Preparation 20 minutes (allow 1¼ hours proving time)
Cooking 15 minutes
Makes 12 croissants

These delicious croissants are surprisingly easy to make.

1 Make the filling: melt the butter in a pan. Sauté the mushrooms in the butter. Cover and cook over a low heat for 2-3 minutes.

2 Add the tamari, garlic, ginger and basil and cook for a further 1-2 minutes until the mushrooms are cooked.

3 Remove from the heat. Stir in 200 g (7 oz) of cheese, reserving the remainder for putting on top of the croissants. Leave to cool.

4 Make the dough: in a bowl, dissolve the yeast in the milk.

5 Put all but 2 handfuls of the flour into a large mixing bowl. Rub the butter into the flour with your fingers. Mix in the salt.

6 Make a well in the middle of the flour and break the eggs into it. Beat the eggs roughly with a fork and begin to mix gently with a wooden spoon.

7 Gradually add the milk and yeast and mix together until you have a sticky dough.

8 Using your hands, work in the remainder of the flour and set aside. The dough should be slack but not wet.

9 Cover the bowl and set aside in a warm, draught-free place for 30-45 minutes until the mixture has risen visibly.

10 Gently knead the dough into a smooth, compact mass. Cover and set aside in a warm, draught-free place for 30-45 minutes until the dough has doubled in size.

11 Knead the dough again. Flour it on both sides and carefully roll it out into a sheet measuring 90 cm × 30 cm (36 in × 12 in). Divide this into twelve 15 cm (6 in) squares. (You may find it easier to halve the dough and roll out 2 sheets measuring 45 cm × 35 cm (18 in × 12 in) and divide these into six 15 cm (6 in) squares each.)

12 Divide the filling into 12 portions: it may still be warm but it should not be hot. Place in a diagonal strip along each square.

13 Starting from one corner, roll up each croissant, taking care not to tear the dough. Pinch the ends together. Bend them around into crescent shapes, giving each a twist as you do it.

14 Heat the oven to 240°C (475°F/Gas 9).

15 Place the finished croissants on an oiled baking tray at least 2.5 cm (1 in) apart. Brush the top of each croissant with milk and sprinkle a little grated cheese on top. Set the croissants aside in a warm place for another 15 minutes to rise.

16 Bake the croissants for 12-15 minutes until the tops are a rich golden brown. Serve warm.

Making the croissants

1 Divide the rolled-out sheet of dough into 12 squares. Place a spoonful of the filling on to each square, and spread out so that it stretches diagonally across the pastry.

2 Take hold of one corner of the pastry square and fold it diagonally over the filling.

3 Take hold of the opposite corner of pastry and fold it over the first corner. Press down securely, then pinch the two ends together firmly and bend into a croissant shape.

Cheese & Herb Bread

20 g (¾ oz) fresh yeast or 5 ml (1 tsp)
   dried
275 ml (½ pt) warm water
5 ml (1 tsp) salt
500 g (1 lb 2 oz) wholewheat flour

Filling
450 g (1 lb) cheese, grated
5 ml (1 tsp) paprika
10 ml (2 tsp) finely chopped fresh basil
   or 5 ml (1 tsp) dried
10 ml (2 tsp) finely chopped fresh
   oregano or 5 ml (1 tsp) dried
15 ml (1 tbsp) finely chopped
   fresh parsley

**Preparation 20 minutes (allow 2 hours
proving time)
Cooking 40-45 minutes
Makes 2 × 400 g (14 oz) loaves**

**Great care should be taken in handling the freshly baked loaf, as
the cooked cheese inside it will make it softer than a regular loaf.**

1 In a large bowl, dissolve the yeast in the water.

2 Stir in a little over half the flour until the mixture has a porridge-like consistency.

3 Mix thoroughly with a hand whisk, then cover and stand to prove in a warm, draught-free place for 30-45 minutes, until the mixture has risen visibly.

4 Stir in the salt with a wooden spoon, then gradually work in more flour until you have a dough that you can knead.

5 Knead the dough thoroughly and methodically until a smooth texture is achieved.

6 Cover and stand to prove in a warm, draught-free place for 30-45 minutes until the dough has doubled in size.

7 Knead again, then divide and mould into 2 individual loaves.

8 Prepare the filling: mix the cheese and paprika with the herbs.

9 On a lightly oiled surface, roll out the 2 pieces of dough into strips about 10 cm × 30 cm (4 in × 12 in), and spread with the cheese and herb mixture, reserving about a quarter of the mixture for the topping. Roll up the 2 strips as tightly as possible.

10 Oil two 15 cm × 9 cm × 7.5 cm (6 in × 3½ in × 3 in) loaf tins. Press the roll firmly down into the tins and top with the remaining cheese and herb mixture.

11 Stand to prove in a warm, draught-free place for 30-45 minutes, until the loaves have almost doubled in size, rising to fill the tins.

12 Meanwhile, heat the oven to 220°C (425°F/Gas 7).

13 Bake for 40-45 minutes until the loaves ring hollow if tapped.

◆

Dervish Barley Bread

15 ml (1 tbsp) honey
350 ml (12 fl oz) water
250 g (9 oz) fine oatmeal
good pinch of salt
250 g (9 oz) barley flour

**Preparation 10 minutes (allow 30
minutes standing time)
Cooking 15 minutes
Makes 8 breads**

1 Mix together the honey, water, oatmeal and salt in a large mixing bowl. Beat into a smooth batter with a hand whisk. Leave to stand for 10 minutes until the oatmeal has absorbed some of the liquid.

2 Add the barley flour and work into a wet sticky dough with a spoon. Allow to stand for another 20 minutes until the dough is soft but workable.

3 Divide into 8 roughly equal pieces. Mould each piece carefully into a compact flat oval shape and place on a lightly oiled surface.

4 Heat the oven to 200°C (400°F/Gas 6).

5 Roll each piece of dough out into a strip approximately 18 cm × 4 cm (7 in × 1½ in). Arrange the strips on a lightly floured baking tray and put straight into the oven.

6 Bake for 15 minutes or until a golden crust has formed. Cool on a rack before serving.

◆

Fruit & Malt Bread

20 g (¾ oz) fresh yeast or 5 ml (1 tsp) dried
250 ml (9 fl oz) warm water
500 g (1 lb 2 oz) wholewheat flour
5 ml (1 tsp) salt
15 ml (1 tbsp) soya oil
45 ml (3 tbsp) malt extract
175 g (6 oz) raisins, currants or other dried fruit

Preparation 20 minutes (allow 2 hours proving time)
Cooking 45 minutes
Makes 2 × 400 g (14 oz) loaves

1 In a large bowl, dissolve the yeast in the water.

2 Stir in a little over half the flour until the mixture has a porridge-like consistency.

3 Mix thoroughly with a hand whisk, then cover and stand to prove in a warm, draught-free place for 30-45 minutes until the mixture has risen visibly.

4 Add the salt, oil, malt extract and dried fruit and stir together, then gradually work in more flour until you have a dough that you can knead.

5 Knead the dough thoroughly and methodically until a smooth texture is achieved.

6 Cover and stand to prove in a warm, draught-free place for 30-45 minutes until the dough has doubled in size.

7 Knead again on a lightly oiled surface, then divide and mould into 2 individual loaves.

8 Oil two 15 cm × 9 cm × 7.5 cm (6 in × 3½ in × 3 in) loaf tins. Place the loaves in the tins. Stand to prove for a further 30-45 minutes or until they have approximately doubled in size, rising to fill the tins.

9 Meanwhile, heat the oven to 200°C (400°F/Gas 6).

10 Bake for 40-45 minutes until the loaves have a dark, even crust.

11 Remove from tins and stand on rack to cool.

◆

Granary-style Bread

20 g (¾ oz) fresh yeast or 5 ml (1 tsp) dried
275 ml (½ pt) warm water
225 g (8 oz) wholewheat flour
5 ml (1 tsp) salt
250 g (9 oz) malt blend or granary-style flour

1 In a large bowl, dissolve the yeast in the water.

2 Stir in the wholewheat flour until the mixture has a porridge-like consistency.

3 Mix thoroughly with a hand whisk, then cover and stand to prove in a warm, draught-free place for 30-45 minutes until the dough has risen visibly.

Continued, page 154.

Granary-style Bread, continued from page 153.

Preparation 20 minutes (allow 2 hours proving time)
Cooking 40 minutes
Makes 2 × 400 g (14 oz) loaves

4 Add the salt and stir in, then work in the granary-style flour.

5 Knead the dough thoroughly and methodically until a smooth texture is achieved.

6 Cover and stand to prove in a warm, draught-free place for 30-45 minutes until the dough has doubled in size.

7 Knead again on a lightly oiled surface, then divide and mould into 2 individual loaves.

8 Oil two 15 cm × 9 cm × 7.5 cm (6 in × 3½ in × 3 in) loaf tins. Place the loaves in the tins. Stand to prove for 30-45 minutes or until they have approximately doubled in size, rising to fill the tins.

9 Meanwhile, heat the oven to 220°C (425°F/Gas 7).

10 Bake for 40 minutes until the loaves sound hollow when tapped.

11 Remove from tins and stand on a rack to cool.

Rye Bread

Rye bread can be given an attractive striped finish by dusting the tops of the loaves with rye flour just before they are put into the tins, and then giving them a series of diagonal cuts, which open as the loaves rise.

about 500 g (1 lb 2 oz) wholemeal rye flour
570 ml (1 pt) warm water
30 g (1 oz) fresh yeast or 7.5 ml (1½ tsp) dried
10 ml (2 tsp) salt
15 ml (1 tbsp) soya or other oil
15 ml (1 tbsp) molasses
5 ml (1 tsp) caraway seeds (optional)
about 500 g (1 lb 2 oz) wholewheat flour

Preparation 20 minutes (allow 12 hours standing time and 1½ hours proving time)
Cooking 45 minutes
Makes 2 × 800 g (1 lb 12 oz) loaves

1 In a large bowl, mix the rye flour with the water. Beat together with a hand whisk until the mixture has a porridge-like consistency and leave to stand overnight.

2 After overnight standing, thoroughly stir in the yeast to dissolve. Cover and stand to prove in a warm, draught-free place for 30 minutes until the mixture has risen visibly.

3 Add the salt, oil, molasses, and the caraway seeds, if liked, and then gradually work in the wholewheat flour until you have a dough that you can knead.

4 Knead the dough thoroughly and methodically until a smooth texture is achieved.

5 Cover and stand to prove for 30-45 minutes. (The dough may not have quite doubled in size, but should have risen visibly.)

6 Knead again, then divide and mould into 2 individual loaves.

7 Oil two 18 cm × 11.5 cm × 8.5 cm (7¼ in × 4½ in × 3½ in) loaf tins. Place the loaves in the tins. Stand to prove for a further 30 minutes, or until they have approximately doubled in size, rising to fill the tins.

8 Meanwhile, heat the oven to 220°C (425°F/Gas 7).

9 Bake for 40-45 minutes until the loaves ring hollow if tapped.

10 Remove from tins and stand on a rack to cool.

Note: This method may also be followed using entirely rye flour: about 1 kg (2 lb 3 oz). The bread will not rise quite as much, of course, but can be delicious, and provided you do not omit the stage of leaving a porridge of rye flour and water to stand overnight, you should be able to achieve an acceptable result. Some cracked rye, or soaked or partially cooked whole rye grains may also be used. They should be added at the first stage, and allowed to steep overnight in the porridge.

Sunflower Seed Bread

20 g (¾ oz) fresh yeast or 5 ml (1 tsp) dried
275 ml (½ pt) warm water
500 g (1 lb 2 oz) wholewheat flour
5 ml (1 tsp) salt
15 ml (1 tbsp) soya oil
15 ml (1 tbsp) honey
150 g (5 oz) sunflower seeds

Preparation 20 minutes (allow 2 hours proving time)
Cooking 45 minutes
Makes 2 × 400 g (14 oz) loaves

1 In a large bowl, dissolve the yeast in the water.

2 Stir in a little over half the flour until the mixture has a porridge-like consistency.

3 Mix thoroughly with a hand whisk, then cover and stand to prove in a warm, draught-free place for 30-45 minutes until the dough has risen visibly.

4 Add the salt, oil, honey and sunflower seeds and stir in, then gradually work in more flour until you have a dough that you can knead easily.

5 Knead the dough thoroughly and methodically until a smooth texture is achieved.

6 Cover and stand to prove in a warm, draught-free place for 30-45 minutes, until the dough has doubled in size.

7 Knead again on a lightly oiled surface, then divide and mould into 2 individual loaves.

8 Oil two 15 cm × 9 cm × 7.5 cm (6 in × 3½ in × 3 in) loaf tins. Place the loaves in the tins. Stand to prove for a further 30-45 minutes or until they have approximately doubled in size, rising to fill the tins.

9 Heat the oven to 200°C (400°F/Gas 6).

10 Bake for 45 minutes until the loaves sound hollow when tapped.

11 Remove from tins and stand on a rack to cool.

Three-seed Bread

20 g (¾ oz) fresh yeast or 5 ml (1 tsp)
  dried
275 ml (½ pt) warm water
500 g (1 lb 2 oz) wholewheat flour
5 ml (1 tsp) salt
15 ml (1 tbsp) soya oil
15 ml (1 tbsp) malt extract
50 g (2 oz) sesame seeds
50 g (2 oz) poppy seeds
50 g (2 oz) linseeds

Preparation 20 minutes (allow 2 hours proving time)
Cooking 45 minutes
Makes 2 × 400 g (14 oz) loaves

1 In a large bowl, dissolve the yeast in the water.

2 Mix in a little over half of the flour until the mixture has a porridge-like consistency.

3 Mix thoroughly with a hand whisk, then cover and stand to prove in a warm, draught-free place for 30-45 minutes until the dough has risen visibly.

4 Add the salt, oil, malt extract and seeds and stir together, then gradually work in the rest of the flour until you have a dough that you can knead.

5 Knead the dough thoroughly and methodically until a smooth texture is achieved.

6 Cover and stand to prove in a warm, draught-free place for 30-45 minutes, until the dough has doubled in size.

7 Knead again on a lightly oiled surface, then divide and mould into 2 individual loaves.

8 Oil two 15 cm × 9 cm × 7.5 cm (6 in × 3½ in × 3 in) loaf tins. Place the loaves in the tins. Stand to prove for a further 30-45 minutes, until they have approximately doubled in size, rising to fill the tins.

9 Heat the oven to 200°C (400°F/Gas 6).

10 Bake for 45 minutes, until the loaves sound hollow when tapped.

11 Remove from tins and stand on a rack to cool.

INDEX